Translation an[...]
of Power

MIX
Paper from
responsible sources
FSC® C014540
www.fsc.org

TRANSLATION, INTERPRETING AND SOCIAL JUSTICE IN A GLOBALISED WORLD

Series Editors: Philipp Angermeyer, *York University, Canada* and Katrijn Maryns, *Ghent University, Belgium*

Translation, Interpreting and Social Justice in a Globalised World is an international series that welcomes authored monographs and edited collections that address translation and interpreting in settings of diversity, globalisation, migration and asylum. Books in the series will discuss how translation and interpreting practices (or their absence) may advance or hinder social justice. A key aim of the series is to encourage dialogue between scholars and professionals working in translation and interpreting studies and those working in other linguistic disciplines, such as sociolinguistics and linguistic anthropology. Books in the series will cover both translation and interpreting services provided by state and corporate entities, as well as informal, community-based translation and interpreting. We welcome proposals covering any combinations of languages (including Sign languages) and from a wide variety of geographical contexts. A guiding aim of the series is to empower those who may be disadvantaged by their lack of access to majority or official languages, and as such proposals which bridge the gap between theoretical and practical domains are particularly encouraged.

Topics which may be addressed by books in the series include (but are not limited to):

- Medical settings (including care settings and provision of public health information)
- Legal settings (law enforcement, court, prison, counselling)
- Educational settings (including community-based education)
- Asylum and migration procedures
- Access to democracy and citizenship
- Interactions with business and private-sector institutions
- The media and minority-language broadcasting and publishing
- Ethical and political considerations in translation
- Cultural translation
- Translation and language rights
- Translation and intercultural relations and conflict

Intended readership: academic and professional.

All books in this series are externally peer-reviewed.

Full details of all the books in this series and of all our other publications can be found on http://www.multilingual-matters.com, or by writing to Multilingual Matters, St Nicholas House, 31–34 High Street, Bristol BS1 2AW, UK.

TRANSLATION, INTERPRETING AND SOCIAL JUSTICE IN A
GLOBALISED WORLD: 3

Translation and Global Spaces of Power

Edited by

**Stefan Baumgarten and
Jordi Cornellà-Detrell**

MULTILINGUAL MATTERS
Bristol • Blue Ridge Summit

DOI https://doi.org/10.21832/BAUMGA1817
Library of Congress Cataloging in Publication Data
Names: Baumgarten, Stefan, editor. | Cornellà-Detrell, Jordi, editor.
Title: Translation and Global Spaces of Power/Edited by Stefan Baumgarten and
    Jordi Cornellà-Detrell.
Description: Blue Ridge Summit, PA: Multilingual Matters, 2018. |
    Series: Translation, Interpreting and Social Justice in a Globalised World: 3 |
    Includes bibliographical references and index.
Identifiers: LCCN 2018026960| ISBN 9781788921817 (hbk : alk. paper) |
    ISBN 9781788921800 (pbk : alk. paper) | ISBN 9781788921848 (kindle)
Subjects: LCSH: Translating and interpreting--Social aspects. |
    Intercultural communication.
Classification: LCC P306.97.S63 T697 2018 | DDC 418/.02--dc23 LC record available
    at https://lccn.loc.gov/2018026960

British Library Cataloguing in Publication Data
A catalogue entry for this book is available from the British Library.

ISBN-13: 978-1-78892-181-7 (hbk)
ISBN-13: 978-1-78892-180-0 (pbk)

Multilingual Matters
UK: St Nicholas House, 31–34 High Street, Bristol BS1 2AW, UK.
USA: NBN, Blue Ridge Summit, PA, USA.

Website: www.multilingual-matters.com
Twitter: Multi_Ling_Mat
Facebook: https://www.facebook.com/multilingualmatters
Blog: www.channelviewpublications.wordpress.com

Copyright © 2019 Stefan Baumgarten, Jordi Cornellà-Detrell and the authors of
individual chapters.

All rights reserved. No part of this work may be reproduced in any form or by any
means without permission in writing from the publisher.

The policy of Multilingual Matters/Channel View Publications is to use papers that
are natural, renewable and recyclable products, made from wood grown in sustainable forests. In the manufacturing process of our books, and to further support our
policy, preference is given to printers that have FSC and PEFC Chain of Custody
certification. The FSC and/or PEFC logos will appear on those books where full
certification has been granted to the printer concerned.

Typeset by R. J. Footring Ltd, Derby.
Printed and bound in the UK by Short Run Press Ltd.
Printed and bound in the US by Thomson-Shore, Inc.

Contents

Contributors

Editors

Stefan Baumgarten is Lecturer in German Language Studies at Jacobs University in Bremen, Germany. His current research centres on critical translation theories and the role of translation as an ideological practice. He is co-editor with Jordi Cornellà-Detrell of the special issue 'Translation in Times of Technocapitalism' of the journal *Target* (2017) and of *Translating the European House: Discourse, Ideology and Politics – Selected Papers by Christina Schäffner*, with C. Gagnon (Cambridge Scholars Publishing, 2016). Some of his recent journal articles include 'The crooked timber of self-reflexivity: Translation and ideology in the end times' (*Perspectives*, 2016), 'Translation and hegemonic knowledge under advanced capitalism' (*Target*, 2017) and 'Adorno refracted: German critical theory in the neo-liberal world order' (*Key Cultural Texts in Translation*, 2018).

Jordi Cornellà-Detrell is Senior Lecturer in Hispanic Studies at the University of Glasgow. His research interests focus on censorship and translation during Franco's regime, the Spanish post-war publishing industry and multilingual literature. He has published several articles, including 'The afterlife of Francoist cultural policies: Censorship and translation in the Catalan and Spanish literary market' (*Hispanic Research Journal*, 2013), and two monographs: *El plurilingüisme en la literatura catalana* (Vitel·la, 2014) and *Literature as a Response to Cultural and Political Repression in Franco's Catalonia* (Tamesis, 2011). Together with Stefan Baumgarten, he co-edited the special issue of *Target* entitled 'Translation in Times of Technocapitalism' (2017).

Authors

Özlem Berk Albachten is Professor in the Department of Translation and Interpreting Studies at Boğaziçi University, Istanbul. Her primary area of research has concentrated on Turkish translation history and intralingual translation, focusing mainly on issues such as modernisation, identity formation and cultural policies. Her more recent research interests include translingual writing, Turkish women translators and autobiography/life writing. She is the author of *Translation and Westernization in Turkey:*

From the 1840s to the 1980s (2004) and *Kuramlar Işığında Açıklamalı Çeviribilim Terimcesi* (*Theoretical Translation Terminology*, 2005) and the co-editor of two forthcoming books on retranslation to be published by Routledge and Springer.

Roger Baines is Senior Lecturer in Translation Studies and French at the University of East Anglia, UK. He has published on sport and translation, stage translation, translator training, subtitling taboo language, and personal and ritual insults in French, and is the author of a monograph on the work of Pierre Mac Orlan. He co-edited *Staging and Performing Translation: Text and Theatre Practice* (2011). Recent publications include: 'Employability as an ethos in translator and interpreter training' (with Cuminatto and Drugan, *The Interpreter and Translator Trainer*); 'Subtitling taboo language: Can the cues of register and genre be used to affect audience experience?' (*Meta*, 2015); and 'Translation, globalization and the elite migrant athlete' (*The Translator*, 2013).

Karen Bennett is Assistant Professor in Translation at Nova University in Lisbon and a researcher with the Centre for English, Translation and Anglo-Portuguese Studies (CETAPS), where she coordinates the Translationality strand. Within Translation Studies, she is interested in translation history, the transmission of knowledge, performativity, multilingualism, linguistic hybridity and (inter-)semiotics. Her most recent publications include a special issue of *The Translator* (2017) entitled 'International English and Translation', co-edited with Rita Queiroz de Barros; 'Translation and the desacralization of the western world: From performativity to representation' (*Alif*, 2018); and 'Foucault in English: The politics of exoticization' (*Target*, 2017).

M. Cristina Caimotto is Assistant Professor of English Language and Translation at the University of Turin, Italy. Her research interests include Translation Studies, Political Discourse and Environmental Discourse. She is a member of the editorial board of *Comunicazione Politica*, *Il Mulino* and *Synergies Italie*. Recent publications include: 'Political and ideological translation practice: Italian and English extracts of Hitler's *Mein Kampf*' (in *Translation und 'Drittes Reich': Menschen – Entscheidungen – Folgen*, 2016, co-authored with S. Baumgarten) and 'The alter-globalist counter-discourse in European rhetoric and translation: Women's rights at the European Parliament' (in *Discourses and Counter-discourses on Europe, from the Enlightenment to the EU*, 2017, co-authored with R. Raus).

Luc van Doorslaer is Chair Professor for Translation Studies at the University of Tartu (Estonia), director of the Centre for Translation Studies at KU Leuven (CETRA, Belgium) and Vice-President of the European Society for Translation Studies. He is a Research Associate at Stellenbosch

University (South Africa). Together with Yves Gambier, he is the editor of the *Translation Studies Bibliography* and the four volumes of the *Handbook of Translation Studies* (2010–13). Recent edited books include *The Known Unknowns of Translation Studies* (2014), *Interconnecting Translation Studies and Imagology* (2016) and *Border Crossings: Translation Studies and other Disciplines* (2016). His main research interests are the institutionalisation of Translation Studies and the links between journalism, ideology, imagology and translation.

Cristina Gómez Castro is Lecturer of English at the University of León, having previously taught at the University of Cantabria, Spain. Her main research interests include theoretical and methodological approaches to translation, the interaction between ideology, translation and gender and the way (self)-censorship and manipulation impinge on the rewritings of texts. Currently, she is working on the reproduction and representation of identities transmitted by North American television series in translation. She has extensively published on translation and censorship and is an active member of the TRACE (TRAnslation & CEnsorship) research team.

José Lambert has been Professor at the Katholieke Universiteit Leuven (Belgium, 1970–2006), at the Universidade Federal Santa Catarina (2011–15) and at the Universidade Federal do Ceará (2015–17), Brazil. He has played a key role in the birth and dissemination of Translation Studies; milestones include organising the historical conference 'Literature and Translation: New Perspectives in Literary Studies' (Leuven, 1976), co-founding the journal *Target* (1989), founding and directing the Leuven Centre for the Study of Translation and Cultures (CETRA) (1989), becoming the first Vice-President of the European Society for Translation Studies (1992) and co-founding the *Translation Studies Bibliography*. He has published 150 articles and edited several volumes in Comparative Literature and Cultural and Translation Studies.

Marion Löffler has lived in Wales since 1994. Having gained her doctorate at Humboldt University, Berlin, she was appointed a Research Fellow at the University of Wales Centre for Advanced Welsh and Celtic Studies, Aberystwyth, where she contributed to the pioneering projects 'A Social History of the Welsh Language' and 'Wales and the French Revolution'. She now lectures in Welsh History at Cardiff University's School of History, Archaeology and Religion. Her latest volumes are *Welsh Responses to the French Revolution: Press and Public Discourse, 1789–1802* (2012) and *Political Pamphlets and Sermons from Wales, 1790–1806* (2014).

Pei Meng is currently Lecturer in the School of Foreign Languages at Shanghai University of International Business and Economics, China. She obtained her MA and PhD in Translation Studies at the University of

Birmingham and the University of Edinburgh. She has carried out research and written on the sociology of translation, audiovisual translation and the discourses of literary reviewing. Other interests include stylistic approaches to translation and the translation of children's literature. She has also translated two English biographies into Chinese: *Nine Lives of William Shakespeare* and *Lincoln and Shakespeare*.

Agnieszka Pantuchowicz teaches literature, gender studies and translation at the University of Social Sciences and Humanities in Warsaw, Poland. She has edited several volumes and published numerous articles on literary criticism, on theoretical aspects of translation, as well as on cultural and ideological dimensions of translation in the Polish context. She is engaged in research within the field of gender studies and the work of contemporary Polish women writers. Her research interests are translation and cultural studies, comparative literature and feminist criticism.

Jonathan Ross studied German and Politics at the University of Edinburgh and completed his doctorate in East German Literature at King's College London. He is now based at the Department of Translation and Interpreting Studies at Boğaziçi University, Istanbul, where he teaches both practical and research-oriented courses. His research interests include telephone interpreting, community interpreting in Turkey, audio-visual translation, the translation of songs and the translation of film titles. Articles by him have appeared in *The Translator*, *Target* and *Across Languages and Cultures*. He has also published numerous Turkish–English translations, including eight books and several short stories and articles, and has produced two films.

Christina Schäffner is Professor Emerita at Aston University, Birmingham. Until her retirement in September 2015 she was the Head of Translation Studies at Aston, teaching courses in translation studies, interpreting, and supervising masters dissertations and PhD students. Her main research interests are: political discourse in translation, news translation, metaphor in translation and translation didactics, and she has published widely on these topics. Major publications include *Political Discourse, Media and Translation* (edited with S. Bassnett, 2010), *Translation Research and Interpreting Research: Traditions, Gaps and Synergies* (2004) and *Politics as Text and Talk. Analytic Approaches to Political Discourse* (edited with P. Chilton, 2002).

Maria Sidiropoulou is Professor of Translation Studies and Chair of the Department of English Language and Literature (School of Philosophy), at the National and Kapodistrian University of Athens. She was Director of the Interuniversity and Interdepartmental Coordinating Committee of the Translation–Translatology MA Programme (2009–11) and Director of the Language and Linguistics Division of the Department of English (2004–06). Her recent publications focus on intercultural issues manifested through translation in the press, in advertising, in academic discourse, in European Union documentation, in literature, on stage and screen.

Acknowledgements

We are grateful to many friends and colleagues who have helped the development of this volume. Specifically, the authors would like to thank Dr Yan Ying for involvement during the early stages of this project and the fantastic team of people at Multilingual Matters who worked hard to produce this volume, particularly the series editors, who provided very detailed and constructive feedback, and the commissioning editor, Laura Longworth, for her encouragement and patience while the manuscript developed. The editors also wish to thank the anonymous reviewers for their support and all the contributors, without whose interest and dedication this book could not have been completed.

General Introduction

Stefan Baumgarten and Jordi Cornellà-Detrell

In the novella *Story of Your Life* (1998), writer Ted Chiang describes the efforts of a linguist to decode the language of an alien civilisation that has just landed on Earth. The story was adapted – or, indeed, semiotically translated – into a movie under the title *Arrival* (2016). What is most remarkable about this science fiction tale is that the word 'translation' is mentioned only once, and in passing, towards the end, and even then it does not refer to the linguist's daunting task but to the fact that she had done some translation work for the military in the past. Translation in its multiple meanings, therefore, is almost absent from a text where the central theme is cross-cultural – indeed, cross-species – communication. Yet, translation is undoubtedly key to the power struggles unleashed by the unexpected arrival: from the frantic efforts spent to comprehend the alien's technology to the military's urge to understand a mysterious gift that the aliens have promised. This glaring disregard of translation's centrality to all acts of communication – and the fact that linguistics takes the spotlight – is hardly news to translation scholars. Since the early 2000s, research in the field has shown time and again that translation practice plays a key role in social, economic and cultural processes, but translation tends to remain in the background, invisible and unacknowledged. As shown by many of the contributions in this volume, it is precisely this invisibility which historically has granted translation the capacity to intervene – albeit covertly – in the public sphere. But, with the rising profile of the discipline in the humanities and social sciences, it is perhaps time to engage in a more sustained manner with the ways in which the manifold facets of power are refracted and reflected in translation processes.

Power is evident at every junction of translation. The translation process, the product, its distribution and its consumption, are shot through with subtle and not so subtle relations of power. The omnipresence of power relations in daily life, the ubiquity of power in academic practice and the absence of a robust conceptual distinction between the concepts of power and ideology might account for the lack of a convincing integrated approach towards questions of power in our discipline. Translation moves across space and time, across culture and history; it is a relational social practice linked to local and global(ised) structures and discourses of power. Translation bears the potential to connect and reveal, to divide and disguise; it is linked to a multitude of structures and discourses that have the power to transform values and behaviour (Bielsa & Hughes, 2009; Tymoczko & Gentzler, 2002). It is, of course, instrumental in the creation and circulation of knowledge, and it may be complicit with political, symbolic and cultural regimes of power. In this edited volume, we aim to underline the complexity of power from the perspective of four social spaces – agency, history, news media, business – that bear their imprint on the act of translation. More to the point, we examine the complex interconnections across power and translation against the backdrop of capitalist globalisation, technological progress and institutional politics.

It is a well known truism that translation is caught up in structural and discursive relations of dominance, and that its analysis requires a historical-hermeneutic and sociological perspective. The different contributions in this book will further sharpen our awareness of translation as being subject to intense hegemonic pressures and dominant institutions or individuals. Translation practitioners and researchers in translation studies never act in an ideological vacuum. They will, to be sure, always have the option to champion the myth that their actions can be free of ideological influence and ignore the existence of an established hegemonic order upheld by state and corporate interests. But both these professional groups may also attempt to bring to light, question or resist the myriad (unequal) relations of power which operate through the medium of translation.

Power is a relational and complex self-generating force. In its various manifestations, transformations and disguises, it remains *the* underlying premise of all research that is devoted to the interpretation of history, culture and society. Translation means that someone has power and thus occupies an ideological position (Fawcett, 1995) and translation is always a child of its own 'ideological' time, as proven by a multitude of translation traditions across the centuries. The traces of such textual traditions can be empirically observed through the investigation of normative translation behaviour (Toury, 2012), which in turn can be linked to dominant historical and political forces at play. The power of (and through) translation is based on the conscious decision to choose and make available a text for a readership in a different language, and this power extends further, into the conscious and subconscious interpretations made on the textual level, all of which can facilitate or prevent social change.

The papers gathered in this volume seek to acknowledge the manifold layers of power play impinging on translation practices, products and effects. They pay attention to a large array of contextual and textual factors, ranging from regional, global and institutional power relations to the linguistic, stylistic and rhetorical implications of translation decisions. In this volume, translation is largely conceptualised as a socially situated and decision-making activity embedded in fluctuating and often conflict-ridden networks of power. The 13 main chapters are broadly organised into four thematic parts, and they are all united by a desire to sharpen our knowledge on the multiple ways in which power relations and ideological positions affect cross-cultural communication.

The three initial contributions combined under the heading 'Translation and the Spaces of Power' set the scene for some of the recurring themes throughout the book. Our introductory Chapter 1 constitutes an attempt to shift the analytical perspective of translation research on power into the realm of the economy. We acknowledge the ubiquity of power and the significance of material needs for our daily lives and propose a quasi-historical-materialist approach to the social analysis of translation. Conceptualising translation alongside diverse but interconnected 'economies of translation' allows us to highlight the extent to which the material relations and forces of production impinge on translation activity and its products. For too long, postmodern translation research has been dominated by a culturalist bias, so we find it necessary to place more attention on how translation, as a commodity, circulates in global markets, and on how it can be used to promote social justice and sustainability. Agnieszka Pantuchowicz in Chapter 2 then looks at the spaces of power from an intriguing philosophical perspective. She argues that translation has the potential to act as an antidote to those hegemonic discourses that present language as a transparent and ideology-free tool whose only function is to express certain preconceived truths. Pantuchowicz contends that the capacity of our interdiscipline to question the apparent transparency and fixity of meaning may neutralise those positivist ideologies that claim to have direct access to the world and to represent it in an accurate manner. The continual fluctuation of values across time and space, however, should not cause new anxieties, but inspire us to engage creatively with the products of language and their intertextual connections. Such an awareness reaffirms the power of knowledge and the ever-present horizon of potentially liberating cultural, political and socio-economic change. Luc van Doorslaer in Chapter 3 focuses on the links between multilingualism, translation and state power in German-speaking Belgium. Heilbron and Sapiro (2007: 95) claim that, in order to grasp translation as a true 'space of international relations', we should first 'analyse it as embedded within the power relations among national states and languages'. In this vein, van Doorslaer sets out to investigate the visible manifestations of power within the context of language planning, language policies and translation in the German-speaking areas of Belgium. Language is a key factor in the cohesion of human societies, but it is rarely acknowledged that translation plays a crucial role in managing linguistic diversity. The unwillingness of the Belgian state to comply with translation policies devised for the German-speaking minority is a good example of one of this book's underlying themes, which considers translation as a response to inequalities across cultures and languages born out of ideological, socio-economic or political factors.

The chapters in Part 2, 'Domination and Hegemony in History', shed light on how translation has functioned in the formation and suppression of worldviews within various historical settings and on the ways in which translation has participated in the reshaping of collective memories. Through their involvement in power struggles, translators have often acted as modernising agents, and consequently their actions allow us to trace the history and development of discursive formations. Chapter 4, by Karen Bennett, provides a fresh look at the history of Bible translation, which since time immemorial has been a site of ideological struggle over the 'correct' interpretation of certain passages. Bible translation has frequently served to secure religious domination by banning unwelcome interpretations, but opposition has also emerged throughout history, in the form of alternative renderings. Nevertheless, if the Bible is supposed to contain God's eternal truth, then any kind of rewriting or reinterpretation becomes a falsification. Bennett asks whether new translations in the wake of two significant historical events – the Protestant Reformation and the advent of feminism – resulted from conscious individual initiative or whether they may also be explained by discursive and historical 'changes in the socio-economic and political infrastructure' (p. 61). Marion Löffler, in Chapter 5, examines the political relations between England and Wales (effectively an internal colony) at the end of the 18th century. By examining the ideological pressures between English state power, national belonging and Welsh political dissidence, Löffler demonstrates how politically charged translations from English into Welsh managed to defy English state power. The translation and manipulation of religious and political texts show how subordinate groups have created dissident sub-cultures by reconfiguring dominant systems of meaning. Significantly, the analysed Welsh translations pursued domesticating translation strategies, both to counteract English colonial domination *and* to maintain Welsh sociocultural identity. In Chapter 6, Maria Sidiropoulou's and Özlem Berk Albachten's analysis of the Greek and Turkish versions of Bruce Clark's *Twice a Stranger* highlights the potential of translation for reframing geopolitical narratives and reshaping collective memory. Clark's historical account of the 1923 population exchange between Greece and Turkey, a highly traumatic experience in the collective consciousness of both nations, was reinterpreted in both target texts in order to steer clear of painful memories and the most controversial aspects of the event. Translational operations, of course, always have the power to transform cultural representations, but it is intriguing to see how translations manipulated the discursive and symbolic systems at their disposal in order to emphasise intercultural affinities and diffuse any potential for conflict. Cristina Gómez Castro, in Chapter 7, on the impact of censorship on bestsellers during Franco's dictatorship in Spain, provides the most evident example of power if understood as top-down domination. Gómez Castro examines the ways in which the publishing sector and translation activities were subordinated to the political field as a consequence of the authoritarian regime's attempt to regulate all cultural production. In time, the accommodation of the cultural establishment to market imperatives and political impositions resulted in a gradual naturalisation of self-censorship on the part of literary practitioners. A set of values initially imposed by sheer political force, therefore, became so ingrained that they caused the gradual transformation of translation practices and the rules of the literary field.

Part 3, entitled 'Media Translation in the Global Digital Economy', explores the ways in which the intensification of communications across cultural boundaries has established translation as a key practice in the production and dissemination of global information. The international flows of translated communications generated by the mass media take the form of hybrid cultural assemblages that are continuously being reframed and reconstructed to serve a variety of political and ideological purposes (Gambier & Gottlieb, 2001). Translation practices in the media cannot be studied in isolation because they form only a small, yet multilayered, component of the vast network of institutions, discourses and technologies that contribute to the construction of public narratives for local and global consumption. José Lambert's Chapter 8 is a revision of a seminal article written in French that was originally published in *Target* in 1989. He maintains that societies continue to generate new systems and technologies of communication, which in turn give rise to new communities of practice. In them, translation functions as a tool for cultural reinvigoration, but also as a potentially destabilising force that may solidify structures of domination or naturalise hegemonic relations. As the author states, contemporary investigations of media translation and mass communication should give more attention to the homogenisation of messages as well as to the strategies that are used to conceal the planning and production of translations on a global scale.

Christina Schäffner in Chapter 9 explores the hidden and visible power complexities of translation and interpretation in mediatised political settings. The cross-cultural mediation of political discourse for the media and state institutions tends to be aligned with institutional values, ideological interests and political objectives. In such official settings, bureaucratic procedure, ideology and politics tend to overrule the translator's and interpreter's agency. When looking at specific situations and textual examples, it emerges that translated and interpreted political discourse is routinely revised, reshaped and recontextualised by various media professionals at several processing stages. Traditional conceptions of power cannot account for the decision-making processes underlying these texts, which reflect socio-economic interests and complex (but largely hidden) power struggles between various stakeholders. In Chapter 10, drawing on critical discourse analysis, Cristina Caimotto explores how translation choices regarding deictic markers may indicate ideological preferences. Her detailed textual analysis demonstrates that the translation of a speech by Barack Obama for Italian newspapers triggered quite different audience assumptions about the US-American 'war on terror'. In political discourse, deictic markers subtly communicate spatial and social proximity and distance, and they are often geared to reinforce narratives of fear and insecurity. The application of deictic markers differs widely across languages, and it is interesting to see how this communicative divergence can help researchers to uncover underlying discursive strategies. Some Italian translations of Obama's speech, for instance, inadvertently foregrounded the source text's ideological and political contradictions due to unavoidable differences in structure and deictic positioning between English and Italian.

The fourth and final part, entitled 'Commercial Hegemonies in the Global Political Economy', explores the role of translation within the commercial circuits of commodity exchange. Also here, translation agents can no longer be seen at the centre of cultural power relations, but at the centre of socio-economic networks and processes that shape the production of meaning. These chapters provide fascinating insights into translation practices in three globalised industries, showing the extent to which translations are affected not just by cultural factors but mainly by global marketing strategies in elite sports, the film industry and international publishing. The three chapters demonstrate not only that translational decision-making may be subject to expectations within target cultural environments (cf. Jauss, 1982; Toury, 2012) but also that translation practice strongly depends on market demands and their accompanying ideological narratives. An exploration of the ways in which translation is embedded in all sorts of professional services and the international flow of consumer commodities will therefore help us to determine its role in market-driven power dynamics. In his analysis of interpreting and translation practices in elite football, Roger Baines argues in Chapter 11 that cross-cultural communication plays a key role in protecting the reputation and wealth of football clubs and their players. Media managers and press officers exert various kinds of pressure on interpreters to preserve the interests of a club, but interpreting can also be used by players to challenge official narratives and to advance their own professional and economic interests. Football as a global commodity is an increasingly deregulated free market in which the objectives of clubs and players are not always shared, and translation can become a bargaining tool in the political economy of professional sports. In Chapter 12 Jonathan Ross explores institutional networks and translational processes at play in the Turkish film industry. Film titles are crucial for marketing purposes and sales strategies, and their translation (or indeed non-translation) into Turkish becomes a site of struggle over economic resources between dominant US-American multinationals and other commercial players in the international film distribution sector. But, while the financially powerful US-American corporations tend to have the last word in deciding on a particular film title, Ross demonstrates that local companies often feel the need to assert themselves in order to protect their own economic interests. It emerges that, once again, the interests of translation agents located in both the source *and* the target cultures play a decisive role in the shaping of the final product. Finally, in Chapter 13 Pei Meng examines selection and publishing procedures within the context of Chinese autobiographical writings, with reference to the British and North American literary markets. By employing a Bourdieusian framework of analysis, and with particular reference to economic capital and the professional habitus of one influential literary agent, she argues that the selection of these texts for the British literary field was largely determined by the literary agent's skilfulness in creating a reading public for a new genre. Meng's discussion highlights the domination of economic capital within the globalised Anglophone literary market, where translations into English are being 'framed as market commodities, with commercial revenue over-riding literary value' (p. 220). An important observation that unites the three chapters in Part 4 is that translation in the global(ising) economy appears to be more decisively influenced by top-level management or marketing experts than by translators themselves.

Finally, the conclusion aims to be a substantive chapter in its own right that brings the different contributions into a broader perspective. In the face of current imbalances of power and the adverse effects of market-driven ideologies on knowledge, diversity and ecological balance, this final contribution explores the ways in which the analysis of power in translation can advance a positive agenda that contributes to the promotion of both social justice and ecological sustainability.

All the chapters in this volume show that relations of hegemony, domination and resistance are ever present within and across what we describe in our first chapter as the 'libidinal', 'digital' and 'political' economies of translation (p. 14). This tripartite conceptualisation, of course, constitutes only a heuristic tool with which to somehow come to terms with the endless complexities of translation and power. The emphasis on the concept of the *economy*, however, might inspire scholars and translators to give this underlying force much more recognition than it has hitherto been granted. Human relations, human–object relations and the ethical prerogatives of social organisation are ultimately founded on the material conditions that we depend upon for our survival (Harvey, 2001: 208). This book demonstrates that these economies of translation constitute arenas for discursive struggles over a variety of socio-economic resources. The case studies and examples presented here not only describe and assess various libidinal, digital or political economies of translation, but also show how the actions of translation agents may reinforce or erode hegemonic relations and dominant beliefs. Translation is situated at the intersection of ideological positions and unequal relations of power, and it is charged with the task of reconstituting narratives through a medium – language – that admits no fixity or closure, a medium that can never be totally overpowered. To conclude on a positive note, despite the multifarious and complex myths, ideologies and norms that are constantly generated by whatever dominant order, the economies of translation will remain privileged spaces that carry opportunities for the development of alternative worldviews, since, after all, they are spaces of power from which new ways of thinking and action will continuously emerge.

References

Bielsa, E. and Hughes, C. (eds) (2009) *Globalization, Political Violence and Translation.* Basingstoke: Palgrave Macmillan.

Chiang, T. (1998) *Story of Your Life.* New York: Tor Books.

Fawcett, P. (1995) Translation and power play. *The Translator* 1 (2), 177–192.

Gambier, Y. and Gottlieb, C. (eds) (2001) *(Multi)Media Translation: Concepts, Practices, and Research.* Amsterdam: John Benjamins.

Harvey, D. (2001) *Spaces of Capital: Towards a Critical Geography.* Edinburgh: Edinburgh University Press.

Heilbron, J. and Sapiro, G. (2007) Outline for a sociology of translation: Current issues and future prospects. In M. Wolf and A. Fukardi (eds) *Constructing a Sociology of Translation* (pp. 93–107). Amsterdam: John Benjamins.

Jauss, H.R. (1982) *Toward an Aesthetic of Reception* (T. Bahti, trans.). Minneapolis, MN: University of Minnesota Press.

Toury, G. (2012) *Descriptive Translation Studies and Beyond* (revised edn). Amsterdam: John Benjamins.

Tymoczko, M. and Gentzler, E. (eds) (2002) *Translation and Power.* Boston, MA: University of Massachusetts Press.

Villeneuve, D. (dir.) (2016) *Arrival.* Paramount Pictures.

Part 1

Translation and the Spaces of Power

1 Translation and the Economies of Power

Stefan Baumgarten and Jordi Cornellà-Detrell

The Economies of Translation in a Globalised World

Power is everywhere: it pervades social formations, mediates our relationships with the physical world and regulates our relationships with each other. One of the ironies of research on power in translation studies is that translators and academics remain caught within hierarchical and thus oppressive regimes of power that are increasingly determined by a relentless rationalisation and technologisation of modern life (Adorno & Horkheimer, 2002; Feenberg, 2002). These forces bear a strong imprint on the subconscious, and they tend to become evident as instances of normative behaviour on the textual level only when we empirically investigate a large number of translations. While such investigations have come to fruition in corpus-based translation studies (Olohan, 2004), most research has been devoted to conceptualising translation as a generator of knowledge across cultures. The cultural turn, with its focus on intertextual relations, however, does not tend to regard texts as commodities that are produced and consumed according to the rules of a hierarchically structured market, and this is why we feel compelled to make a case for an integrated cultural-economic focus concerning the analysis of translation and power. A primarily cultural view is flawed to the extent that it ignores the underlying structural and institutional conditions which allow elites to reproduce their privileges and dominant positions in society. An overly cultural perspective also tends to overlook the fact that globalisation is increasingly determined by communication technologies and commercial interdependencies (Samir, 2014). It is time to balance this over-reliance on cultural epistemology by an approach on translation that is more firmly grounded in the material and technologically mediated dynamics of everyday life (Cronin, 2003). In other words, it is time to take a much closer look at the ways in which the products, processes and functions of translation are embedded in the markets of commodity exchange. The new buzzword for us is the reality of the *economy* as the foundation of our existence. Let us therefore make an attempt to conceptualise the intricacies of power and translation across libidinal, digital and political dynamics within a globalised world. The importance of each domain will be exemplified with three case studies which highlight (1) the impact of translation on the (social) body, (2) the effects of automated translation on practitioners and languages themselves, and (3) the need for a more sustained analysis of the economics of translation.

The flows of power across time are delineated by a multitude of epochal labels. Currently, the most widely used is postmodernism, symbolising an era where traditional certainties in stable sexual, national or political identities have become increasingly eroded (Lyotard, 1984). Postmodernist thought rejects grand ideological narratives, fixed categorisations and stable identities, and concentrates its analytical energies on subjectivity and discursive practices at the expense of material factors. Transformations in the regimes and forces of power are of course underpinned by the transformation of dominant belief systems. Research in translation studies, however, has not yet sufficiently acknowledged that epistemological shifts tend to be driven by the vicissitudes of the economy and capital. Moreover, power evolves alongside scientific and technological change, a historical dynamic with its very own effects on the human condition. Future translation research, indeed, might position itself under the label of posthumanism, an intellectual paradigm that aims to transcend culturalism by problematising taken-for-granted ideas about what it actually means to be human in a world dominated by capital, science and technology (Braidotti, 2013). The cultural turn that was inspired by postmodernism's power of subversion – for instance, the critique of colonial translation methods or the advancement of feminist translation strategies – will most likely become enriched by an additional 'posthuman' focus on our reliance on translation technologies and on how these are transforming the nature of cross-cultural communication. At the dawn of the posthuman condition, we begin to ask questions about the extent to which the digital economy, the ever-increasing power of global technological flows, impacts on human subjectivity and social life.

Contemporary translation theory needs to critically acknowledge the genealogy of scientific and technological rationality and its impact on human subjectivity. Yet, a critical engagement based primarily on postmodern ethics and posthuman sensitivities would fail any litmus test in a world that revolves around the logic of economic exchange and consumption. In our discipline, the notion of the *political economy* has received very short shrift, presumably because of its roots in Marxist historical materialism, yet it is evident that the political and the economic are two sides of the same coin. These two dimensions have virtually become symbiotic during the historical transitions of capitalism into a stage where its ideological force has become an unquestioned principle (Jameson, 1991). Hence, it would be interesting to see a future turn towards investigations of translation as embedded in local and global political economies. It is clear, after all, that the power of capital plays a significant role in the history of translation (Liu, 1999; Milton, 2008). A new focus on the political economy, therefore, would complement activist research and practices, and would create a stronger awareness of the ways in which the politics of cultural exchange is bolstered by economic principles.

Advanced capitalism has spawned new forms of oppressive power that have become internalised by large swathes of the global population as unquestioned principles of conduct. The fetishisation and uncritical acceptance of the imperatives of capital and technology have generated a multitude of cultural identities and practices, including a blind belief in global market forces and the prerogatives of private competition, wealth accumulation and bureaucratic efficiency. An important task for translation theory, therefore, remains a systematic critical assessment of the acceptance of neoliberal imperatives to the detriment of intercultural understanding, social justice and environmental sustainability. A transla- tion theory that seriously attempts to think through the reciprocal effects across translation and power needs to reflect upon translational flows within the context of (global) commercial operations and their complicity with technology-driven biopolitics (Nakai & Solomon, 2006: 27). The emphasis within postmodern and post-colonial research on operations of culture, however, has resulted in a certain depoliticisation of academic theory and the relegation of *socio-economic* structures and processes to the analytical margins (Baumgarten, 2016: 121–124). It is important to take these aspects into account because, as Jacquemond (1992: 139) already stated 25 years ago, 'the global translation flux is predominantly North–North, while South–South translation is almost non-existent and North–South translation is unequal: cultural hegemony confirms, to a greater extent, economic hegemony'. Translation studies needs to forge stronger links between critical (economic) theory and critical practice in order to empower our interdiscipline to facilitate change, engage in action and become visible in public discourse.

In the early 21st century, the structural dynamics of capital are strongly interwoven with the onward march of science and technology, engendering ever more complex forms of interdependency. Notions like *hypermodernity* and *hyperreality* capture snapshots of emergent new regimes of power (Baudrillard, 1994; Lipovetsky, 2005), while the neoliberal political paradigm and its techno-scientifc offshoots engender new forms of rationality (Pellizoni & Ylönen, 2012). The emerging new realities in the global political arena call for more finely differentiated accounts of translation and power that can enlighten us about the possibility of new ways of living, not dominated by market forces and state control, new ways of living which will necessarily have to address current social in- equalities and the looming ecological disaster (cf. Hardt & Negri's (2004) concept of the multitude).

The recent surge in sociological translation research has propelled the notion of agency into the scholarly debate (Milton & Bandia, 2009), but actor-centred methodologies tend to insufficiently account for the underlying inequalities generated by the dynamics of capitalist globalisation. Bourdieu's ideas, however, have facilitated a better understanding of the ways in which translation both shapes and is shaped by solidified yet also fluid and emergent regimes of power (Hanna, 2016; Inghilleri, 2005; Vorderobermeier, 2014). The three economies of translation that we wish to highlight in our discussion bear relations to Bourdieu's approach, because (1) an agent's habitus is embedded within a given *libidinal economy*, (2) it is dependent upon forms of capital that are in turn increasingly dependent on the shifting technological provisions within the *digital economy*, and (3) it is ultimately tied to the capitalist logic within the globalised and globalising *political economy*. While it is obvious that translation agents can freely choose their allegiances and participation in wider social struggles, their decisions remain subject to the fluctuations of power within the libidinal, digital and political economies of translation. It is therefore instrumental to identify such newly defined intercultural spaces, and locate them at the junctions of translation studies, in order to better understand how translation shapes and is shaped by emerging new centres and relations of power and their underlying ideologies.

The *postmodern* perspective on human affairs is libidinal to the extent that it considers biopower as integral to all organic life and social reality (Foucault & Gordon, 1980; Hardt & Negri, 2004; Lyotard, 1984, 1993). Translation is, of course, subject to the whims of our feelings and emotions; it is a cognitive and affective-somatic practice (Robinson, 1991; Scott, 2012) that may be envisaged as taking place within the realms of a global *libidinal economy*. The *classical* perspective emphasises power as a centralised resource held by the elites who impose their interests on subordinate groups (Mills, 1956). In this classical sense, translation may be seen as subject to techno-scientific progress, entrenched within a *digital economy* where influential (multi)national and technological players compete within a worldwide marketplace. Finally, the *structuralist* perspective on power underscores its diffused and relational, its conflictive and consensual nature, permitting refined insights into overlapping social and agentive networks of power (Bourdieu, 1990). Here, translation is seen as firmly integrated within the structural fabric of society, within the hustle and bustle of institutional and commercial relations that characterise the *political economy*. To what precise extent, however, do these three socio-economic realms relate to the question of translation and power?

The Libidinal Economies of Translation

We speak of a *libidinal economy of translation* to suggest that the theory and practice of translation are human activities bound to affective and embodied dispositions. Research on translation has tended to locate the sources and effects of power in libidinal conceptualisations such as identity, agency, memory or somatic theory (e.g. Brodzki, 2007; Cronin, 2006; Milton & Bandia, 2009; Robinson, 1991). The spotlight that translation research has placed on the libidinal manifestations of the human condition certainly helps to advance our understanding of translation. Sociological research in particular has taken critical note of Foucault's theory of power (Nakai & Solomon, 2006) and of Bourdieu's conception of the subject as a confluence of socially and perceptually constituted dispositions known as habitus (Vorderobermeier, 2014). The postmodern 'libidinal' perspective has given us much to think about with regard to both identity and agency. The intricacies of translation and biopower, however, need to be unravelled with recourse to a theory that accounts for questions of hegemony and domination against the backdrop of commodified relations of power. Overall, this requires a reorientation of translation studies towards the *materiality* of knowledge and cultural practices, towards a concept which is all too often frowned upon due to its appropriation by hegemonic discourses on consumption and commodification.

The South Korean movie *Okja* (2017, directed by Bong Joon-ho) offers a particularly nuanced exploration of the ways in which libidinal energies, biopower, late capitalism, technology, globalisation and translation intertwine at the beginning of the 21st century. The main issues explored include the power of transnational companies, the morality and immorality of bioengineering, the ecological crisis and the radical structural changes suffered by human societies in the last few decades. In the movie, a local farmer who lives in harmony with nature in a remote Korean village grows a recently created species of giant pig on behalf of an agricultural corporation that intends to mass produce the animal to help alleviate world hunger. In reality, the whole operation is a greenwashing exercise devised to boost the company's profitability. Mija, the farmer's daughter, develops strong emotional ties with the pig, named Okja, and when the animal is reclaimed by the company she embarks on a journey from rural Korea to Seoul and as far as New York to reunite with her friend. Mija is helped by the Animal Liberation Front (ALF), determined to unmask the company's real intentions and to liberate the pig.

Mija communicates with the ALF through an interpreter. On being asked whether she would like the animal to be freed or whether she would like a camera to be implanted in the pig's body to secretly record animal abuse taking place in the company's main facilities, Mija simply answers that she wants to go back to the countryside. The interpreter, though, sensing the disappointment that her answer will cause and given ALF's high moral ground, purposely mis-translates her words. Once the interpreter's dubious translation choice is revealed, the ALF's leader, to make the interpreter realise that treating a person with respect involves respecting his or her language, beats him up while stressing that 'translations are sacred'. The ALF eventually obtains the desired images, but only through

Okja's brutal torture by the agricultural corporation. This reminds us that translation has been used for the subjugation of bodies and human communities, and that this practice ultimately intervenes in organic systems. To redeem himself, the interpreter has the sentence 'translations are sacred' voluntarily tattooed on his arm, an act of self-mutilation that stresses the need to recognise and respect the embodied dispositions present in the enunciations of translation, while also expressing his future commitment to the voice of those he represents. The interpreter's translation decision, taken in a split second, shows how translation is subordinated to libidinal intensities, moved by feelings and desires that act upon the body; in other words, the example shows how libidinal energies impact upon translation decisions. The power of the translator, exerted at the level of life and in the name of life, obviously has an impact on organic life.

In *Okja*, interpreting is also used within the agricultural company, because the managing board and the employees do not speak the same language. The former use English to engage in greenwashing strategies and develop new technologies to impose their industrial food products on a global scale; the latter speak only Spanish and have no other option but to contribute to their own subordination by first producing and then consuming the company's products. Translation, *Okja* suggests, should be used to sustain rather than undermine social and ecological life-support systems. In addition, the fact that in the film Korean and Spanish mainly exist in translation shows that languages, like natural ecosystems, have also been threatened by the socio-economic order, which favours a reduction of linguistic diversity in the name of market profitability. Given that the international market is presently dominated by English and translations out of English, research on translation, power and globalisation cannot evade the question of linguistic imperialism. Here, the global hegemony of English panders to an illusion of immediate and transparent communication which is nourished by Western rationality. The result is that virtually 'every kind of thought must presuppose that it will be translated into English' (Takaaki, 2006: 42), while such translations may indeed be complicit in 'the systematic destruction of rival forms of knowledge' (Bennett, 2007: 154). Translation may threaten the cohesion of social structures, reinforce inequalities and obliterate knowledge and linguistic systems. Human beings integrate translation into their lives; it is a practice which allows us to plan, perform and control intervention in our environment. We should therefore investigate the ways in which the libidinal economies of translation can blossom within and across human communities, not to put our communities at risk or subordinate them, but to guarantee the preservation of cultural diversity, to enhance their self-image and to make sure that they are able to control their own knowledge and ways of life. *Okja*, with its focus on a quasi-sentient bio-engineered animal, hints at the need to develop an ecological method of translation which is less anthropocentric and more life-centred, and which is sensitive to the way the natural world is described, presenting it as an indissociable part of human experience rather than as an external reality that exists mainly to be exploited.

The Digital Economies of Translation

The rise of networked and digital technologies since the second half of the last century has significantly changed the processes and products of translation (Folaron & Buzelin, 2007). It makes sense, therefore, to scrutinise newly emerging yet constantly shifting hierarchies of power within the context of the *digital economy of translation*. While new technologies to some extent foster the erosion of classical 'top-down' relations of power, they nevertheless remain subject to the pressures of increasingly interconnected global markets. For this reason, translation research needs to analyse the ongoing reconfiguration of social identities through the forces of techno-scientific rationality and capitalist globalisation (O'Thomas, 2017). Translation technologies are not just tools subordinated to human interests; rather, we increasingly live in symbiosis with them, to the point that frequently we do not notice their presence. As Alonso and Calvo (2015: 141) point out, 'we find examples of the use of digital tools in even the most traditional forms of translation'. There appears, on the whole, to be no room outside of (capitalist) techno-scientific domination on a global level, because scientific research and technological development are firmly entrenched within public and private sectors, promising endless material riches and prospects for human advancement, often at the expense of social justice and the degradation of the environment.

Dealing with information is becoming ever faster and cheaper, and mobility-enhancing technologies have resulted in the emergence of a truly global marketplace. This has transformed the practice of translation, which now can be carried out in real time by teams located in any part of the world with software that provides a significant input to the final product (Daelemans & Hoste, 2009). Translation processes are progressively mediated by interconnected actors who have specific, self-contained tasks to perform and who often have no access to information on the purposes and results of the job at hand. As a consequence, authorship or ethical responsibility can rarely be claimed by translators working, for instance, in large international institutions such as the European Union (Koskinen, 2008: 24). In the wake of the global expansion of the techno-scientific marketplace, the translation process itself is increasingly explained in the managerial terms of productivity and professional efficiency. This discourse, which contributes to the grand narrative of techno-scientific progress, risks approaching translation from an exclusively rationalist and practical point of view that fosters purely empirical models of analysis. In order to avoid simply absorbing and reproducing these discourses, the discipline needs to pay more critical attention to power relations within the translation industry, composed of a vast number of organisations of very different sizes and with very different objectives and practices. Technology has, to be sure, lowered entry barriers into the profession, but we cannot ignore the fact that translation output is increasingly mediated by a very limited range of tools which determine product quality.

Digital networks have streamlined the translation process, but at the risk of promoting the rise of market-driven technocratic managerialism, homogenising knowledge and creating further inequalities. In May 2017, for instance, a subscriber to the Spanish digital television channel Movistar+ tweeted a still image with Catalan subtitles from the series *Fargo* in which the caption read 'És molts diners. Cent mil galls dindi' ('It's a lot of money. One hundred thousand turkeys'). Catalan speakers immediately realised that the expression 'gall dindi' was a literal translation of the word 'pavos' from Spanish, which only in this language can mean both 'turkey' and, in slang, 'bucks'.

This mistake, obviously a result of automatic translation, irritated Catalan speakers and sparked a heated media debate which had political consequences: Santi Vila, the Catalan Minister of Culture, alarmed by the controversy, contacted Movistar+ and informed his Twitter followers that the company would amend the error (Ara, 2017; *La Vanguardia*, 2017). It soon transpired that Movistar+ and the Ministry of Culture had signed an agreement by which, between 2014 and 2016, the former would subtitle into Catalan 600 films and 60 seasons of different television shows. It was also revealed that, in 2016 alone, Movistar+ had received €300,000 for its subtitling efforts. Movistar+ distanced itself from any responsibility by pointing out that the distributor (Metro-Goldwyn-Mayer) had provided the subtitles, which had been outsourced to an external company. Catalan internet users, shocked by the lack of respect for their language, started circulating similar mis-translations from other shows and films, as well as from newspapers, making it obvious that in Catalonia computer-generated translation is a pervasive phenomenon that extends well beyond subtitling.

Translation or subtitling into Catalan is done not just in the interest of linguistic plurality and out of respect for Catalan speakers, but also because the Catalan government subsidises such initiatives. Everyone involved benefits from this: the government can claim that audio-visual content in Catalan is growing exponentially and that the continuous interest of media corporations provides evidence of the vitality of the language; and media companies receive a small government subsidy, which, while not allowing them to provide a good service, grants them some publicity in the Catalan media and helps them balance their accounts. We could criticise corporate greed and question whether translation into stateless languages should be the sole responsibility of local governments, but the fact remains that €300,000 is a tiny subsidy: how many hours of content could be properly subtitled by a translator earning a decent salary? Not many.

What outsourcing companies do is to employ an editor (whose contractual conditions we can imagine are not particularly good) who quickly scans the automated translation in order to rectify the most glaring errors. This particular mistake spread through social media and thus uncovered the deplorable political, corporate and economic realities of automated translation, but the example also illustrates some of the less obvious consequences of the new digital economy of translation. No matter the original language of the media product, Catalan is systematically translated from the Spanish translations of these media products. Such relay translations distort the lexicon, phraseology, syntax and grammar of Catalan, in a process which renders the language other to itself, gradually transforming it into a mere appendage of Spanish. Ironically, an initiative that in principle should help to promote the use of Catalan among its speakers may end up defacing the language to a point where, if the process persists and intensifies, Catalan may become indistinguishable from the 'source code', thus eliminating the need for translation.

Most automated translation tools rely on so-called pivot languages: instead of translating directly from a source to a target language, they first translate to an intermediary language and then to the target. To be effective, software needs massive amounts of data, which explains why results are poor when it comes to translating less widely spoken languages. As Boleslav (2015) pointed out regarding the disastrous results of automated translation into Irish Gaelic, 'languages are [should be] judged by the quality of what is said and written in them – not by the quantity of what can be cheaply translated into and out of them'. In the face of the catastrophic results that machine translation could have for the ecology of languages, Cronin (2017) has rightly called for a sustainable development of translation which protects languages from massification strategies that corrupt and distort them.

As the above example shows, research needs to investigate the social and cultural implications of the increasing technological mediation of translation (Pym, 2011). Large sectors of the translation profession have quickly shifted from the rhythms of solitary intellectual production to the rhythms of the technological age, with its alienated labour, bureaucratic routines and compulsion for productivity (Moorkens, 2017). The societal drive towards technological rationalism strongly relies on the forces of advanced capitalism, and research on translation and power needs to steer away from an over-reliance on cultural, social and symbolic forms of capital to the benefit of a robust focus on *economic capital* (Bourdieu, 1990).

The New Spaces of Power in the Political Economy

The global spread of capitalism has been facilitated through newly evolving communication technologies and through the artificial creation of consumer needs. It is indeed reasonable to argue that the most significant 'paradigm shift in the global economic and political orders' constitutes the 'unification of the world market, which paradoxically operates through diversity and diversification' (Neilson, 2006: 158). The world's multilingual reality makes up for one significant aspect of this paradox, and it cannot be overemphasised that (linguistic) diversity is mediated through translation *and* capital. When we speak of a *political economy of translation*, we focus on local and global manifestations of power in relation to institutional dynamics, political organisation and economic imperatives. This structural perspective on the topic of power and translation offers insights into the local histories, hierarchical compositions and market objectives of differentiated socio-economic spaces, such as publishing houses, translation agencies, software companies, educational departments, government institutions and so on. By drawing on discourse analysis, terminology research and corpus linguistics, scholars have provided valuable insights into the linguistic challenges of translating business discourse and economic texts, but the focus on 'the translation of economics' should give way to an increased attention to 'the economics of translation' (Biel & Sosoni, 2017).

Logemann and Piekkari (2014), for instance, examine how multinational corporations implement translation and language policies to regulate internal communication, create a common corporate language and reduce internal linguistic diversity. Their study brings to light the importance of invisible practices such as self-translation, the particularly active role of junior employees regarding this practice and the way it is used to solidify or contest power relations within organisations. Another practice that has been analysed from this perspective is that of crowdsourcing, which has shaken the foundations of the translation industry (McDonough Dolmaya, 2012). Advances in technology have blurred the boundaries between professional and amateur translators, which has resulted in fears about the potential de-professionalisation of sectors of the translation practice. Translation services have in any case become widely diversified; they now include not just paid professional translation, but also unpaid raw machine translation, paid post-edited machine translation and paid or unpaid crowd-sourcing (Garcia, 2015). While volunteer translation initiatives can provide training opportunities for graduates or invaluable support in situations such as a humanitarian crisis, for-profit corporations have already explored the use of 'gamification' strategies and canvassed online communities to recruit unpaid volunteers. In 2009, for instance, LinkedIn sent an online survey to thousands of translator members asking whether they would be willing to help to translate material on the company's website for no remuneration (Newman, 2009). The options included translating in exchange of an upgraded account or simply for fun. While a number of translators expressed serious concerns, many others welcomed this initiative as a way of enhancing their CV and thereby potentially securing paid jobs.

It appears that, first and foremost, the problem was one of communication: LinkedIn employs professional translators on a regular basis, and a company whose revenue mainly comes from providing information to human resources professionals surely would not risk jeopardising its reputation with an underdeveloped translation programme. While some feared that the survey was an attempt to cut costs by calling for the unpaid assistance of translators, others argued that the goal was to develop an ambitious crowd-sourcing translation project, but that this was not well explained (Kelly, 2009).

The key role of translation in fostering intercultural communication is obvious to translators and scholars, but examples abound which show that the added benefits of a well-thought-out translation strategy are by no means obvious to the corporate world. In 2015, for instance, Taco Bell's communication strategies floundered in Japan: information from the company was mainly in English, tweets in Japanese were ignored and the company used unmediated machine translation to translate its Japanese website, which gave the impression that Taco Bell was entirely ignoring the local context (Sholl, 2015). The cases of LinkedIn and Taco Bell demonstrate that communication and translation strategies are interlinked but not always developed to the same standard. In order to understand the political economies of translation, it is paramount to explore the ways in which translation is embedded in a company's culture and business practices, to examine its internal communication systems and policies and translation needs, the way it presents itself externally, and how it interacts with clients from different countries.

What needs to be investigated regarding the political economies of translation, however, is not only how translation is embedded in the daily functioning of corporations, but how translation companies themselves operate. Scholars logically side with translators, raising concerns about practices that appear to threaten the profession and highlighting those that seem to empower it. Nevertheless, when a translation company promotes its services by stating that 'Every economic institution, organization and business understands that money is the greatest communicator in the world and that accurate financial translations are indispensable toward making certain that communication is not infringed upon in any way' (York's Translation, 2017), it is obvious that we should be more critical with the rampant industrialisation and commodification of this practice. Similarly, another company states that it 'can help ensure that through a maze of new terminology and regulations [relating to hedge funds, credit default swaps, swaptions, subprime debt, etc.], shades of meaning do not get lost' (Ulatus, 2017). The blind adherence by many specialised translation companies to market principles, with claims that their high-quality services increase profits and ensure growth and security, poses the inconvenient question of whether the role of translation lies not just in promoting intercultural understanding, but also in the (surely also inadvertent) creation of global economic bubbles, the depredation of the environment and the reproduction of social injustice.

Undeniably, the opportunities available for translation researchers and practitioners have grown exponentially in just a few years, but at the cost of a creeping internalisation of hegemonic market values. The rift between humanist and market-driven discourses on translation is echoed in the ways in which scholars address the study of newly emerging technological and economic processes. By leaning on the scepticism of the Frankfurt School regarding technological development and consumerism, there are concerns about the potential capacity of these processes to limit and control the subjectivity of the translator (Dizdar, 2014; Nakai & Solomon, 2006). But it has also been argued that these transformative changes may in fact liberate translators from repetitive and mundane tasks, allowing them to focus on those aspects of their job which demand more creativity (Cronin, 2003: 117; also Pym, 2011). Pessimistic views on the unviability of capitalist relations of production and consumption exist side by side with the idea that advanced capitalism does indeed offer opportunities that empower and free the human subject (Featherstone, 1991: 86). This may be the case, but we should not forget that at the precise moment when translation becomes integrated into the global exchange system of commodities – that is, when a translation is distributed on the consumer market – it becomes part and parcel of the realm of capitalist ideology.

Final Considerations

The demands of the market, which probably represents the most significant locus of power in most spheres of society, have generated both optimism and insecurity in the field of translation studies. This inter-discipline, one of the few recent success stories in the humanities partly due to its large potential for the creation of practice-based knowledge, finds itself in a contradictory position. While it keeps drawing heavily from its humanist-hermeneutic foundations, it is simultaneously drawn towards the private sector, consistently creating links with actors in the corporate world. The tension between these poles has given rise to two divergent dis-courses coexisting side by side in postgraduate courses, conferences and journals. One body of research draws inspiration from cultural studies and the social sciences, whereas the other borrows heavily from the discourses of business administration, international marketing and translation tech-nology (Pym, 2013, 2014). These are discourses that, above all, propagate market ideals such as employability, productivity and skills development. Their influence is evidenced by a growing number of educational training courses whose main aim is to produce translation professionals for the brave new world of (largely corporate) intercultural communication. This techno-managerial approach to translation education tends to give prominence to linguistic structures and technological innovations at the expense of cultural context, and often presupposes the neutrality of both language and translators, favouring an empiricism that 'tends to privilege analytical concepts derived from linguistics, regardless of how narrow or limited they may be in their explanatory power' (Venuti, 2013: 67).

In recent decades, the global spread and availability of information and knowledge have become crucial assets in maintaining stakes in economic and political power. Any knowledge-based modern society crucially rests on the foundations of a socio-economic order overseen by institutional networks of power (Castells, 2000; Rooney *et al.*, 2005). However, keeping an appearance of *order* calls for considerable efforts and resources, because social values, norms and conventions are constantly being challenged and re-evaluated. Translation, as a key factor in the dissemination of knowledge, has the power to consolidate or disturb ideological positions and relations of dominance. The translation process itself can be seen as a moment of structuration (Giddens, 1984; van Rooyen, 2013) in which new discourses are being created and in which multifaceted layers of meaning are being (re)negotiated, shaped and reinforced. During the act of translation, knowledge is in transit, in the making so to speak, and this is often a moment of individual hesitation infused with power, in which critical choices are being made. As a result, uncovering how translation agents make and reshape the text also requires us to direct our attention to the often microscopic and sometimes seemingly trivial choices through which they negotiate power relations. This may then enable us to speculate on the causes and effects of translational decisions in the wider social arena. Translation is instrumental in fostering the reconfiguration of values and wider structural relations, as it participates in the social construction of knowledge and identities. But we should not forget that it is also firmly embedded in processes of (neoliberal) globalisation which promote social inequalities and the depredation of natural resources.

On a positive note, in today's political economy, power is more diffused and fragmented than ever, because the barriers that once granted monopolies to large-scale organisations have been eroded or can be more easily circumvented (Naím, 2013). The last few years, for instance, have seen the emergence of a myriad of small, specialised and very flexible (mostly technology-driven) companies that can deliver services at often very low costs, but we have also witnessed an explosion in phenomena like citizen journalism and 'fansubbing' (Massidda, 2015; Wang & Zhang, 2017). It is obvious that technological developments in communication systems have resulted in the redistribution of global power relations and they have also greatly increased the opportunities for social activism, which pose challenges to corporate, media and state institutions. The growing number of translators organised in close-knit networks across the globe has led to an increasing emphasis on their social responsibility and on opportunities for intervening in public debate (Tymoczko, 2010). Further to this, from the perspective of the sociology of globalisation, proposals have been put forward to engage in 'intercultural translation' in order to preserve cultural heterogeneity and to counteract hegemonic neoliberal globalisation (Cronin, 2017; Santos, 2014). The fact that information produced in any part of the world can today almost instantaneously be made available in any major language, therefore, propels the economies of translation into a position of new political significance, not least because activists and translators are gaining more options to question, outflank, or even sabotage hegemonic and dominant forms of power.

References

Adorno, T.W. and Horkheimer, M. (2002) *Dialectic of Enlightenment: Philosophical Fragments* (E. Jephcott, trans.). Stanford, CA: Stanford University Press.

Alonso, E. and Calvo, E. (2015) Developing a blueprint for a technology-mediated approach to translation studies. *Meta: Journal des Traducteurs* 60 (1), 135–167.

Ara (2017) 'Cien mil pavos' són 'cent mil galls dindis': errors en els subtítols en català de 'Fargo' a Movistar+, 26 May, at http://www.ara.cat/media/Cien-mil-subtitols-Fargo-Movistar_0_1802819801.html, accessed 23 September 2017.

Baudrillard, J. (1994) *Simulacra and Simulation* (S. F. Glaser, trans.). Ann Arbor, MI: University of Michigan Press.

Baumgarten, S. (2016) The crooked timber of self-reflexivity: Translation and ideology in the end times. In M. McLaughlin and J. Muñoz-Basols (eds) 'History, Ideology, Censorship and Translation: Past and Present', special issue, *Perspectives: Studies in Translatology* 24 (1), 115–129.

Bennett, K. (2007) Epistemicide! The tale of a predatory discourse. *The Translator* 13 (2), 151–169.

Biel, L. and Sosoni, V. (2017) The translation of economics and the economics of translation. *Perspectives: Studies in Translation Theory and Practice* 25 (3), 351–361.

Boleslav, M. (2015) Do minority languages need machine translation?, at https://multikulti.wordpress.com/2015/11/13/do-minority-languages-need-machine-translation, accessed 17 August 2017.

Bong Joon-ho (2017) *Okja*, Netflix.

Bourdieu, P. (1990) *The Logic of Practice* (R. Nice, trans.). Stanford, CA: Stanford University Press.

Braidotti, R. (2013) *The Posthuman*. Cambridge: Polity Press.

Brodzki, B. (2007) *Can These Bones Live? Translation, Survival, and Cultural Memory*. Stanford, CA: Stanford University Press.

Castells, M. (2000) *The Rise of the Network Society. The Information Age: Economy, Society and Culture* (Vol. 1) (2nd edn). Malden, MA: Blackwell.

Cronin, M. (2003) *Translation and Globalisation*. London: Routledge.

Cronin, M. (2006) *Translation and Identity*. London: Routledge.

Cronin, M. (2017) *Eco-Translation. Translation and Ecology in the Age of the Anthropocene*. London: Routledge.

Daelemans, W. and Hoste, V. (eds) (2009) 'Evaluation of Translation Technology', special issue, *Linguistica Antverpiensia* 8.

Dizdar, D. (2014) Instrumental thinking in translation studies. *Target* 26 (2), 206–223.

Featherstone, M. (1991) *Consumer Culture and Postmodernism*. London: Sage.

Feenberg, A. (2002) *Transforming Technology: A Critical Theory Revisited*. Oxford: Oxford University Press.

Folaron, D. and Buzelin, H. (2007) Introduction: Connecting translation and network studies. *Meta* 52 (4), 605–642.

Foucault, M. and Gordon, C. (1980) *Power/Knowledge: Selected Interviews and Other Writings, 1972–1977*. New York: Pantheon Books.

Garcia, I. (2015) Cloud marketplaces: Procurement of translators in the age of social media. *JoSTrans: The Journal of Specialised Translation* 23, 18–38.

Giddens, A. (1984) *The Constitution of Society: Outline of the Theory of Structuration*. Cambridge: Polity Press.

Hanna, S. (2016) *Bourdieu in Translation Studies: The Socio-cultural Dynamics of Shakespeare Translation in Egypt*. London: Routledge.

Hardt, M. and Negri, A. (2004) *Multitude: War and Democracy in the Age of Empire*. New York: Penguin.

Inghilleri, M. (ed.) (2005) 'Bourdieu and the Sociology of Translation and Interpreting', special issue, *The Translator* 11 (2).

Jacquemond, R. (1992) Translation and cultural hegemony: The case of French–Arabic translation. In L. Venuti (ed.) *Rethinking Translation: Discourse, Subjectivity, Ideology* (pp. 139–158). London: Routledge.

Jameson, F. (1991) *Postmodernism, or The Cultural Logic of Late Capitalism*. Durham, NC: Duke University Press.

Kelly (2009) Freelance translators clash with LinkedIn over crowdsourced translation, 19 June, at http://www.commonsenseadvisory.com/Default.aspx?Contenttype=ArticleDe tAD&tabID=63&Aid=591&moduleId=391, accessed 23 September 2017.

Koskinen, K. (2008) *Translation Institutions: An Ethnographic Study of EU Translation*. Manchester: St Jerome Publishing.

La Vanguardia (2017) Traducen por error 'cien mil pavos' por 'cent mil galls dindis' en la serie Fargo, 26 May, at http://www.lavanguardia.com/series/20170526/422954358200/ fargo-error-de-traduccion-cent-mil-galls-dindis.html, accessed 23 September 2017.

Lipovetsky, G. (2005) *Hypermodern Times*. Malden, MA: Polity Press.

Liu, L.H. (1999) The question of meaning-value in the political economy of the sign. In L.H. Liu (ed.) *Tokens of Exchange: The Problem of Translation in Global Circulations* (pp. 13–41). Durham, NC: Duke University Press.

Logemann, M. and Piekkari, R. (2014) Localize or local lies? The power of language and translation in the multinational corporation. *Critical Perspectives on International Business* 11 (1), 30–53.

Lyotard, J.F. (1984) *The Postmodern Condition: A Report on Knowledge* (I. Bennington and B. Massumi, trans.). Manchester: Manchester University Press.

Lyotard, J.F. (1993) *Libidinal Economy* (I. Hamilton Grant, trans.). London: Continuum.

Massidda, S. (2015) *Audiovisual Translation in the Digital Age: The Italian Fansubbing Phenomenon*. Basingstoke: Palgrave Macmillan.

McDonough Dolmaya, J. (2012) Analyzing the crowdsourcing model and its impact on public perceptions of translation. *The Translator* 18 (2), 167–191.

Mills, C.W. (1956) *The Power Elite*. Oxford: Oxford University Press.

Milton, J. (2008) The importance of economic factors in translation publication: An example from Brazil. In A. Pym, M. Shlesinger and D. Simeoni (eds) *Beyond Descriptive Translation Studies: Investigations in Homage to Gideon Toury* (pp. 163–174). Amsterdam: John Benjamins.

Milton, J. and Bandia, P. (2009) Introduction: Agents of translation and translation studies. In J. Milton and P. Bandia (eds) *Agents of Translation* (pp. 1–18). Amsterdam: John Benjamins.

Moorkens, J. (2017) Under pressure: Translation in times of austerity. *Perspectives: Studies in Translation Theory and Practice* 25 (3), 464–477.

Naím, M. (2013) *The End of Power: From Boardrooms to Battlefields and Churches to States, Why Being in Charge Isn't What It Used To Be*. New York: Basic Books.

Nakai, N. and Solomon, J. (2006) Introduction: Addressing the multitude of foreigners, echoing Foucault. In N. Sakai and J. Solomon (eds) *Translation, Biopolitics, Colonial Difference* (pp. 1–35). Hong Kong: Hong Kong University Press.

Neilson, B. (2006) The market and the police: Finance capital in the permanent global war. In N. Sakai and J. Solomon (eds) *Translation, Biopolitics, Colonial Difference* (pp. 157–172). Hong Kong: Hong Kong University Press.

Newman, A.A. (2009) Translators wanted at LinkedIn. The Pay? $0 an Hour, 28 June, at http://www.nytimes.com/2009/06/29/technology/start-ups/29linkedin.html?mcubz=0, accessed 23 September 2017.

Olohan, M. (2004) *Introducing Corpora in Translation Studies*. London: Routledge.

O'Thomas, M. (2017) Humanum *ex machina*: Translation in the post-global, posthuman world. *Target* 29 (2), 284–300.

Pellizoni, L. and Ylönen, M. (2012) Hegemonic contingencies: Neoliberalized technoscience and neorationality. In L. Pellizoni and M. Ylönen (eds) *Neoliberalism and Techno-science: Critical Assessments* (pp. 47–74). Farnham: Ashgate.

Pym, A. (2011) What technology does to translating. *Translation and Interpreting* 3 (1), 1–9.

Pym, A. (2013) Translation skill-sets in a machine-translation age. *Meta* 58 (3), 487–503.

Pym, A. (2014) Localization, training, and instrumentalization. In E. Torres-Simón and D. Orrego-Carmona (eds) *Translation Research Projects* 5, at http://isg.urv.es/publicity/isg/publications/trp_5_2014/index.htm, accessed 11 November 2016.

Robinson, D. (1991) *The Translator's Turn*. Baltimore, MD: Johns Hopkins University Press.

Rooney, D., Hearn, G. and Ninan, A. (2005) *Handbook on the Knowledge Economy*. Cheltenham: Edward Elgar.

Samir, A. (2014) *Capitalism in the Age of Globalization: The Management of Contemporary Society*. London: Zed Books.

Santos, B. de S. (2014) *Epistemologies of the South: Justice Against Epistemicide*. London: Routledge.

Scott, C. (2012) *Literary Translation and the Rediscovery of Reading*. Cambridge: Cambridge University Press.

Sholl, J. (2015) The curious case of Taco Bell's translation trouble, 24 September, at http://www.lionbridgeondemand.com/blog/2015/9/24/0udm2h3cftoho6rccx65it039qvnbs, accessed 23 September 2017.

Takaaki, M. (2006) Translation as dissemination: Multilinguality and de-cathexis. In N. Sakai and J. Solomon (eds) *Translation, Biopolitics, Colonial Difference* (pp. 39–53). Hong Kong: Hong Kong University Press.

Tymoczko, M. (ed.) (2010) *Translation, Resistance, Activism*. Boston, MA: University of Massachusetts Press.

Ulatus (2017) Localize to globalize (translation service), at https://www.ulatus.com/banking-finance-translation.htm, accessed 23 September 2017.

van Rooyen, M. (2013) Structure and agency in news translation: An application of Anthony Giddens' structuration theory. *Southern African Linguistics and Applied Language Studies* 31, 495–506.

Venuti, L. (2013) *Translation Changes Everything: Theory and Practice*. London: Routledge.

Vorderobermeier, G.M. (ed.) (2014) *Remapping Habitus in Translation Studies*. Amsterdam: Rodopi.

Wang, D. and Zhang, X. (2017) Fansubbing in China: Technology-facilitated activism in translation. In S. Baumgarten and J. Cornellà (eds) 'Translation in Times of Techno-capitalism', special issue, *Target* 29 (2), 301–318.

York's Translation (2017) Professional translation and voice-over service in China, at http://www.yorkstranslation.com/financial.html, accessed 23 September 2017.

2 Bloodless Academicians and the Power of Translation Studies

Agnieszka Pantuchowicz

> In every possible sense, translation is necessary but impossible.
> Spivak (2000a: 13)

The catchphrase 'bloodless academicians' refers to the disciples and followers of various deconstructivist theories who, owing to their lack of social and political engagement, have absented themselves from the public sphere and retreated to the narrow chinks of the cavern of academia (Žižek, 2011: 212). John Brockman uses the phrase when commenting on Russell Jacoby's book *The Last Intellectuals* from 1987, which bemoans the demise of a 'generation of public thinkers and their replacement by "bloodless academicians"' (Žižek, 2011: 212). Jacoby himself describes what he calls a 'public intellectual' as 'roughly an intellectual who uses the vernacular and writes for more than specialists, an intellectual who remains committed to a public', adding that '[t]hey wrote to be read' (Jacoby, 2000: 40–41). If, for Jacoby, public intellectuals (like Edmund Wilson or Lionel Trilling) have disappeared, Brockman (1996: 17) sees their reappearance within what he calls 'the third culture', a culture which 'consists of those scientists and other thinkers in the empirical world who, through their work and expository writing, are taking the place of the traditional intellectual in rendering visible the deeper meanings of our lives, redefining who and what we are'. What Brockman seems to be articulating is a nostalgia for the gradual unfolding of an ultimate 'truth', the revelation of which, however remote, will materialise as an alternative to the various kinds of scepticism and constructivism that have made their way into the world through all sorts of textual studies, translation studies included.

In Brockman's view, bloodless academicians seem to be those scholars whose intellectual achievements are not geared to a wider readership and who do not offer any deeper exploration or useful explanation of the profundity of human nature. Rather, they ignore the answers to the crucial questions of what, and who, we 'really' are. The alleged bloodless academicians do not spread any true knowledge about the human condition but are among an audience hungry for it, craving facts and scientifically explicit solutions on the level of ontology. This testifies to a certain anaemia of theory, to the lack of power to communicate anything relevant and useful to a public that is alien to academic theorisations and their hermetic textualisations. As I will try to show, however, the seeming weakness of translation studies in the face of 'truth' is precisely what constitutes its empowerment as a critical discourse: by exploring the ways in which (multimodal) textualities may be misread, translation studies points to the ideological rootedness of ostensibly visionary projects such as Brockman's 'third culture'.

Translation studies, which tends to identify itself as an academic 'interdiscipline', seems to constitute a perfect example of powerless academic speculation. As an interdiscipline, it does not even have a properly delimited space to circumscribe the kinds of 'truths' it could possibly communicate. Moreover, by extensively drawing from post-structural and postmodern theory, translation studies disempowers itself by endowing power with negativity, constantly suspecting its object of study of carrying strong potential for ideological manipulation. In looking critically at manifestations of traditional ideas of authorship, patriarchal values or ethnic exclusions in relation to various translational strategies and practices, translation studies seems to be following the postmodernist tendency to uncover the negativity of power mainly in those spheres in which this negativity is too obvious. This is exactly what Terry Eagleton sees as one of the critical reasons for the failure of the postmodernist promise for political change: 'One reason why postmodernism instinc-tively suspects power as negative is that the forms of power which most engage its attention are exactly that. There was never a good word to be said for patriarchy or racial supremacism' (Eagleton, 1996: 56).

Good words for critical concepts such as patriarchy and authori-tarianism, however, seem to be propounded by Brockman's concept of the third culture and its advocates who, as Žižek puts it, 'elevate scientists into a "subject supposed to know"' (2011: 213), into a position of fully knowledgeable individuals whose texts simply reveal and clarify 'the ultimate enigmas ("reading the mind of God", as Hawking was once credited with)' (Žižek, 2011: 215–216). The third culture quite clearly revives the Barthesian 'zero-degree writing', the idea of a transparent, readerly (*lisible*) text whose ultimate truths place it outside the scope of any cultural or ideological manipulation. What is ultimately posited is a certain innocence of language, whose proper use may serve an equally innocent purpose of communication: who speaks, or writes, and the places from which one speaks, are just as irrelevant as the medium of communication itself. What is crucial, and what carries power within the social world in which we live, therefore, is *what* we say. The *how*, the manner, the style, the fashion, the mode of speaking and the context, become disempowered, and it is only the bloodless academicians who, for some reason, make a fuss over their relevance. What translation studies to a certain extent reveals, however, is that the *how* is always already involved in any act of communication, thereby rendering the power of language crucial in thinking about what and who we are. Nevertheless, translation scholars tend to reject the possibility of offering eventual answers to those questions. The repudiation of this power reflects a certain 'uncanniness of the ordinary', described by Stanley Cavell as 'the capacity, even desire, of ordinary language to repudiate itself, specifically to repudiate its power to word the world' (Cavell, 1988: 154).

Translation studies, very much like ordinary language, rejects the illusion of the 'mastered tongue' (Cavell, 1988: 154) which transparently words the world, ideally without traces of its having been used. In a sense, this disclaimer makes translation studies powerless, but this powerlessness carries along a constant threat to the purported innocence of language, a threat which can be rebutted only by way of attempting to ignore it as irrelevant, marginal, powerless or bloodless. Such a marginalisation, in turn, empowers translation studies with a repressed discourse that becomes one of the voices of subalternity. Unlike other 'sanguinary' academic disciplines which produce a kind of knowledge which 'is itself involved in the "othering" of the subaltern' (Beverley, 1999: 2), translation studies 'de-others' knowledge; it helps to reveal that the actual fluidity and instability of 'sanguinary' knowledge is hidden in seemingly neutral translational practices. Translation studies does not answer the unanswerable ontological questions of what or who we really are, but at least it points to the ways in which certain meanings that affect the human condition are negotiable and disputable across languages and cultures. The problematisation of the question of who or what we 'really' are, and more broadly of the question of identity, clearly positions translation studies within the wider realms of cultural studies. This, as Sherry Simon puts it, 'principally means that the terms "culture", "identity" and "gender" are not taken for granted but are themselves the object of inquiry. They are no longer self-explanatory notions which can be used unquestioningly' (Simon, 1996: x). And their questioning simultaneously puts in motion what Lawrence Venuti calls 'the identity-forming power of translation', which is the power of changing rather than surrendering to established and institutionalised forms of identity. For Venuti, this power seems to be subversive, as it 'always threatens to embarrass cultural and political institutions because it reveals the shaky foundations of their social authority' (Venuti, 1998: 68).

A few recent turns within translation studies which focus on the social impact of translation make this discipline an important link between intellectual isolation and the public sphere of discursive exchange. Translation studies opens up a possibility for recovering individual human agency behind texts which became 'de-authored' in the modern era, when, as claimed by Michel Foucault, authentication 'no longer required reference to the individual who had produced them; the role of the author disappeared as an index of truthfulness' (Foucault, 1977: 126). Yet, the recovery of the translator's agency does not naïvely try to ascribe intention and purpose to individual actions. Readers, indeed, have become increasingly aware of the decisive role of ideology in the configuration of any text, and they are less willing to tolerate instances of ideological 'manipulation'. For instance, the ideological distortion in the first English translation of Bertolt Brecht's *Mother Courage* from 1941, which weakened 'the obvious connection between war and commerce' (Lefevere, 2000: 244), would hardly go unnoticed today.

A crucial issue in this respect remains the questioning of the invisibility of the translator, which problematises strongly established notions such as authorial intention and textual transparency in relation to their alleged capacity to communicate truths. These concepts are part and parcel of dominating 'cultural trends' according to which 'it seems inevitable that transparency would become the authoritative discourse for translating, whether the foreign text was literary or scientific/technical' (Venuti, 2004: 6). By challenging the transparency of the text and the demand for the translator's invisibility, translation studies seems to be working against the alleged power of language to express final truths. The interdiscipline appears to remain powerless, indeed anaemic and bloodless, when confronted with truth(s) and meaning(s) traditionally conceived as somehow located 'inside' an 'original' text. This ultimate truth/knowledge is always already 'lost in translation', and the idea of the author's 'authentic' intention turns out to be an ideological manipulation. To be sure, such manipulation echoes a strong belief in the completeness of authorial intention, which may thus become compromised through translational losses. In this respect, the metaphysical conception of an authentic truth conveyed by pre-linguistic meaning carries significant disadvantages for any practising translator: 'On the one hand, translation is defined as a second-order representation: only the foreign text can be original, an authentic copy, true to the author's personality or intention, whereas the translation is derivative, fake, potentially a false copy' (Venuti, 2004: 6–7).

In his numerous writings on language and translation, Jacques Derrida, perhaps bloodlessly, has pointed to the fragility and vagueness of the notion of the original and to the inevitability of translation in any kind of communicative practice. In *The Ear of the Other*, and commenting on Walter Benjamin's essay 'The Task of the Translator', Derrida relates the idea of the original to a phantasmatic and untouchable kernel which can be identified as desire itself: 'This desire for the intact kernel', he writes, 'is irreducible – despite the fact that there is no kernel' (Derrida, 1988: 42). What this desire evokes is a sense of loss, a sense of having lost something which, in fact, has never existed. The idea of losing something in translation is paired with a paradoxical nostalgia which conjures up the desired object and simultaneously posits it as lacking something. This brings into play the transactional dimension of translation, an economy of translation that largely operates in the sphere of hypothetical and imaginary losses and gains, and which engenders 'a desire for meaning as value': 'The act of translation thus hypothesizes an exchange of *equivalent* signs and makes up that *equivalence* where there is none perceived as such' (Liu, 1999: 34; original emphasis).

The translational economy of imaginary equivalence, therefore, 'translates' loss into an equally imaginary category. Something that is lost is perceived as absent, and this perception is, according to Slavoj Žižek, a result of a certain melancholic interpretation. If desire is driven by a sense of lack, of incompleteness and non-fulfilment, because it does not correspond to anything attainable, 'melancholy interprets this lack as loss, as if the lacking object was once possessed and then lost' (Žižek, 2000: 659–660). Loss is produced by the phantasmatic idea of once having possessed what has been lost – despite its non-existence. Translation studies, however, by challenging the myth of transparent communication, has questioned the 'translation' of lack into loss, disengaging the pairing which, as Žižek (2000: 660) puts it, under the regime of transparency, 'enables us to assert our possession of the object'.

The object, in the case of idealised visions of translation, is the original: the original meaning, the original intention. For Žižek, it is merely an object of fixation of a melancholic who 'possesses it in its very loss' (Žižek, 2000: 660). This melancholic possession of the original constitutes the fragile origin of the conceptual possibility of loss in translation, which places translation in the sphere of economic and commodities exchange. But the fear of loss, which is grounded in economic principles, need not be the attitude motivating the practice of translation and, in fact, it could be argued that translation studies has opened up a new perspective by way of also considering the possibility of gain in translation. According to Susan Bassnett, this became possible thanks to the questioning of the idea, or the principle, of sameness between languages:

> Once the principle is accepted that sameness cannot exist between two languages, it becomes possible to approach the question of *loss and gain* in the translation process. It is again an indication of the low status of translation that so much time should have been spent on discussing what is lost in the transfer of a text from SL to TL whilst ignoring what can also be gained, for the translator can at times enrich or clarify the SL text as a direct result of the translation process. (Bassnett, 2013: 39; original emphasis)

The phrase 'authentic copy' with reference to an original, which Venuti uses in the already quoted fragment – 'only the foreign text can be original, an authentic copy, true to the author's personality or intention' – clearly signals the crisis of the mere possibility of possessing an authentic object that is not a copy. The oxymoron 'authentic copy' communicates the possibility of a coexistence of copy and original which does not mark the original as lost, but which saturates the copy with originality. According to Žižek, melancholic desire conceals 'that the object is lacking from the very beginning, that its emergence coincides with its lack, that this object is *nothing but* the positivization of a void or lack, a purely anamorphic entity that does not exist in itself' (Žižek, 2000: 660; original emphasis). The object, though lacking, is not simply lost or missing, and its lack only marks it as imperfect, perhaps unfinished. What this puts in question is the full presence of the original. From Venuti's perspective, the entrance of translation into the fray questions the copy's secondary status and allows for its conceptualisation not in terms of the original's lost 'truth', but rather in terms of mutual contamination: the act of translation inscribes lack into the original while the original inevitably renders the translation as lacking. What may get lost in translation is only Venuti's 'authentic copy', which discloses a lack within the 'authentic' original, the lack of an allegedly undistorted message whose existence can only be the melancholic reconstruction of the possession of the original. Žižek rightly calls the translation of lack into loss a 'deceitful translation', since 'what we never possessed can also never be lost' (Žižek, 2000: 660). Since this illusory possession results from the melancholic 'unconditional fixation on the lost object' (Žižek, 2000: 660), the melancholic presence of the original in its very loss is reminiscent of the act of mourning, which forms a crucial part of Derrida's phenomenology of meaning and presence.

For Derrida, reading demands – as does any act of interpretation and translation – an act of mourning, a reference to an absent presence, to a dead author, in an attempt to somehow endow this absence with a presence and commemorate it in the act of interpretation. 'This mourning', writes Derrida, 'provides the first chance and the terrible condition of all reading' (2001: 220). Without mourning there is no readability; reading, like mourning, always involves a melancholia whose linguistic existence is produced through what Walter Benjamin calls 'overnaming', a secondary language that impotently tries to recover, or revive, the originary language of things:

> Things have no proper names except in God. For in his creative word, God called them into being, calling them by their proper names. In the language of men, however, they are overnamed. There is, in the relation of human languages to that of things, something that can be approximately described as 'overnaming' – the deepest linguistic reason for all melancholy. (Benjamin, 1996: 73)

As pointed out by Martin Jay, overnaming has frustrated the project of regaining the lost language of God after the destruction of Babel and has produced 'the melancholy of a disenchanted world of nature, no longer at one with its original names' (Jay, 2009: 173), named not from the one blessed paradisiacal language of names, but from the hundred languages of man, in which name has already withered, yet which, according to God's pronouncement, have knowledge of things. (Benjamin, 1996: 73)

Benjamin's overnaming is linked to the problematics of translation through its reference both to the idea of original meaning and to its secondary, repeated and thus derivative rendition in some different language which mourns over the loss of something that it simultaneously recalls and which cannot be simply reduced to lack or absence. This absence is in fact an apparition, a spectre, a trace of the utopian full presence of the author, whose message should remain 'unmediated by trans-individual determinants (linguistic, cultural, social) that might complicate authorial originality' (Venuti, 2004: 7). Though Venuti does not refer to Benjamin in this respect, his criticism of the view of translation as second-order representation implicitly evokes mourning. Like mourning, which melancholically evokes the lost object, the second-order translation evokes the author without reducing him or her to absence, but also without allowing him or her to speak in a fully articulated voice. The translator thus accepts what Venuti calls 'weird self-annihilation', a reduction to invisibility which constitutes 'a way of conceiving and practicing translation that undoubtedly reinforces its marginal status in Anglo-American culture' (Venuti, 2004: 8).

In this way, translation becomes a repetition which hides its own failure, a manipulation whose ideal task is to translate loss into presence. From the perspective of translation studies, this task could be viewed as an attempt to return to the time *prior* to Roland Barthes's announcement of the death of the author (Barthes, 1977), an attempt to bring back the authoritative voice of an untranslated truth. Translation, however, evokes what is lost and brings it to spectral visibility. Spectres are, or at least seem to be, bloodless: they cannot speak their own language and, perhaps like the nymph Echo, can produce only an aura of reverberation. Like Brockman's bloodless academicians, spectres cannot reveal anything authentic; they cannot produce any strong statements and communicate them directly to others. The spectres evoked by the melancholy discourse of mourning appear as the effects of what Milad Doueihi recognises as a 'phantasm of incorporation', which she analyses in the context of the funerary meal as a way of dealing with the experience of death (Doueihi, 1997: 5–11). The meal, and the accompanying speeches, evoke the dead and rhetorically set up a relationship of phantasmagoric communion with the dead person, a relationship whose expression in language simultaneously bids farewell to its possibility: 'The speaker, in the case of the phantasm of incorporation', writes Doueihi (1997: 8), 'utters words that are his words but that are also not his, words that ultimately belong to an other who cannot be recognized or named because it has, once and for all, disappeared, faded away under its own skin'.

The weakness, or bloodlessness, of overnaming is posited against, and in opposition to, the power of naming, represented among others by Brockman's idealised third culture.[1] It is a project opposed to the 'increasingly reactionary' (Brockman, 1991) culture of (American) intellectuals who replace true, empirically supported statements with an endless jargon of words about words, of commentaries about commentaries, and so on, which do not really mean anything. The culture of these 'old' intellectuals, according to Brockman, 'dismisses science, is often non-empirical. It uses its own jargon and washes its own laundry. It is chiefly characterized by comment on comments, the swelling spiral of commentary eventually reaching the point where the real world gets lost' (Brockman, 1996: 17). In our discipline, the original is the empirical object of the 'real' world, which the intellectuals, those bloodless academicians, leave behind in their commentaries and theorisations. Reality is lost in translation as a running commentary; it figures as a lack which the third culture will eventually make up for. Even though Brockman seems not to be engaged in thinking about translation, he implicitly evokes the possibility of an ideal rendition of the world, an actually thoroughly translational question. Translation studies, on the other hand, refrains from looking at translation as a means which brings one closer to an idealised original, because it sees the distance between the original and its expression as irreducible, be it on the intralingual or the interlingual level. The recognition of this irreducible distance, an empirical fact, if you wish, puts those who recognise it, for instance attentive students of translation, in the position of a public enemy of sorts, as someone who – rather than being 'a synthesizer, a publicist, a communicator' (Brockman, 1991), which is what a 'proper' third culture intellectual should be – obstructs the smoothness of communication and does not participate in moulding the intellectual *Zeitgeist* of their generation: 'The role of the intellectual includes communicating. Intellectuals are not just people who know things but people who shape the thoughts of their generation' (Brockman, 1996: 19). What seems to be at stake here is more than the communication of truth. Lurking in Brockman's projection are some masters of truth who, very much like Freud's leaders of the lazy rabble,[2] ought to think for others and guide them to a better future. 'Throughout history', Brockman tells his readers, 'only a small number of people have done the serious thinking for everybody else', and today we can observe 'a passing of the torch from one group of thinkers, the traditional literary intellectuals, to a new group, the intellectuals of the emerging third culture' (Brockman, 1991).

The hoped for re-emergence of the third culture appears to be threatened by the bloodless powerlessness of those who do not think, and do not even think about thinking, 'for everybody else'. The fear of bloodless academicians, clearly discernible in Brockman's text, points to the existence of significant power, if only the power of knowledge, attached to textual studies and its practice. The power of translation studies is located in its ability to estrange, to defamiliarise gridlocked ways of thinking and behaviour, or simply to question the presuppositions of originality and the apparent fixity of meanings. One aspect of this power seems to be a strong text-based motion against the totalitarianism (and in the case of Brockman quite rightly so) of cultural, ideological and political strategies that convey a melancholic nostalgia for ultimate truths.

The questioning of this nostalgia for truth may result in deference to the text, and hence the relationship between the text and the translator may be that of surrender rather than conquest: 'I surrender to the text when I translate', writes Gayatri Spivak in 'The Politics of Translation' (Spivak, 2000b: 370). Rather than mastering the text, the translator takes up a position in which the text is given the upper hand, which somehow limits the creative freedom of the translator. By means of surrender, however, 'the translator earns permission to transgress' (Spivak, 2000b: 370), a permission to recalibrate the text in a relationship which is not that between enemies, but rather a loving, even erotic, relation between friends: 'To surrender in translation is more erotic than ethical' (p. 373). Such a surrender to the Other is the position which translation studies seems to have chosen. The surrender is not passive, since it may work by means of surrendering one's home to the guest, in accordance with the law of hospitality in which the guest is welcome though does not fully master the home. This hospitality, or perhaps the power of hospitality, is also reflected in the possibility of looking at translation as rewriting, a rewriting which is not simply a passive repetition but an active and creative engagement in which another text, the rewritten text, participates rather than dictates what should, or must, be rewritten.

Translation seen as rewriting inevitably implies ideological decisions. Susan Bassnett and André Lefevere notice in the general editors' preface to Venuti's *The Translator's Invisibility* that '[a]ll rewritings, whatever their intention, reflect a certain ideology and a poetics and as such manipulate literature to function in a given society in a given way' (Venuti, 2004: vii). In view of the power of any social authority, the effects of such a manipulation can be blindly accepted as obvious, real or true, or they can be critically evaluated and studied along with their contextual determinations and historical repercussions. A critical look may point to the totalitarian threat within seemingly innocent discursive formations that appear to 'over-empower' the dictating author, and in so doing it may increase an awareness of the manipulative nature of texts. Bassnett and Lefevere quite rightly use the word 'awareness' rather than 'knowledge' with reference to the potential outcomes of studying translational rewritings:

> Rewritings can introduce new concepts, new genres, new devices, and the history of translation is the history also of literary innovation, of the shaping power of one culture upon another. But rewriting can also repress innovation, distort and contain, and in an age of ever increasing

manipulation of all kinds, the study of the manipulative processes of literature as exemplified by translation can help us toward a greater awareness of the world in which we live. (Venuti, 2004: vii)

An awareness of the changeable milieu in whose construction we partici- pate as its translators results in the awareness of this milieu's complexity, its overwritten status, which is graspable only as a melancholy spectre of what preceded it. The alleged power of knowledge is the power to stabilise this changeability. From such a perspective, the fact that we, inevitably, translate can be used as a proof of the existence of translation's haunting predecessor, of a constant presence which avoids and evades loss in the fun-house of translation. For Stanley Rosen, for example, it is the very existence of translation which constitutes the proof of there being a universal and unchangeable 'something' to which the potentiality of translation testifies: 'despite the fears of some philosophers', he points out in his book on the possibility of philosophy, 'we can translate one natural language into another. This is enough to render entirely plausible the belief in some constancy of human nature that persists across linguistic change and serves as the basis for the intelligibility of translation' (Rosen, 2002: 226). The survival of the constancy of human nature seems to be the proof of the possibility of philosophy. What is translated/overwritten only revives something beyond it, a permanence of the world which philosophy will embrace, cherish and protect. It is a permanence that cannot be presented other than in a silence whose disruption inescapably brings change.

Even though bloodless, the academicians involved in translation studies are at least aware of the absurdity of certainty. If *translation changes everything*, as apparent from the title of Venuti's recent essay col- lection, then the power of translation studies may consist in its strength to overcome the 'fear of change' (Venuti, 2013: 10) on which the instrumental model of translation depends, along with its insistence 'on the existence of a source variant' (Venuti, 2013: 8). Power, therefore, speaks itself through translation, whose simultaneous necessity and impossibility indicate that its loss does not necessarily entail its lack. Translation is necessary, because all communication depends on it. It is also impossible, because it is always too weak to communicate. This weakness, however, is not a defect; it is merely a sign of a certain powerlessness of power which indicates that meaning is always negotiable across languages and cultures.

Notes

(1) While Brockman does not write about mourning or overnaming, his idea of a third culture virtually epitomises the Derridean 'metaphysics of presence', Derrida's well known umbrella term for the belief in a transcendental, self-present *logos* which precedes any expression. An approximate equivalent of 'metaphysics of presence' is

Derrida's term 'logocentrism'. Derrida wrote a lot about translation and its philosophical and cultural aspects. An invaluable source of information about Derrida's impact on translation studies is Kathleen Davis's (2001) *Deconstruction and Translation*, which also features an extensive bibliography.

(2) 'It is only through the influence of individuals who can set an example and whom masses recognize as their leaders [*Führers*] that they can be induced to perform the work and undergo renunciations on which the existence of civilization depends' (Freud, 1961: 9–10).

References

Barthes, R. (1977) The death of the author (S. Heath, trans.). In *Image, Music, Text* (pp. 142–148). New York: Hill and Wang.

Bassnett, S. (2013) *Translation Studies*. London: Routledge.

Benjamin, W. (1996) On language as such and on the languages of man (E. Jephcott, trans.). In M. Bullock and M.W. Jennings (eds) *W. Benjamin, Selected Writings: Volume 1, 1913–1926* (pp. 62–74). Cambridge, MA: Harvard University Press.

Beverley, J. (1999) *Subalternity and Representation: Arguments in Cultural Theory*. Durham, NC: Duke University Press.

Brockman, J. (1991) The emerging third culture, at http://www.edge.org/the-third-culture, accessed 22 June 2016.

Brockman, J. (1996) *Third Culture: Beyond the Scientific Revolution*. London: Simon and Schuster.

Cavell, S. (1988) *In Quest of the Ordinary: Lines on Skepticism and Romanticism*. Chicago, IL: Chicago University Press.

Davis, K. (2001) *Deconstruction and Translation*. London: Routledge.

Derrida J. (1988) *The Ear of the Other: Otobiography, Transference, Translation* (P. Kamuf, trans.). New York: Schocken Books.

Derrida, J. (2001) *The Work of Mourning* (P.-A. Brault and M. Naas, eds). Chicago, IL: University of Chicago Press.

Doueihi, M. (1997) *A Perverse History of the Human Heart*. Cambridge, MA: Harvard University Press.

Eagleton, T. (1996) *The Illusions of Postmodernism*. Oxford: Blackwell.

Foucault, M. (1977) What is an author? In D.F. Bouchard (trans. and ed.) *Language, Counter-Memory, Practice: Selected Essays and Interviews by Michel Foucault* (pp. 113–138). Ithaca, NY: Cornell University Press.

Freud, S. (1961) *The Future of an Illusion* (J. Strachey, trans.). New York: Norton.

Jacoby, R. (2000) Intellectuals and their discontents. *Hedgehog Review*, fall, 36–52.

Jay, M. (2009) Magical nominalism: Photography and the re-enchantment of the world. *Culture, Theory and Critique* 50 (2–3), 165–183.

Lefevere, A. (2000) Mother Courage's cucumbers: Text, system and refraction in a theory of literature. In L. Venuti (ed.) *The Translation Studies Reader* (pp. 233–249). London: Routledge.

Liu, L. (1999) The question of meaning-value in the political economy of the sign. In L. Liu (ed.) *Tokens of Exchange: The Problem of Translation in Global Circulations* (pp. 13–41). Durham, NC: Duke University Press.

Rosen, S. (2002) *The Elusiveness of the Ordinary: Studies in the Possibility of Philosophy*. New Haven, CT: Yale University Press.

Simon, S. (1996) *Gender in Translation: Cultural Identity and the Politics of Transmission*. London: Routledge.

Spivak, G.C. (2000a) Translation as culture. *Parallax* 6 (1), 13–24.

Spivak, G.C. (2000b) The politics of translation. In L. Venuti (ed) *The Translation Studies Reader* (pp. 369–388). London: Routledge.

Venuti, L. (1998) *The Scandals of Translation: Towards an Ethics of Difference*. London: Routledge.

Venuti, L. (2004) *The Translator's Invisibility: A History of Translation*. London: Routledge.

Venuti, L. (2013) *Translation Changes Everything: Theory and Practice*. London: Routledge.

Žižek, S. (2000) Melancholy and the act. *Critical Inquiry* 26, 657–681.

Žižek, S. (2011) *Did Somebody Say Totalitarianism? Five Interventions in the (Mis)Use of a Nation*. London: Verso.

3 Turning Minorities and Majorities Upside Down

Luc van Doorslaer

Language and/or Translation Policy

Language policy is a topic that has been extensively researched in political science and sociolinguistics. For practical and organisational reasons, we divide the world into smaller parts (continents and sub-continents; states, countries and regions; provinces, cities and districts), out of which may emerge complex multilingual situations. In an attempt to deal with linguistic diversity, authorities and policy-makers have developed language policies at very different levels: in multi-state organisations (such as the United Nations or the European Union), at the national or federal level of officially multilingual countries (such as South Africa, Canada, Switzerland or Belgium), and even at the lower regional or local level (e.g. city regulations about language use in local museums). These different types of language policy can be characterised as *top-down*: authorities impose a given policy by making use of laws or other types of regulation. Most modern language policies (at least in democratic societies) take into account, to a greater or lesser extent, local or regional sensitivities. Obviously, there are also many historical examples of non-democratic, totalitarian imposition of languages, particularly in situations of colonialism, cultural domination, ideological unification or political authoritarianism. Emily Apter discusses the work of the French linguist Louis-Jean Calvet, who has studied the historical cultural domination of the French and Russian languages, as examples of top-down linguistic intervention:

> Calvet shows how this French linguistic colonization of itself was extended to the colonies, documenting the application of French language policies *outre mer*, and the consequent consolidation of a dominant French culture in territories outside the Hexagon. He also examines the lack of tolerance for minority languages in Russia – both before and after the Revolution. The doctrine of 'One Tsar, one religion, one language' is transformed by the Soviet regime into the mandate of a society without frontiers or

nations. This 'unique culture' was supposed to evolve in stages, from 'rastvet' (the flowering of different cultures), to 'sblizheniye' (their coming together), to 'sliyaniye' (the emergence of harmonious unity in a single world language). (Apter, 2006: 136–137)

Recently, researchers have started to pay more attention to *bottom-up* language practices, which may also implicitly impact on the formation of language policies. Such research often focuses on dynamic multilingual situations created by immigration in urban areas, examining everyday language-related experiences in modern cities, such as menus in several languages, texts on display windows, and so on. Jan Blommaert defines this bottom-up approach as typical of 'a discipline that digs into the smallest details of momentary events, but propels them towards the highest levels of contextual determination' (2013: 119). In his book *Ethnography, Superdiversity and Linguistic Landscapes*, which focuses on contemporary Antwerp, Blommaert applies a 'nano-sociolinguistic approach' to the failure of the gentrification policies developed by local or city authorities (2013: 116). This case study shows that social and linguistic transformations are highly complex and lack synchronicity in particularly diverse, or 'superdiverse', city areas. Whereas in Antwerp the use of standard Dutch once used to be a sign of the social upgrading of a given district, this is no longer necessarily true. Partly independent from class stratification and upward social mobility, several types of Dutch with thick immigrant accents are now being used as 'ecumenical Dutch' (Blommaert, 2013: 77). This form of 'ecumenical' Dutch fulfils similar pragmatic functions both in new high-end businesses and in budget stores, and is therefore proving itself as an adequate sociolectal variety in this particular urban area. In terms of local governance, however, the constant social evolution and complex language characteristics of a given district, which are part of wider changes in attitudes, lifestyles and values typical of gentrification, make it difficult for local authorities to develop traditional language or (non-)translation policies.

Another recent publication on 'nano-sociolinguistics', which could be described as the context-sensitive interpretation of smaller-scale linguistic phenomena, is Pennycook and Otsuji's (2015) monograph *Metrolingualism: Language in the City*, which deals with urban linguistic diversity in places like markets, restaurants, shops, cafés and streets. It is interesting to note that sociolinguists like Blommaert or Pennycook and Otsuji approach urban multilingual life without paying attention to the centrality and omnipresence of translation, which is most likely a consequence of the traditional view in the field of linguistics that translation is a text-bound activity based on the concept of equivalence. In contrast to such a narrowed-down idea of translation, sociolinguistic research investigates context-bound linguistic diversity, and as such it has developed conceptual categories and analytical tools that are able to describe much more complex and dynamic processes than 'simple' translation. Pennycook and Otsuji, for instance, abundantly use the term *translanguaging*, defined by Ofelia García as the '*multiple discursive practices* in which bilinguals engage in order to *make sense of their bilingual worlds*' (quoted in Pennycook & Otsuji, 2015: 180–181; original emphasis). This analytical concept refers to codeswitching in multilingual and migrant urban settings, but is also used in language education. In a similar vein, yet with a sustained focus on the centrality of non-professional acts of translation in diverse metropolitan contexts, Flynn and van Doorslaer (2016) explore the links between migration, urban life and non-institutionalised translation. Their study shows how monolingual and monocultural biases, as well as a persistent focus on national languages, have prevented us for a long time 'from taking urban multilingualism seriously and examining its dynamics more pertinently, particularly from a translational perspective' (Flynn & van Doorslaer, 2016: 88). Pennycook and Otsuji's notion of metrolingual 'translanguaging spaces' shows a clear resemblance to Michael Cronin's discussion of 'translation spaces' (Cronin, 2006: 68), to the point that it can be argued that translation spaces 'are further manifestations of translanguaging spaces that have incorporated various degrees of language brokering [...], ad hoc interpreting or translation' as well as further crosslinguistic varieties 'that have become part of the local economy in all its various aspects' (Flynn & van Doorslaer, 2016: 79).

Sherry Simon's study of the role of multilingualism in city contexts from a cross-cultural and translation perspective is another example of how sociolinguistics can contribute to the debate on translation policies (Simon, 2006, 2012, 2014). Simon investigates the key role played by immigrants in the linguistic dynamics of metropolitan areas, particularly in relation to the phenomenon of self-translation, focusing on her home town of Montreal, but also on other linguistically diverse cities, like Calcutta, Trieste or Barcelona. Although translation policy (in the 'political' sense of the word) is not explicitly present in her work, several of her ideas can be used to better understand translation practices in city life. This would apply to ideological questions concerning the (in)equality of languages where translation is involved, especially against the backdrop of (economic) globalisation, cultural imperialism, migration and citizenship, social alienation as well as modernisation and grassroots empowerment. Pennycook and Otsuji (2015) briefly mention Simon's work, but only because her ideas can be connected to cultural and linguistic diversity and not because translation (let alone translation policy) plays a crucial role in the linguistic dynamics of modern urban settings.

Michael Cronin (2012) has shown that the different stages of linguistic integration in modern immigration societies, as well as the sociological genealogy of intercultural understanding, can also be described in translational terms, in relation to both professional and non-professional practices. He describes a three-stage level of translational interaction:

Phase 1 interaction is heteronomous translation, which involves relying on someone to do the translation for you, whether it is the interpreter in an outpatients' clinic or a Polish personal assistant negotiating with local suppliers in Warsaw for a foreign businessperson. Interpreting, no matter how proficient, takes time and already there is a sense in which time is beginning to 'thicken' in phase 1 translation exchange. Phase 2 is the shift towards semi-autonomous translation, where subjects want to begin to learn the language themselves and, in a sense, do their own translation. They begin to invest a certain amount of time in the process so that the durational reality of time begins to take precedence over the instantaneous. [...] Phase 3 is full-autonomous translation, where subjects become fully functioning bilinguals or plurilinguals whose competence involves extensive expenditure of time either as a result of circumstance (being brought up in bilingual/multilingual environments, working and living in a foreign country) or acquisition (formal language study). All three phases involve the acknowledgement of the state of dwelling with the shift from the heteronomous to the autonomous modes of translation [...]. (Cronin, 2012: 187)

These three interactional phases illustrate the extent to which translation often plays a pivotal role in institutional language policies and urban language practices. Under such conditions, real-time language transfer and interaction become more prominent and visible, and inevitably more time is invested in elements of the communication process that in more unproblematic monolingual settings remain below the surface. Cronin's approach has parallels with Blommaert's research on sociolinguistic complexity and the constant change and non-synchronicity of linguistic development in small-scale sociolinguistic phenomena. It makes the 'disturbing' elements of translational interaction in multilingual settings explicit and raises awareness of the intermediary position of translation in language transfers. Whereas in earlier work on translation policy Cronin (1995) focused on more traditional social groups and their relationships with multilingualism, language and power, specifically in view of minority languages and translation flows, his more recent work develops similar lines of thinking, but now predominantly applying them to the micro-levels involved in multiculturalism and the struggles for language difference. In both cases the common theme is 'the persistent misreadings of European cultural history through neglect of its plurilingual nature' (Cronin, 1995: 99).

If we accept that language policies are developed as a response to language conflict, then translation is the most important instrument for moderating this conflict. Based on this assumption, Reine Meylaerts wrote that 'there is no *language* policy without a *translation* policy' (2011: 744; original emphasis). The resolution of conflicts by means of translation and language policies, however, 'involves accepting that there is no final, definitive reconciliation of opposites but that any arrangement is a provisional, unstable equilibrium which does not rule out further conflict in the future' (Cronin, 2012: 182). It is obvious that the concept of translation is used here in a broad, non-stable sense, in constant interplay with societal and political changes. It includes differing acts of linguistic and communicative mediation and is not limited to Roman Jakobson's (1959) notion of interlingual transfer ('translation proper'), since it extends to different types of intralingual transfer (rewording, rewriting and paraphrasing) as well as intersemiotic translation (transmutation and transfer to another semiotic system).

Translation Policy in Translation Studies

There has been surprisingly limited attention to the topic of translation policy in the field of translation studies. A search (in July 2018) conducted in the online *Translation Studies Bibliography* (Gambier & van Doorslaer, 2014) produced many more results for 'language policy' (131 hits) than for 'translation policy' (55 hits). It could be argued that the neglect of the central role of translation in language policies is in part a result of the Romantic paradigm, according to which a nation, a language, a literature and a culture should coincide. Language policies, however, are usually a result of language contact situations, and complex multilingual contexts and interactions cannot be understood through the lens of traditional source–target dichotomies. Post-national and post-colonial approaches have explored and challenged such binary oppositions. Examples can be found in research on the role of orality (e.g. Bandia, 2008) or on complex multilingual production and reception settings of translations (e.g. Kruger, 2012). Since the so-called power turn, translational power relationships in societies where multilingualism now is more present and accepted than only a couple of decades ago have attracted increasing attention from scholars (Snell-Hornby, 2006). Translation is nowadays studied as an instrument with political, cultural and/or linguistic impact, and translators themselves have become a prominent object of sociological research, being increasingly conceptualised as agents capable of developing their own political, cultural or linguistic agenda (cf. Chesterman, 2009, who calls for a 'translator studies').

Reine Meylaerts (2010, 2011) has differentiated four models of translational regimes in relation to communicative interactions between the authorities and citizens, ranging from absolute institutional multilingualism (and translation) to complete institutional monolingualism (and non-translation):

(1) complete institutional multilingualism with obligatory multidirectional translation in all languages for all (e.g. the European Union's translation policy for its 24 official languages);
(2) institutional monolingualism and translation into minority languages

(e.g. the translation of some US administrative documents, usually occasional and temporary);

(3) institutional monolingualism combined with institutional multi-lingualism (e.g. federal countries such as Canada or Switzerland, which offer institutional multilingualism at the federal level, but institutional monolingualism at the regional or local level);

(4) complete institutional monolingualism and non-translation (e.g. nation-states such as the Netherlands, but also states with a multi-lingual population yet in practice only one official language, such as 19th-century Belgium).

In social, economic or political situations where more than one language is being used, ideological interests collide and explicit or implicit power relationships develop, often as a result of the opposition between majority and minority populations.

The definition of minority languages is neither obvious nor static, as it can depend on changing circumstances. Alternatives have been suggested, such as 'lesser used languages' or 'state' versus 'non-state languages'. Baumgarten and Gruber (2014: 31), for instance, point out that these terms show a historically evolving reality, whereas the concept of 'minority language' is 'located within an artificially framed national milieu'. In 1992, the Council of Europe (a cross-national and inter-governmental organisation which does not belong to the European Union) drew up the European Charter for Regional or Minority Languages with the objective of protecting and even promoting those European languages which, for different historical or national reasons, have not become state languages, such as Catalan, Frisian or Welsh. Three main criteria were used for the delineation of the complex term 'minority language': first, it should not presently be an official state language in Europe; second, it should be a language that has been 'traditionally' used by a minority in a given territory; and third, it should not be a dialect or a language of a recently established migrant community.

In spite of the centrality of institutionalised multilingualism in many states and public organisations, the interplay between minority languages and translation has merited limited attention from scholars. The edited volume *Less Translated Languages* (Branchadell & West, 2005) is one of the few concerted scholarly efforts in which the issue of minority languages is explicitly connected to translation (but see also a special issue of the journal *Translation Studies*, 'Translation in Wales' – Miguélez-Carballeira *et al.*, 2016). In their introduction, the editors state that their aim is to study minority languages in translation against the background of nation-building processes and of the culture and power turns in modern translation studies (Branchadell & West, 2005: 1). One of the contributors, Oscar Díaz Fouces (2005), develops the concept of 'minority language' within the European Union by distinguishing three different levels: the 24 official EU languages; non-official (regional) EU languages; and migrant languages. Obviously, these levels have a direct impact on the relative translational relevance – and thus institutional legitimacy – of a language, especially with regard to the number and frequency of translations carried out. Yet, being recognised by one of the member states as an official language plays a more important role than any quantitative criterion such as numbers of native speakers. The current EU territory, for instance, is inhabited by more native speakers of Turkish than of Latvian, but only the latter is an official EU language. Categories like majority and minority, then, are relative and largely depend on a given institutional and (geo)political context.

Michaela Wolf's (2012) historical research on the former Habsburg dual monarchy (also known as the Austro-Hungarian Empire) and its multilingual interactions is an important example of how translation policies and practices can be studied from a historical and sociological point of view. Wolf bases her research on a large amount of statistical data with translational relevance which illustrates, among other examples, that it was a considerable challenge for the state to achieve a balanced national composition among railways staff, since there were even boycotts because of the translation – or rather non-translation – of train tickets and stamps. This case study shows that, in the 19th century, part of the population was already sensitive to issues of translation and its relation with social discrimination and linguistic marginalisation. Wolf also pays attention to obvious but non-institutionalised translation practices, which she calls *habitualisiertes Übersetzen* (translation that has become a habit or that has become 'habitualised'). This is a phenomenon that has hardly ever been investigated, especially in the ways in which it relates to everyday, non-institutionalised translation practices among members of the (mostly) lower social classes, such as maids, servants, craftsmen or prostitutes. On the other hand, institutionalised translation in the dual monarchy was characterised by its legal foundations, drawn up in order to cope with linguistic diversity, mainly in the education system, the army and the civil service. Wolf convincingly demonstrates how intra-monarchic migration and translation were closely intertwined in the Habsburg monarchy, and how complex views on translation policy and practices in a multi-ethnic state entered into conflict with bipolar thinking about source text and target text, or even source culture and target culture.

The experiential diversity of the previous examples shows that translation policy can relate to and impinge on diverging linguistic practices and institutional situations. The wide range of the use of the concept of translation policy is also thematised and partly problematised by Gabriel González Núñez (2016: 92), who understands it, in broad terms, 'as encompassing translation management, translation practice, and translation beliefs'. This definition serves as a transition to the case study analysed in the present chapter, the situation of the German-language community in Belgium. The analysis will show that there is an intense interaction and overlap between bottom-up and top-down approaches, as it is by no means the case that only institutionalised translation policies determine concrete translation practices. Be that as it may, the lack of such practices will also impact on the attitude of the population to political translation management, and, by extension, on political well-being in general.

Maxi–Min Concepts

Research on translation policy has been limited and typically on countries with more than one official state language, Belgium being a case in point, where the focus has been either historical or on the relationship and conflicts between Dutch and French as the two main language groups (e.g. Meylaerts, 2007; van Doorslaer, 2010). However, it is little known that German is the third official language in Belgium, which makes it worthwhile exploring the application of official translation policies within the small German-language community, particularly through the innovative lens of the Belgian philosopher Philippe van Parijs. In public discourse, Belgium is often presented as a prime example of a multilingual state. In an earlier article, I questioned 'Belgium's multilingualism myth' (van Doorslaer, 2013: 63), a phenomenon that tells us more about national processes of image-building or uncritical thinking on the part of the general media than about the country's political and linguistic realities. At an institutional level at least, Belgium decided to opt for a model that combines its individual monolingualisms, with the smaller but more densely populated northern part (Flanders) being Dutch-speaking, the southern part (Wallonia) French-speaking, and two eastern German-speaking parts (see Figure 3.1). There is only one significant exception to this institutionalised monolingualism: the capital city, Brussels, is officially bilingual (French and Dutch), but in reality it has now become a multilingual metropolis where only 50.3% of its inhabitants still use one of the two official languages as their home language (BRIO, 2013). The small German language community is located in two small territories in the Walloon region near the border with Germany (see Figure 3.1). By way of comparison, Flanders has approximately 6.5 million inhabitants, Wallonia 3.5 million, Brussels 1.1 million and the German-speaking community 80,000. It should be noted that the German-speaking territories are not strictly monolingual and that French-speakers have some limited rights (the so-called 'facilities'), which means that certain local services can also be offered in French (for instance official street signs). Similar administrative facilities for Dutch- or French-speakers also exist in a limited number of municipalities in geographical areas close to the Dutch–French language border; the situation of the exceptional municipalities with linguistic 'facilities' has been described more extensively by van Doorslaer (2010: 207) and Meylaerts (2011: 752).

Figure 3.1 Map of language areas in Belgium (from https://www.polgeonow.com/2016/12/what-is-wallonia-in-belgium.html)

The German community has a somewhat ambiguous status within the Belgian state. At the Congress of Vienna (1815) it was decided that the region belonged to the Rhine provinces of Prussia, and therefore it was integrated into the German Empire. It joined Belgium only in 1920, almost a century after Belgium's creation as a sovereign state. During the post-war negotiations in Versailles, Belgium claimed territories belonging to Luxemburg, the Netherlands and Germany as a form of compensation for the suffering and destruction experienced during World War I, but eventually received only territories around the towns of Malmédy, Eupen and Sankt-Vith. Following the Treaty of Versailles, a plebiscite was organised among the local population, but since it was not secret – voters had to register and there was a strong pressure from the authorities to vote in favour of Belgium – hardly anyone participated. At the beginning of World War II, in 1940, the territories were immediately annexed by the Nazis, and in 1945 the situation was reversed. As Belgian attempts to 'de-Germanise' the region were not successful, it was gradually accepted that the German language would have to become institutionalised. Today, Malmédy belongs to the French-speaking territory, while the other two German-language territories are recognised as a German-speaking cultural community, with German functioning as the third official state language in Belgium. However, there exists no officially recognised monolingual German region: Eupen and Sankt-Vith fully belong to the region of Wallonia. From the point of view of a translation studies researcher, hybrid linguistic areas like Brussels as well as the 'facilities' legislation lend themselves well to bottom-up, or 'micro-linguistic', metrolingual approaches. From a pragmatic and political point of view, however, institutional monolingualism based on the top-down territoriality principle, which is a type of monolingualism that tends to avoid translation, shows a higher degree of conflict prevention.

The conceptual framework developed by Philippe van Parijs in his book *Linguistic Justice for Europe and for the World* (2011) is relevant to research in translation policy. Van Parijs is a highly esteemed multilingual Belgian philosopher and political economist who has mainly concentrated on matters of basic income, ethics and linguistic justice; in the aforementioned monograph, he investigates the tensions between internationalisation, linguistic minorities, as well as the territoriality and heterogeneity principles in language policy. His work bears considerable relevance for translation research, since he proposes an approach that combines 'an accelerated worldwide democratization of competence in English with the territorial protection of a large number of languages' (van Parijs, 2011: 4). One important concept introduced by van Parijs is that of the *maxi–min language*: the language of the maximal minimal competence. At international academic conferences, the use of English has become an implicit norm, even during conversations in smaller groups, because we try to *minimise* exclusion and thus linguistic discrimination in order to achieve *maximally* effective communication (van Parijs, 2011: 14–15). The maxi–min language principle is a well known mechanism that comes into play at a micro-level (such as during conferences), but also at a larger communicative level, for instance when developing and implementing language policies in some countries. South Africa is a valid macro-level example: it is a multilingual country with 11 official languages, yet despite presenting itself as English-speaking, there is hardly any region where English is the dominant mother tongue. There is nonetheless a maxi-min language mechanism at work similar to the situation at conferences: because the potential for the exclusion of all other languages is larger than that of English, English functions as the lingua franca of South Africa, and hence English minimises exclusion and maximises effective communication. Van Parijs, however, asserts that we have to consciously reflect on the political and cultural consequences of such a communicative mechanism. As has happened with English, it is very likely that the axiom of a maxi–min principle will generate a *maxi–min dynamic* (van Parijs, 2011: 15–16). It is clear that the rewards gained by learning and using English are high, so the motivation for learning it is high. While there is of course nothing wrong with high rewards and high levels of motivation, it is also apparent that a maxi–min dynamic can easily lead to a pattern of convergence towards one single standard (even if a single standard can consist of several varieties, such as the constellation of today's so-called 'world Englishes' – the localised varieties of English worldwide). In terms of linguistic power relations, therefore, the Darwinian principle of the survival of the fittest can be readily invoked. Van Parijs mentions three examples of cities where this power effect has taken place: the Anglicisation of Montreal, the Hispanisation of Barcelona and the Frenchification of Brussels (van Parijs, 2011: 152). The three maxi–min languages in these examples are also the main colonial languages of world history: English, Spanish and French. The principle of maxi–min dynamics, combined with the history of colonialism, has cemented the hegemonic position of these three languages. It goes without saying that post-colonial linguistic policies also affect the ideological position of translation and translation policies. Whereas many African states nowadays have French as one of the state languages, meaning that many official documents are officially translated into French, which in effect leads to further institutionalisation of the ideological and political significance of the colonial language, other former French colonies in Africa no longer use French as a state language, with totally different consequences concerning the dynamics of translation and institutionalisation practices.

Another key principle for van Parijs in the achievement of linguistic justice is the notion of 'parity of esteem' (2011: 117). Because of the unbalanced and unequal power relationships between languages, it is the task of authorities and public institutions to enforce parity of esteem, and the best possible model to achieve this is a 'territorially differentiated coercive regime' (van Parijs, 2011: 133), which is the model adopted in Belgium. The alternative to such a coercive regime, an 'accommodating linguistic regime', appears less adequate, as it will eventually lead to the domination of the colonising language. So, if public authorities want to achieve a 'parity of esteem' in linguistic matters, they will have 'to impose specific constraints on the conduct of the inhabitants of a territory' (van Parijs, 2011: 138). Linguistic justice may be achieved by imposing constraints on language use, just as constraints are imposed in the school curricula or in the payment of taxes. The alternative model, to accommodate individually expressed preferences, would not be acceptable in the education system nor the payment of taxes, just as in linguistic matters this would lead to everything but 'parity of esteem'.

Such balances and imbalances between parity and imparity of esteem can be observed in language policies in many countries. The Baltic states, for instance, regained their independence in the 1990s. Estonia and Latvia have their own 'national' language, but as a consequence of the post-war Soviet occupation they also have to take into account a considerable minority of Russian-speakers. Estonian- or Latvian-speakers defend the principle of linguistic territoriality, whereas Russian-speakers defend the 'personality principle', meaning that the usage of a particular language should be adapted to what an individual prefers. This again illustrates the relativity of concepts such as majority and minority, in addition to the complexity of achieving parity of esteem, in other words linguistic justice. Estonian and Latvian are majority languages in their own countries, but the rights of the large Russian minority cannot be debated without considering the powerful Russian neighbour. Every attempt to develop a translation policy or translation practices has to be seen against this complex historical, political and linguistic background. The territoriality principle, to be sure, is certainly not the perfect solution, yet the other alternatives have riskier consequences. As van Parijs puts it, 'a territorially differentiated coercive linguistic regime is the best that can be done to secure parity of esteem – to avoid it always being the same group who do the linguistic "bowing" – consistently with fundamental individual freedoms and with the unavoidably inegalitarian need for a lingua franca' (van Parijs, 2011: 141).

The language policy of Belgium, which consists of a sum of mono-lingualisms, is mainly based on the territoriality principle, with the important exception of the relatively small areas with 'facilities', where individuals are granted the option not to adopt the local official language and let their individual preferences prevail. These administrative facilities, based on the personality principle, are a partial compensation for the prevalent territoriality principle.

Translation Policy in German-Language Belgium

This section will focus on translation policies regarding the majority–minority binary in German-language Belgium. While in an earlier study I analysed the *legal and administrative context* in this part of Belgium (van Doorslaer, 2013), Anneleen vanden Boer (2011) has focused on issues of *linguistic conflict* in a region that has belonged to Germany or Belgium at different times in its history. Having conducted the widest survey on the topic so far, vanden Boer has examined the causal interconnections between language conflict, identity development and degrees of personal satisfaction in the German-speaking part of Belgium. The popular stereo-type according to which German-speaking Belgians are 'more Belgian' than Dutch- or French-speakers served as the analytical starting point. Even though this popular myth keeps being peddled by the Belgian media, it may have been relevant only for the first post-war generation, which felt reluctant to be associated with Germany; today's younger German-speakers are much more critical of Belgium and have a much less pronounced sense of Belgian identity (vanden Boer, 2011: 154). The difference in perceptions of national belonging is indeed so significant that vanden Boer points to the existence of a *Generationskluft* (generation gap) caused by a growing discontent of younger German-speaking generations with Belgium, due to shortcomings in the application of language legisla-tion (vanden Boer, 2011: 138). No longer willing to share the traditional views of their parents and grandparents, younger German-speakers publicly deplore the political impotence and linguistic invisibility of the German-language community and criticise the inaccurate implementation of language laws. One of the numerous criticisms relates to several types of local application documents supposed to exist in German translation yet often available only in French. This is a clear case of 'Unzufriedenheit mit der Anwendung der Sprachgesetzgebung' (dissatisfaction with the application of the language laws; vanden Boer, 2011: 139). If translation does not help to put abstract language policies into practice, the result may be a loss of national identity and a disconnection from the state.

Whereas vanden Boer focused on the relationship between identity and language policy, Esther de Fijter (2012) scrutinised *translation policies* in German-language Belgium. De Fijter's study reveals that German-language media in Belgium are rife with complaints about non-compliance with language legislation (e.g. as frequently reported in the daily newspaper *Grenz-Echo* or on the public radio and television station Belgischer Rundfunk). This kind of public discontent reflects power asymmetries regarding state reforms for the German-speaking group. A kind of political autonomy exists at the level of the community (e.g. in education, culture and sports), but German-language Belgium has never been officially granted the status of a region (like Flanders, Wallonia or Brussels), which of course is a much more influential level of political participation. The absence of a political voice at the regional level no doubt has an impact on the community's ability to enforce legislative and administrative measures. This discontent with the federal Belgian level, just as in Dutch-language Flanders, has crystallised in the presence of an important regionalist party, initially called Partei der Deutschsprachigen Belgier (Party of the German-Speaking Belgians), later renamed Pro Deutschsprachige Gemeinschaft (Pro German-Speaking Community). Pro Deutschsprachige Gemeinschaft was elected into communal government for the first time in 2014, and it aims to create a fourth region in Belgium with equal political and linguistic rights.

Over the past few decades, various Belgian state reforms have brought about comparable language rights (achieved through the medium of translation) for the three language groups (Dutch, French and German). For the German-language community, this means that documents have to be translated at three administrative levels:

(1) the federal level – a translation service for the production of German translations is based in Malmédy in the French-language area of Wallonia, close to the two small German-language areas (the Zentrale Dienststelle für Deutsche Übersetzungen);
(2) the regional level – the region of Wallonia (where the large majority is French-speaking, but with a German-language minority);
(3) the provincial level – the province of Liège (where the large majority is French-speaking, but with a German-language minority).

The website of the translation service located in Malmédy contains the German translations of parts of the Belgian legislation and is trilingual (German–French–Dutch), although the URL exists only in the French version (Service central de traduction allemande, http://www.scta.be/; accessed 30 January 2016). De Fijter lists three main reasons why not many of the texts that from a legal point of view should be available in German – for instance, local authority application documents for obtaining a hunting licence – are actually translated. These reasons are not exclusively linked to a specific administrative level, but to all of them. The first reason is financial, since, at the time of de Fijter's research, the federal translation service in Malmédy employed 29 translators, but many more would have been needed to translate all the relevant documentation in accordance with the requirements of the law (see http://www.scta.be/Wer-wir-sind/Wer-wir-sind.aspx, accessed 30 January 2016). The second reason relates to the question of labour, since each administrative level appears to struggle to attract good candidates due to the scarcity of civil servants with an adequate command of German. And thirdly, there seems to be a certain degree of open and tacit unwillingness, given that quite a number of institutional decisions exclude German and that translating into German is not considered a priority. This (institutional) unwillingness is mainly found at the federal Belgian level (de Fijter, 2012: 69). It is worth emphasising that at the time of de Fijter's investigation a large number of federal websites existed in three languages, but not in the country's three *official* languages. Dutch and French versions are sometimes complemented by an English version, but not by a German one.

Vanden Boer's research on language policy and de Fijter's work on translation policy neatly complement each other, as vanden Boer's conclusions about the potential for conflict in German-language Belgium can be connected to the German-language minority's discontent with linguistic matters. Such new research on language and translation policy is significant in that it highlights an instance of official non-compliance with federal legislation, the greater political awareness of younger generations and the development of an identity that is much more critical of Belgium than in previous years. According to vanden Boer, the levels of political satisfaction and tolerance on the part of Belgium's German-speaking population are closely connected to their linguistic rights:

Es liegt hauptsächlich Konfliktpotential vor zur politischen Sichtbarkeit der deutschsprachigen Belgier und zur Anwendung der Sprachgesetzgebung für Deutschsprachige. Die Mündigkeit der jüngeren Generationen Belgier und die Identitätsentwicklung beeinflussen das Konfliktpotential erheblich. Eine künftige Zunahme des Konfliktpotentials zwischen der nicht-deutschsprachigen und der deutschsprachigen Bevölkerung ist deswegen wahrscheinlich. Anscheinend werden sowohl die Toleranz und die Zufriedenheit hinsichtlich Aspekten [sic] der Position der deutschsprachigen Belgier im belgischen föderalen System abnehmen. Außerdem ist das Zufriedenheitsniveau der deutschsprachigen Bevölkerung bereits nicht besonders hoch. (vanden Boer, 2011: 149)

Conflict potential exists mainly with regard to the political visibility of the German-speaking Belgians and the application of the language laws for German-speakers. Awareness among the younger Belgian generations and their identity development have a considerable impact on this conflict potential. For that reason, there is a possibility of a future increase in conflict potential between the non-German-speaking and the German-speaking population. It seems that the degree of both tolerance and satisfaction with regard to aspects of the position of German-speakers within the Belgian federal system will diminish. Moreover, the actual level of satisfaction of the German-speaking population is not particularly high. (Translation by the present author)

Contradictions as Conclusion

Research on translation policies and translation practices in German-language Belgium is still in its infancy. The few existing studies, however, highlight four interrelated contradictions, or at least paradoxes, in the realisation of language policies, particularly when seen against the backdrop of linguistic and territorial power relationships and multilingual situations. Smaller language groups such as the German-language community in Belgium are defended by a well developed legal framework, yet there is the possibility of a contradiction between the idealism of linguistic legislation and actual translation practice. The discontent of the German-speaking population is not related to the legislation itself but, rather, to its non-implementation in (some) governmental and linguistic practice(s).

Secondly, striving for multilingualism seems to be a characteristic of smaller or minority-language areas, since in majority-language areas the tendency veers towards the opposite. Education policies in the small German community in Belgium are clearly directed towards a better knowledge of the 'majority' languages of the country (Dutch and French), whereas knowledge of the third 'national' language – German – is not stimulated in the education policies of either the Flemish or the French communities: a drive towards 'Belgian' multilingualism, therefore, is not taking place in the two major language communities. Traditional linguistic power relationships, then, still seem to function well within national frameworks, and the maxi–min dynamic as described by van Parijs appears to persist.

A third paradox relates to political legislation and linguistic equality in the context of historically determined national image-building and border construction. The introduction of German as a third national language, and the language and translation policies developed later, are a direct result of the territorial expansion of nation-states at the beginning of the 20th century, and a consequence of Germany's defeat in World War I, when Belgium demanded large areas of foreign territory during the post-war negotiations but in the end received only two small regions.

A fourth paradox for linguistic legislation concerns the tension between strict nationalist thinking and the modern desire to think in 'transnational' terms. German in Belgium is considered a minor language, but geographically the German-speaking area borders on the largest linguistic community in the European Union, with almost 100 million native speakers. As such, traditional nationalistic thinking about borderlines has a considerable impact on linguistic rights and democratic efficiency. Although the European Union boasts a clearly developed language policy, linguistic and cultural (im)balances within member states mean that the same language can sometimes require significantly different policies. Over a period of several decades, Belgium has developed a legal framework and a language and translation policy for a relatively small number of inhabitants. For a variety of reasons, however, the different administrative, mainly geographically determined, levels of the Belgian state are not implementing and enforcing the laws sufficiently. The contradiction is all the greater in view of the fact that Belgium's German-speaking inhabitants, though few in number, belong to the largest linguistic community in the European Union. From a supranational European perspective, a level with a highly developed translation policy itself, this is quite paradoxical.

It is challenging for translation studies and linguistics to get to grips with the fact that translation policies within national borders can turn linguistic relationships upside down. The marginalisation of German at various levels in the Belgian administration is an illustration of the political reality that, in matters of language and translation, the supranational European level is subordinate to categories of national (in this case Belgian) thinking. Within a national framework, even the largest EU mother tongue can be treated as a minority language. National thinking seems to be counterproductive – and sometimes highly inefficient – in matters of language and translation policy. Studying the interconnection between language/translation policy and different levels of administrative decision-making (including minority–majority relations), therefore, opens up new perspectives for translation studies. Translation and translation policy are traditionally perceived as emancipating tools, but it seems that they can also be developed for more conservative purposes, for maintaining and confirming nation-state thinking. Future research on language and translation policies will have to deal with the four contradictions and paradoxes discussed in these concluding remarks, which may serve as a starting point for the analysis of new case studies.

References

Apter, E. (2006) *The Translation Zone: A New Comparative Literature*. Princeton, MA: Princeton University Press.

Bandia, P.F. (2008) *Translation as Reparation: Writing and Translation in Postcolonial Africa*. Manchester: St Jerome.

Baumgarten, S. and Gruber, E. (2014) Phenomenological asymmetries in Welsh translation history. *The Translator* 20 (1), 26–43.

Blommaert, J. (2013) *Ethnography, Superdiversity and Linguistic Landscapes: Chronicles of Complexity*. Bristol: Multilingual Matters.

Branchadell, A. and West, L.M. (eds) (2005) *Less Translated Languages*. Amsterdam: John Benjamins.

BRIO (Brussels Informatie-, Documentatie- en Onderzoekscentrum) (2013) *Taalbarometer 3: Diversiteit als Norm*, at http://www.briobrussel.be/assets/onderzoeksprojecten/brio_taalbarometer_3_brussel_2013.pdf, accessed 15 February 2013.

Chesterman, A. (2009) The name and nature of translator studies. *Hermes* 42, 13–22.

Cronin, M. (1995) Altered states: Translation and minority languages. *TTR* 8 (1), 85–103.

Cronin, M. (2006) *Translation and Identity*. London: Routledge.

Cronin, M. (2012) Who fears to speak in the new Europe? Plurilingualism and alterity. *European Journal of Cultural Studies* 15 (2), 182–194.

de Fijter, E. (2012) 'Bedauerlicherweise nicht auf Deutsch verfügbar.' Een drietalige case study over het vertaalbeleid voor Duitstalig België. MA thesis, Lessius Antwerp.

Díaz Fouces, O. (2005) Translation policy for minority languages in the European Union: Globalisation and resistance. In A. Branchadell and L.M. West (eds) *Less Translated Languages* (pp. 95–104). Amsterdam: John Benjamins.

Flynn, P. and van Doorslaer, L. (2016) City and migration: A crossroads for non-institutionalized translation. *European Journal of Applied Linguistics* 4 (1), 73–92.

Gambier, Y. and van Doorslaer, L. (eds) (2014) *Translation Studies Bibliography*, 11th online release, approx. 26,000 items. Amsterdam: John Benjamins, at http://www.benjamins.nl/online/tsb, accessed 22 December 2015.

González Núñez, G. (2016) On translation policy. *Target* 28 (1), 87–109.

Jakobson, R. (1959) On linguistic aspects of translation. In R.A. Brower, *On Translation* (pp. 144–151). Cambridge, MA: Harvard University Press. Reprinted in L. Venuti (ed.) (2004) *The Translation Studies Reader* (pp. 138–143). London: Routledge.

Kruger, H. (2012) *Postcolonial Polysystems: The Production and Reception of Translated Children's Literature in South Africa*. Amsterdam: John Benjamins.

Meylaerts, R. (2007) 'La Belgique vivra-t-elle?' Language and translation ideological debates in Belgium (1919–1940). *The Translator* 13 (2), 297–319.

Meylaerts, R. (2010) Multilingualism and translation. In Y. Gambier and L. van Doorslaer (eds) *Handbook of Translation Studies* (vol. 1, pp. 227–230). Amsterdam: John Benjamins.

Meylaerts, R. (2011) Translational justice in a multilingual world: An overview of translational regimes. *Meta* 56 (4), 743–757.

Miguélez-Carballeira, M., Price A. and Kaufmann, J. (eds) (2016) 'Translation in Wales: History, Theory and Approaches', special issue, *Translation Studies* 9 (2).

Pennycook, A. and Otsuji, E. (2015) *Metrolingualism: Language in the City*. London: Routledge.

Simon, S. (2006) *Translating Montreal: Episodes in the Life of a Divided City*. Montreal: McGill-Queen's University Press.

Simon, S. (2012) *Cities in Translation: Intersections of Language and Memory*. London: Routledge.

Simon, S. (2014) The city in translation. Urban cultures of central Europe. In E. Brems, R. Meylaerts and L. van Doorslaer (eds) *The Known Unknowns of Translation Studies* (pp. 155–171). Amsterdam: John Benjamins.

Snell-Hornby, M. (2006) *The Turns of Translation Studies: New Paradigms or Shifting Viewpoints?* Amsterdam: John Benjamins.

vanden Boer, A. (2011) Sprachkonfliktforschung in Sprachkontaktgebieten: Die öffentliche Meinung zu Aspekten der Position der deutschsprachigen Belgier im belgischen föderalen System. PhD thesis, University of Leuven.

van Doorslaer, L. (2010) The Belgian conflict frame: The role of media and translation in Belgian political ideologies. In C. Schäffner and S. Bassnett (eds) *Political Discourse, Media and Translation* (pp. 198–210). Newcastle: Cambridge Scholars.

van Doorslaer, L. (2013) Belgian translation policy: The case of the German-language community. In P. Cuvelier, T. du Plessis, M. Meeuwis, R. Vandekerckhove and V. Webb (eds) *Multilingualism for Empowerment: Studies in Language Policy in South Africa* (pp. 60–71). Pretoria: Van Schaik.

van Parijs, P. (2011) *Linguistic Justice for Europe and for the World*. Oxford: Oxford University Press.

Wolf, M. (2012) *Die vielsprachige Seele Kakaniens. Übersetzen und Dolmetschen in der Habsburgermonarchie. 1848–1918*. Vienna: Böhlau. Translated by K. Sturge (2015) as *The Habsburg Monarchy's Many-Languaged Soul: Translating and Interpreting, 1848–1918*. Amsterdam: John Benjamins.

Part 2

Domination and Hegemony in History

4 Where the Devil Sneaks In: Power and Agency in Radical Bible Translation

Karen Bennett

> [...] As when a prowling wolf,
> Whom hunger drives to seek new haunt for prey,
> Watching where shepherds pen their flocks at eve
> In hurdled cotes amid the field secure,
> Leaps o'er the fence with ease into the fold:
> Or as a thief bent to unheard the cash
> Of some rich burgher, whose substantial doors,
> Cross-barred and bolted fast, fear no assault,
> In at the window climbs, or o'er the tiles;
> So clomb this first grand thief into God's fold.
> (John Milton, *Paradise Lost*, Book IV: 183–192)

Translation as Will-to-Power

For most translator organisations, the notion that their members might intervene in the texts that they translate for political or ideological reasons is anathema. All translators' charters include clauses that bind them to some form of fidelity to the source text, on the understanding that their role is to transmit its sense as accurately as possible. Failure to do so may result in expensive court cases and professional disgrace, depending upon the perceived severity of the damage caused. However, such clauses are based upon a rather naive understanding of translation activity itself. They assume that meaning is simple, unitary, unproblematic, that there is a one-to-one relationship between signs and their referents, and that meaning can be transferred smoothly from one language to another without any loss or distortion. This is a theory of language that, while dominant in the Anglo-Saxon world, does not take account of the complexities of the process, nor of the interpretative role of the translator.

A more sophisticated theory of language recognises that meaning does not accrue to any objective extralingual 'reality', but is an effect of language (Derrida, 1972: 61; Saussure, 1916: 117–118), generated through an interplay of differences and oppositions that encodes the worldview of the particular linguistic community. According to this perspective, translation is inherently ideological (on ideology, language and essentialism, see Baumgarten, 2012: 62). As it is almost never possible simply to map a stretch of discourse in one language onto another without alteration or loss, the final outcome will depend upon the aspects that translators, and their publishers, patrons and so on decide (consciously or unconsciously) to privilege and the structures available in the target language for expressing them. Hence, even when the aim is to replicate the original as faithfully as possible, the result will inevitably be flawed. Not only are there likely to be lacunas, but the translation may also contain dimensions of meanings that were not present in the original, new nodes of signification that gesture off into the thickets of semantic proliferation beyond the boundaries of the individual text. This has been theorised by Lecercle (1990: 182) as 'the remainder', a notion also mobilised by Venuti (1998).

The gap between languages and cultures not only permits unintentional cross-fertilisation from other discourses but also allows the devil to sneak into the garden of pure referentiality – the devil understood as the conscious *will to power* in all its various manifestations. By will to power, I understand the primordial need of the self, individual and collective, to assert itself in the world on its own terms, writing its own script rather than passively accepting the parts that have been attributed to it by dominant others. As Nietzsche (1901: 340) put it:

> every specific body strives to become master over all space and to extend its force (its will to power) and to thrust back all that resists its extension. But it continually encounters similar efforts on the part of other bodies and ends by coming to an arrangement ('union') with those of them that are sufficiently related to it: thus they then conspire together for power. And the process goes on.

The will to power is the desire to make a mark on the world by getting our voice heard and influencing others. But it is also the desire to escape the kind of symbolic violence that occurs when we are forced to become the Other for someone else. Power and empowerment are thus two faces of the same devil, who brings conflict and unrest, but also newness, into the world.

The Bible has been the site of devilish activity and unintentional cross-fertilisation since it first began to be written down, possibly as early as the 8th century BCE (Sweeney, 2010: 183). Having served as an identity vehicle for many different peoples over the ages, it is natural that different interpretations should have been imposed and challenged at different times, meanings fought over. Hence, an analysis of the tussles that have occurred over the interpretation of key passages can tell us a great deal not only about the values and beliefs of the communities involved, but also about the way that human understanding has evolved in line with changing sociopolitical circumstances.

This chapter is concerned with some of the power issues involved in Bible translation in the context of two ideological struggles: first, the Protestant Reformation of the 16th century, which called into question the age-old power of the Church of Rome; and second, the feminist cause of the present era, which has sought to overturn some of the most cherished assumptions of Judaeo-Christian tradition in the interests of gender equality. In each case, I shall attempt to gauge whether the new versions resulted from a conscious attempt on the part of discerning individuals to impose a fresh meaning on the ancient text, or whether they emanated spontaneously from a new way of seeing, generated by cultural mechanisms that were themselves triggered by changes in the socio-economic and political infrastructure.

In some cases, the new ideology actually seems to have emerged unbidden from the textual work in an interesting illustration of Foucault's (1969) notion of the 'author' as a function of discourse. For example, we will see how Martin Luther's key tenets of *sola scriptura* (by scripture alone) and *sola fide* (by faith alone) seem to have developed out of textual strategies mobilised for other purposes, including translation, while some of William Tyndale's perceived excesses may have resulted from his getting carried away by his own discourse. On the other hand, many of the alterations implemented under the rubric of modern feminism seem to have been fully conscious attempts to challenge the status quo through semantic engineering.

These questions thus contribute to the ongoing debate in translation studies about *translator agency*, understood as the translator's capacity to consciously intervene in texts in order to bring about social change (e.g. Kinnunen & Koskinen, 2010; Milton & Bandia, 2009; Tyulenev, 2016). Borrowed from the social sciences (e.g. Giddens, 1984), the notion of agency made its appearance in the translation studies lexicon in the early years of the 21st century, challenging the prevailing post-structuralist conviction that the concept of the author was defunct (Barthes, 1968; Foucault, 1969). Although new insights into this question have come from related disciplines, such as Greenblatt's 'new historicism' and Bourdieu's 'habitus' (both acknowledged by Milton and Bandia in the introductory essay to their 2009 volume *Agents of Translation*; see also Chapters 7 and 13 of the present volume, respectively by Cristina Gómez Castro and Pei Meng), the question of how much control the translator has over meaning continues to be as intractable as the Church's interminable tussles over destiny and free will. But before plunging into the swirling paradigms of cultural history, let us look first at some of the textual and political implications of Bible translation. Where better to start than at the very beginning?

The Archetype: *Logos*

> In the beginning was the Word, and the Word was with God and the Word was God.

Thus begins the Gospel of St John, a compelling affirmation of what phenomenologists of religion (e.g. Eliade, 1954, 1957; Otto, 1923) call the 'sacred' mindset. From this perspective, everything that is meaningful in life is subsumed into a symbolic order that is all-encompassing ('totalitarian' according to Auerbach, 1953: 15), a primal state of linguistic unity where sign and referent are one and the same, with their origin and their end in God. The breakdown of this unity is conceived in Jewish and Christian mystical traditions as a state of loss and confusion, realised historically in the linguistic chaos of the Tower of Babel but also experienced at first hand in the more immediate sphere of religious ritual and practice whenever the archetype, which embodies the godhead, is debased. According to Mircea Eliade, in the sacred domain, 'an object or act becomes real only insofar as it *imitates or repeats an archetype*. Thus, reality is acquired solely through repetition or participation; everything which lacks an exemplary model is "meaningless", i.e. it lacks reality' (1954: 34; emphasis added). Consequently, failure to reproduce the *exact words* of an incantation or prayer is perceived as a profanity that distorts the sacred *logos* and contaminates the hierophany, disturbing the fundamental equilibrium of the self-referential system.

The importance of this notion of the archetype for translation cannot be underestimated. For if the sacred text is understood to be primarily a 'vehicle of revelation' (Frye, 1983: 29) that effectively summons the hierophany into existence (Bennett, 2002), then any kind of rewriting, even intralinguistic, becomes a falsification (Robinson, 1996: 64–70). This is why Bible translation has always been such a fraught activity. The community whose soul it embodies will experience the new version as a diabolical desecration, analogous to the destruction of a shrine, and this produces distress on a level that is barely conceivable to post-Enlightenment 'rational' man.

Yet, since earliest times, the Bible has been repeatedly translated, often at great cost. Some of these translations have been intralinguistic attempts to modernise a text that seems linguistically or culturally outmoded, or to establish an authoritative version from among several competing 'originals' (this is what happened between the 7th and 10th centuries CE when the Jewish Masorete scribes updated and fixed the Hebrew Bible, introducing sentence and chapter divisions, as well as a vowel notation system into what had previously been a consonant-only language). Others are properly interlinguistic versions to serve peoples who do not know the language of the original, either because they have 'forgotten' it – as with the Jews of Alexandria in the 3rd century BCE, believed to have been the original targets of the Septuagint (see below) – or because they have never learned it. There have also been numerous re-translations, usually to correct perceived inaccuracies in the preceding version or to make the text more accessible to a specific readership. In all cases, power is of course a tremendously important issue, as the religious text becomes a site of struggle for the imposition of meaning and identity.

Some of the translations that were initially considered radical and controversial have subsequently acquired the status of a new archetype as religious heritage is reinvented in line with changing sociocultural conditions. The Judaeo-Christian tradition has, as we know, undergone a number of major paradigm shifts over the millennia and in all cases translation has played a significant role (Robinson, 1991: 65–69). The Hebrew Bible of the Jews was overwritten by the Greek Septuagint in the context of the Diaspora and then reinterpreted and supplemented to become the archetype of the early Christian Church. This Greek Bible was then supplanted during the Roman Empire by the Latin Vulgate, which became the archetype of Western Christianity throughout the medieval period. All three of these archetypes were then used as source texts for the various vernacular Bibles produced by Protestant Reformers in Europe during the early modern period, which in turn became archetypes in their respective cultures. Many of those ultimately ended up being transported to other parts of the globe during the colonial era to become the source text for new translations into other languages. Hence, the biblical artefact that has come down to us today is actually an elaborate palimpsest, made up of many different texts superimposed upon one another. It makes no sense, therefore, to use the conventional binaries of 'original' versus 'translation' to speak about it, as almost every version that we know of is, in some sense, both a source and a target text.

Given the complexity of the power issues involved in the overwriting process, translators have had to position themselves very carefully. On the one hand, they have had to be able to show that they were being faithful to God's word, or else their text would not achieve the authoritative status of the new archetype that was needed for it to function adequately in the sacred domain. On the other hand, they have also had to cultivate a meta-discourse that justifies the move away from the current archetype (usually either by emphasising the incumbent's inadequacies or by focusing on the need for a version that is intelligible to a specific target community with distinct requirements). In translational terms, this has meant steering a narrow course between the conventional dichotomies of faithful versus free, literal versus idiomatic, word-for-word versus sense-for-sense, in order to kill the political and the sacred birds with the same stone.

In the earliest Bible translations, the issue was resolved through recourse to mythopoeia. The translation of the Hebrew Bible into Koinê Greek in the 3rd century BCE, known as the Septuagint, was instigated by Ptolemy II Philadelphus, partly because he wanted a copy for his library, and partly to serve the Jews of Alexandria, who no longer spoke the language of their forebears yet wished to have access to the texts that were so central to their religious and ethnic tradition. The motivation was, thus, overwhelmingly political. However, it was, as we know, accompanied by the creation of a myth that 70 translators, all working separately, managed to produce exactly the same text in just 70 days. This claim can be traced back to the first-century Alexandrian philosopher Philo Judaeus (see Yonge, 1854–1890), who elaborated on the more realistic account given in the earlier 'Letter of Aristeas' (c. 130 BCE) to facilitate the incorporation of the Platonic notion of *logos* into the Jewish worldview, and was perpetuated by Epiphanius of Constantia in the 4th century (Epiphanius, 392: 22) and then Augustine in the 5th (Augustine, 426: 820–821). The effect of it was to enable the Greek text to assume the role of the archetype over and above the Hebrew original; and of course the Septuagint remains the canonical version of the Old Testament for Orthodox Christians today.

A similar mechanism seems to have been in operation with the Vulgate, the Latin translation by St Jerome, which replaced the Greek Bible as the archetype for Catholics. Jerome was of course famous for advocating a translation policy that was above all target-oriented, in line with the prescriptions of Cicero, from whom he drew inspiration; and, although in his famous 'Letter to Pammachius' (c. 398: 23) he appears to exempt Bible translation from this prescription in recognition of its opacity, he did not always follow a rigorously source-text-oriented strategy in his own translation of the Bible (Hammond, 1980: 106–110). Once again, the status of this translation as a new archetype was ensured by mythopoeic means. Jerome was, as we know, canonised for his labours, thereby ensuring that his version was endowed with a mystical aura of a hallowed text. As such, it too became the archetype for Christians throughout the medieval period, and was officially adopted as the official version of the Catholic Church in the 16th century.

By the early modern period, however, the public had probably become too discerning to be easily fobbed off with myths. The Protestant translators who impelled the Reformation chose instead to appeal to reason in their attempts to make their versions stick, producing complex arguments of a forensic nature to 'prove' that their reading of the scriptures was the correct one. In the next section I shall analyse how Luther and Tyndale negotiated this complex question by examining some of the metatexts that have accompanied their works, while, at the same time, keeping my eyes open for glimpses of the devil, who of course had something of a field day in this most turbulent period of history.

Reformist Bibles

Translation had a tremendously important role to play in the great paradigm shift that occurred in the early modern period with the Protestant

Reformation. The return to the scriptures seems to have been both a symptom and a source of disgruntlement with the established Church, as critics claimed that the original Christian message had been falsified over the centuries by an institution that had become corrupt and lost touch with its roots. The urge to re-translate was, therefore, only partly about making that message accessible to ordinary people who did not know Latin. In a changing socio-economic context marked by the breakdown of feudalism, rise of nationalism and development of a print culture that gave the written word an authority that it had not had before, there was also the need to renegotiate the archetype in order to bring it into line with a whole new set of social values.

This becomes clear in the protracted debate between William Tyndale and Thomas More concerning, among other things, the original source of the Christian message to which each side laid claim. Tyndale, as a follower of Luther, naturally defended the primacy of the scriptures, arguing (in *The Obedience of a Christian Man*, 1528) that the Church's authority rested on a series of mis-translations (which he himself had attempted to rectify in his own version of the New Testament, published in its complete form in Worms in 1526). Thomas More, the Catholic, retorted not only that the gospels had been transmitted by word of mouth long before they had been written down, but also that Tyndale's translations were misleading and heretical. In particular, he criticised (in the *Dialogue Concerning Heresies*, 1529) Tyndale's use of 'congregation' to translate the Greek *ekklesia* (usually 'church'), 'elder' for *presbuteros* (usually 'priest'), 'repent' for the verb *metanoeite*, 'to do penance'), 'love' for *agape* ('charity'), 'favour' for *charis* ('grace') and 'knowledging' for *homologia* ('confession'), mobilising sophisticated philological arguments to dispute both their accuracy and contextual appropriacy (De Coursey, 2010: 22–26).

In the *Confutation of Tyndale's Answer* (1532–1533), More also took issue with Tyndale's translation of John 5:34 concerning the nature of Jesus's testimony (this had appeared in the 1526 Worms Bible as 'And Cryste also sayth hym selfe [...] I receave no recorde of man' (cited by Fabiny, 2008: 13). More claimed that Tyndale had deliberately omitted the definite article in order to give the impression that Christ rejected all kinds of human witness, when in fact it was referring to a particular instance:

> And therefore I saye that Tyndale sholde in his englysh translacyon not haue lefte oute that article the / but sholde at the leste wyse haue translated yt thus, I receuye not the recorde of man [...] And thys hathe he done not of ignoraunce but of malyce, to make yt seme that Cryste vtterly refuseth and reiecteth all maner wytnesse of man, in testyfycacyon and wytnessynge of hym and his trouth. And this translacyon therefore deuyseth Tyndale / because he wold haue vs wene that Cryste wolde haue the wytnesse of all his chyrche vtterly serue of nought. (More, *Confutation*, 234/19–35; cited by Fabiny, 2008: 14)

The question of translator agency is interesting here. Fabiny (2008: 14) points out that Tyndale actually reworked this sentence in his 1534 revision of his New Testament and inserted the missing definite article in accordance with More's prescription ('I receive not *the* record of man'; emphasis added), although there is no evidence that he had actually read the *Confutation*, or that he would have heeded it if he had. This suggests that it had been a genuine lapse rather than a deliberate distortion of the text for ideological purposes, as More had claimed. It may well be that Tyndale had got carried away on a wave of reforming fervour, to the extent of allowing it to cloud his vision. However, the fact that he moved to correct the mistake effectively reinforces his agency in the case of the other, rather radical translation options that he left unchanged, many of which effectively enact the Protestant doctrines of the 'invisible Church' and 'priesthood of all believers'.

The debate about the source of religious authority had its immediate origin in Luther's 1520 treatise *The Babylonian Captivity of the Church*, which was when the doctrine of *sola scriptura* ('by scripture alone') appears to have taken shape. In it, Luther uses the scriptures as ammunition to attack the sacraments in a treatise which, like the earlier 95 *Theses*, seems primarily designed to prove Church corruption. Much as a lawyer might do today, he offers biblical passages almost as empirical evidence to support his case – a highly unusual discursive practice at a time when the disputational techniques of scholasticism were still in vogue. For example, on the matter of the Eucharist, Luther analyses John 6 in detail in order to 'prove' that it cannot be interpreted as offering support for the sacrament:

> In the first place, the sixth chapter of John must be set aside altogether, as not saying a single syllable about the sacrament; not only because the sacrament had not yet been instituted, but much more because the very sequence of the discourse and of its statements shows clearly that Christ was speaking – as I have said before – of faith in the incarnate Word. For He says: 'My words, they are spirit and they are life'; showing that He was speaking of that spiritual eating, wherewith he who eats, lives [...]. A sacramental eating does not give life, for many eat unworthily, so that Christ cannot be understood to have spoken of the sacrament in this passage. (Luther, 1520: 147)

Thus, it would appear that the doctrine of *sola scriptura* has almost slipped into the equation by accident, while Luther was focusing on something else. That is to say, the recourse to the scriptures, which ultimately became one of the key tenets of Protestantism, may have begun life as a rhetorical strategy in the service of a different argument before it became a dogma in its own right.

Another of the mantras of Protestantism, the doctrine of *sola fide*, or justification by faith alone, may also have entered the picture obliquely, this time during the course of a translation. This controversy broke out following the publication of Luther's translation of the New Testament in 1522, five years after his nailing of the 95 theses to the church door in Wittenberg. Although the Protestant character of Luther's New Testament is evident throughout the work (Schaff, 1910), it was the specific inclusion of the word *allein* ('only' or 'alone') in a passage of Romans 3 that served as the focus for his detractors. In 'An open letter on translating' (1530), Luther defends the option as a purely linguistic matter, arguing that his target-oriented translation strategy meant that the word was required to make the German text sound natural:

> I know very well that in Romans 3 the word *solum* is not in the Greek or Latin text – the papists did not have to teach me that. It is fact that the letters *s-o-l-a* are not there [...]. In all these phrases, this is a German usage, even though it is not the Latin or Greek usage. It is the nature of the German language to add *allein* in order that *nicht* or *kein* may be clearer and more complete. To be sure, I can also say, 'The farmer brings grain and *kein* money', but the words '*kein* money' do not sound as full and clear as if I were to say, 'the farmer brings *allein* grain and *kein* money.' Here the word *allein* helps the word *kein* so much that it becomes a completely clear German expression. We do not have to ask the literal Latin how we are to speak German, as these donkeys do. Rather we must ask the mother in the home, the children on the street, the common man in the marketplace. We must be guided by their language, by the way they speak, and do our translating accordingly. Then they will understand it and recognize that we are speaking German to them.

If Luther is being sincere here, which is equivocal, it would suggest that, once again, it is the discourse that is propelling the ideology – quite an admission given the importance of *sola fide* for the Protestant cause (in his 'Commentary on Galatians' of 1538, Luther called it 'the chief article of the whole Christian doctrine' and 'the rock upon which the Church will stand or fall' – Bouman, 1955: 801). Hence, we are left wondering just where the boundaries between the linguistic and the theological lie. Were the two so tightly bound up together in Luther's mind that they were indistinguishable? Or was he himself being 'written' by his discourse to such an extent that he allowed a purely linguistic question to influence the whole course of European history? This consideration will concern us again in the next section, on the feminist translations of the Bible.

Feminist Bibles

From the gender perspective, the Bible is, as Gomola (2010: 193–194) puts it, a *skandalon*. Not only does it belittle women, with its relentless parade of devious seductresses, and excludes them through a systematic use of patriarchal language, it has also served to legitimise a whole range of misogynistic social orders (thereby offering a clear example of how a canonised text feeds a discursive order, which in turn becomes the matrix for the production of new texts). Feminist critiques of the Bible have thus involved not only an assessment of the way these misogynistic meanings were generated in the first place, but also the preparation of new translations that seek to compensate for the imbalances of the earlier ones.

Some of the findings made by these feminist biblicists are indeed startling. We learn, for example, that God was not unequivocally male in the Hebrew Bible, but was often referred to using forms that were grammatically feminine or which in some way connoted activities associated to the female domain. These include: a feminine noun meaning 'breath', 'wind' or 'spirit', which in Genesis 1:2 (i.e. 'the Spirit of God was hovering over the surface of the waters') collocates with a participle usually used to evoke the presence of a female bird as she hovers protectively ('fluttering', 'brooding') over her eggs (Korsak, undated); the Hebrew form *El Shaddai*, which could be etymologically related to the word for 'breast', implying a god of fertility that is feminine rather than masculine (Mollenkott, cited in Gomola, 2010: 196); and the conceptualisation of 'God as Wisdom', a noun that is feminine in both Hebrew and Greek, generating a range of feminine connotations (Mollenkott, cited in Gomola, 2010: 196–197). There are also plural conceptualisations, such as *El Elohim*.

We also learn that the word 'adam' in Genesis 1–3 was not in the first instance a name, nor did it refer to man in the masculine sense, but suggests instead some generic proto-human creature moulded out of the earth. This argument rests on the fact that the Hebrew word *adam* is etymologically related to the word for 'ground' (*adamah*), which suggests that sexual differentiation takes place only later, when the gendered concepts of *ish* and *isha* are created (Korsak, 1992: 196–197; Korsak, undated; Simon, 1996: 117–120). Neither was the first female human actually called Eve (the word *hawwa* means 'life' in Hebrew), and she was not formed from man's rib but rather from the 'side' (*sela*) of this 'adam' (Korsak, 1992: 196).

As for Jesus's mother Mary, the notion that she was a virgin probably rests on a mis-translation. There are no references to her virginity in the New Testament (von Flotow, 2012: 139); instead, the attribute derives from a prophesy in Isaiah 7:14 (subsequently interpreted by Christians as referring to Jesus) in which the Hebrew word *almah*, meaning a young woman of marriageable age, was translated into Greek in the Septuagint as παρθένος (*parthenos*, i.e. 'virgin'). The fact that it did not technically mean the same thing is shown by the fact that the word *almah* is also used about Dinah in Genesis 34 after she has been raped (Rogerson, 1999: 14–15). Interestingly, the discrepancy is signalled in the Spanish Ferrara Bible of 1553, which used 'virgin' in its Christian version and 'young woman' in the Jewish one (Simon, 1996: 113).

Why all these were rendered first in Greek, then in Latin and the European vernaculars in such a patriarchal fashion is a moot point. Was this part of a generalised conspiracy to impose omnipotent male divinities at a time when ancient matrilineal societies were giving way to patrilineal ones, as some feminist commentators have asserted (Leeming & Page, 1996; Spretnak, 1978: 26–28)? Was it a rhetorical or aesthetically motivated gesture designed to bring cohesion and unity to a disparate body of scriptures by different authors and from different times? Or might it simply be that the translators were working within the categories that were available to them in their target languages, and interpreting the untranslatables in the way that seemed most obvious to them in the light of the cultural mores of the day?

This question of translator agency is obliquely broached by von Flotow (2000) in her consideration of two Bible translations commonly labelled 'feminist': Julia Evelina Smith's Holy Bible of 1876 and Mary Phil Korsak's 1992 version of Genesis. Both claim to be 'literal' renderings of the biblical texts, systematically using one English word for each occurrence of a particular Hebrew word. However, as von Flotow shows by comparing their very different treatments of chosen passages, Smith is much more conservative than Korsak on both the gender and the environmental fronts, even 'resolutely patriarchal' (von Flotow, 2000: 16) on many of the most significant issues. 'If both Smith and Korsak claim to produce a literal work', she asks, 'how can we reconcile their very different versions?' (von Flotow, 2000: 15–16).

Von Flotow answers this question indirectly, with recourse to the discourse of perception. She several times suggests that Smith actually failed to 'see' things that would have been evident to Korsak, possibly because she was focusing on different things. For example, Smith 'not only maintains the "rib" but doesn't "see" that, like the translators of the King James Bible, she uses one English word "man" for two Hebrew words "adam" and "ish"', while Korsak, who is very focused on the status of women, 'sees' the literal meaning of *sela* ('side') and also works on the gap in meaning between *adam* and *ish* (von Flotow, 2000: 16). On the environmental issue, Smith, as a gentleman farmer's daughter in the 1840s, would scarcely have felt the ecological urgency that motivates Korsak: 'yet Korsak does not impose a politics of environmentalism on the text, she simply "sees" differently' (von Flotow, 2000: 17).

This explanation owes much to the post-structuralist approaches to textual production and reception that were popular in the closing decades of the 20th century, according to which the author (and by extension translator) is at the mercy of their discourse and effectively 'written' by it (cf. Barthes, 1968; Foucault, 1969). According to this, our very perceptions are constrained by the categories that exist in our language, to the extent that we may effectively fail to see something for which there is no word. Hence, Smith, whose version 'never aspired to any ideals of the suffrage movement or feminism' (von Flotow, 2000: 16) but was motivated by other concerns, will not have been focusing on the same issues as Korsac. Thus, she simply fails to see them.

Curiously, von Flotow seems to abandon this post-structuralist stance later on. In her 2012 article 'Translating Women', she seems to have become a particularly forthright defender of active conscious translator agency. 'Translation is deliberate', she states roundly. 'It is intentional, and usually done for a purpose' (2012: 129). In the same article, she goes on to claim that biblical materials suffered 'deliberate twists and mis-translations' at the hands of the patriarchal translators, and that this has been 'confirmed' by Mary Phil Korsac's exposée. It is unclear if this shift in her position reflects a growing radicalisation of her ideological position as a feminist or if it results from the decline of interest in post-structuralism since the turn of the millennium and the concomitant resurgence of the notion of active agency in textual production.

Certainly the feminist translations that have appeared in recent years seem to be very deliberate in their attempts to adjust the balance (see Gomola, 2010; Simon, 1996: 111–133; von Flotow, 2012: 129–130). There are now feminist translations of the Bible in English, German and French which seek (controversially) not only to introduce more inclusive language (Gomola, 2010: 202–205; Simon, 1996: 124–131), but also to grapple with some of the thorny issues caused by the incommensurability of languages. Ingenious solutions have been proposed. Korsak in her version of Genesis (1992) translates *adam* as 'groundling' (p. 196) in order to emphasise the etymological link with the ground (*adamah*) and remove the masculine bias, and renders *hawwa* (traditionally 'Eve') as 'Life', for similar reasons (p. 197). Mollenkott (cited in Gomola, 2010: 196) suggests that 'El Shaddai', one of the names for 'God', usually translated as 'the Almighty', should become 'the breast of Jesus' or 'the God with breasts' in recognition of the word's associations with that part of the female body, while the Inclusive New Testament (2006, cited in Gomola, 2010: 201) avoids gender bias by using 'the Only Begotten' instead of 'Son', and 'the Chosen One' instead of 'the Son of Man'. It is too soon to say what effect these versions will have upon the reception of the Judaeo-Christian Bible in the long term. We know that ideological changes implemented by translators usually acquire general acceptance only if they are supported by 'hard' (i.e. political and economic) power, and that has not yet been forthcoming as far as these feminist Bibles are concerned. But it is probably only a matter of time. A long period of turmoil and conflict was required before the Protestant translations of Luther and Tyndale found their way into the mainstream, but versions based upon them are today installed as archetypes within their respective language communities. As such, they remain lasting testimonies to the capacity of translation to change the world.

Conclusion

The devil as the will-to-power is nowhere more explicit than in the colourful revolutionary created by John Milton in his epic poem *Paradise*

Lost, whom we encountered in the epigraph to this chapter as he prepared to sneak into the Garden of Eden. For the Romantics, Milton's Satan was a heroic figure. Shelley, in the *Defence of Poetry* (1821), lauds his 'energy and magnificence', calling him a moral being 'far superior to his God'; while Blake in *The Marriage of Heaven and Hell* (1793) considers him a 'Messiah' whose role is to re-energise a stultified universe which, 'being restrained', has by degrees become passive 'till it is [now] only the shadow of desire'. In this chapter, I have suggested, with Evan-Zohar (1979: 16), that translation has a similar function to play with regard to sacred texts like the Bible, which are eminently self-referential in their worldview, and resistant to change. We know from thermodynamics, as well as from Blake, that all systems tend to entropy if not revitalised by injections of energy: the pristine garden becomes overgrown with weeds unless a reaper is allowed in to clear away the undergrowth. Whether from individual initiative or urged on by the devil in the discourse, the translator plays havoc in Eden, slashing away at the vegetation and scattering new seedlings. This naturally stirs anger and resentment among those who have invested their whole identities in the status quo. But it also opens up the sacred precinct to new currents and, in doing so, enables it to adapt to a changing world and avoid sinking into oblivion.

References

Aristeas (c. 130 BCE) *Aristeas to Philoctetes (Letter of Aristeas)* (M. Hadas, trans.). New York: Krav Publishing (1973).

Auerbach, E. (1953) *Mimesis: The Representation of Reality in Western Literature*. Princeton, NJ: Princeton University Press.

Augustine (426) *City of God* (H. Bettenson, trans.). London: Penguin (2003).

Barthes, R. (1968) The death of the author (S. Heath, trans.), in *Image, Music, Text* (pp. 142–148). New York: Hill and Wang (1977).

Baumgarten, S. (2012) Translation and ideology. In L. van Doorslaer and Y. Gambier (eds) *Handbook of Translation Studies* (vol. 3, pp. 59–65). Amsterdam: John Benjamins.

Bennett, K. (2002) Mediating between God and man: Towards a poetics of sacred discourse. *Máthesis* 11, 109–123.

Bouman, H.J.A. (1955) The doctrine of justification in the Lutheran confessions. *Concordia Theological Monthly* 26 (11), 801–809.

De Coursey, M. (2010) *The Thomas More/William Tyndale Polemic: A Selection*. Hong Kong: Early Modern Literary Studies.

Derrida, J. (1972) Différance (A. Bass, trans., 1982). In P. Kamuf (ed.) *A Derrida Reader: Between the Blinds* (pp. 61–69). New York: Columbia University Press (1991).

Eliade, M. (1954) *The Myth of the Eternal Return* (W.R. Trask, trans.). Princeton, NJ: Princeton University Press (1971).

Eliade, M. (1957) *The Sacred and the Profane: The Nature of Religion* (W.R. Trask, trans.). New York: Harcourt, Brace and World (1959).

Epiphanius (392) *On Weights and Measures* (M. Hadas, trans.), in D. Robinson (ed.) *Western Translation Theory from Herodotus to Nietzsche*. Manchester: St Jerome (2002).

Evan-Zohar, I. (1979) Polysystem theory. *Poetics Today* 11 (1) (1990), 9–45.

Fabiny, T. (2008) Scripture versus Church in the debate of More and Tyndale. *Thomas More Studies* 3, 9–17.

Foucault, M. (1969) *What Is an Author?* (D.F. Bouchard and S. Simon, trans.), in D.F. Bouchard (ed.) *Language, Counter-Memory, Practice* (pp. 124–127). Ithaca, NY: Cornell University Press (1977).

Frye, N. (1983) *The Great Code: The Bible and Literature*. Toronto: Penguin.

Giddens, A. (1984) *The Constitution of Society: Outline of the Theory of Structuration*. Cambridge: Polity Press.

Gomola, A. (2010) Feminist thought in Bible translations. *Przekładaniec: A Journal of Literary Translation* 24, 193–208.

Hammond, G. (1980) The evolution of English Bible narrative: A study of Tyndale's translation methods in the Book of Genesis. *English Studies* 61 (2), 104–118.

Jerome (c. 398) Letter to Pammachius (K. Davis, trans.). In L. Venuti (ed.) *The Translation Studies Reader* (2nd edn) (pp. 21–30). London: Routledge (2004).

Kinnunen, T. and Koskinen, K. (eds) (2010) *Translators' Agency*. Tampere: Tampere University Press.

Korsak, M.P. (undated) The Bible: A controversial translation, at http://publishingcentral. com/subject.html/subject.html?sid=24&si=iptoiklag, accessed 29 March 2000.

Korsak, M.P. (1992) *At the Start ... Genesis Made New: A Translation of the Hebrew Text*. Louvain: Leuvense Schrijversaktie.

Lecercle, J-J. (1990) *The Violence of Language*. London: Routledge.

Leeming, D. and Page, J. (1996) *Goddess: Myths of the Female Divine*. Oxford: Oxford University Press.

Luther, M. (1520) On the Babylonish captivity of the Church. In H. Wace and C.A. Buchheim (eds) *First Principles of the Reformation, or The 95 Theses and the Three Primary Works of Dr. Martin Luther* (pp. 141–245). London: John Murray (1883).

Luther, M. (1530) An open letter on translating (G. Mann, trans.; revised and annotated by M.D. Marlowe, 2003), at http://www.bible-researcher.com/luther01.html, accessed 5 July 2015.

Milton, J. (1667) *Paradise Lost* (ed. A. Fowler). London: Longman (1971).

Milton, J. and Bandia, P. (2009) Introduction: Agents of translation and translation studies. In J. Milton and P. Bandia (eds) *Agents of Translation* (pp. 1–18). Amsterdam: John Benjamins.

Nietzsche, F. (1901) *The Will to Power* (W. Kaufmann and R.J. Hollingdale, trans.). New York: Vintage Books (1969).

Otto, R. (1923) *The Idea of the Holy* (J.W. Harvey, trans.). Oxford: Oxford University Press (1950).

Robinson, D. (1991) *The Translator's Turn*. Baltimore, MD: Johns Hopkins University Press.

Robinson, D. (1996) *Translation and Taboo*. Dekalb, IL: North Illinois University Press.

Rogerson, J.W. (1999) *An Introduction to the Bible*. Harmondsworth: Penguin.

Saussure, F. de (1916) *Course in General Linguistics* (W. Baskin, trans.). New York: Philosophical Library (1959).

Schaff, P. (1910) Luther's translation of the Bible, in *History of the Christian Church*. New York: Charles Scribner's Sons. Available at http://www.bible-researcher.com/luther02. html#note21, accessed 5 July 2015.

Simon, S. (1996) *Gender in Translation: Cultural Identity and the Politics of Transmission*. London: Routledge.

Smith, J. (trans.) (1876) *Holy Bible Containing the Old and New Testaments: Translated Literally from the Original Tongues*. Hartford, CT: American Publishing Company.

Spretnak, C. (1978) *Lost Goddesses of Early Greece: A Collection of Pre-Hellenic Myths*. Boston, MA: Beacon Press (1992).

Sweeney, M.A. (2010) *The Prophetic Literature*. Nashville, TN: Abingdon Press.

Tyulenev, S. (2016) Agency and role. In C. Angelelli and J. Baer (eds) *Researching Translating and Interpreting* (pp. 17–31). London: Routledge.

Venuti, L. (1998) *The Scandals of Translation: Towards an Ethics of Difference*. London: Routledge.

von Flotow, L. (2000) Women, Bibles, ideology. *TTT: Traduction, Terminologie, Rédaction* 13 (1), 9–20.

von Flotow, L. (2012) Translating women: From recent histories and re-translations to 'querying' translation, and metramorphosis. *Quaderns: Revista de Traducció* 19, 127–139.

Yonge, C.D. (transl.) (1854–1890) On the life of Moses II. VII:37. In *The Works of Philo Judaeus, the Contemporary of Josephus*. London: H.G. Bohn. Available at http://www.earlychristianwritings.com/yonge, accessed July 2018.

5 Challenging the State: Subversive Welsh Translators in Britain in the 1790s

Marion Löffler

Imperial Britain, Ethnic Wales and the Translator

This chapter focuses on the uses of translation from imperial English into colonised Welsh during the Franco-British war of 1793–1802. It explores the complex relationship between political domination and the translator's position as an interpreter of power within the Welsh tradition of Bible translation, which has insisted on fluent target texts (TTs) in order to enrich the Welsh language and culture (Bassnett, 2014: 56–60). One of the main goals is to draw attention to the translation experience in relation to colonised languages within Europe before the 20th century, an issue which, leaving aside the work of Michael Cronin regarding Ireland (Cronin, 1996: 3; Cronin, 2004), remains neglected in translation research.[1] I will argue that domesticating strategies which result in fluent translations do not necessarily amount to the 'ethnocentric violence' which, according to Venuti (2008: 16), characterises such translation *from colonised into colonial* languages, leading him to favour a 'foreignising' strategy. Related to this, I will demonstrate that, during the 1790s, an attempt at foreignising a Welsh TT was rejected by Welsh target language (TL) guardians as a threat to the continuity of the Welsh textual tradition. Last but not least, the chapter will contend that the 'invisibility' of the translator in the TT, rather than ignoring the translator's efforts as is often the case, can save him or her from political persecution by the dominant group.

During the French Revolutionary Wars of 1793–1802, Welsh translators were able to draw on their centuries-old translation tradition (Davies, 2012; Miguélez-Carballeira *et al.*, 2016) to voice specifically Welsh protests against British state ideology and to pursue their own cultural projects. Three case studies from the beginning of the war demonstrate the complex relationships between British imperial state power, the Welsh nation and the cultural and ideological aims of Welsh translators. First, in 1793, the official translator of liturgies appointed by the Anglican Church (i.e. the British state church), which supported the British war effort, used his position between political centre and internal colony in order to further his Enlightenment-inspired aim of modernising the Welsh language. He achieved this by publishing his translation in an orthography he had devised himself. His attempt, however, foundered on the opposition of Welsh intellectuals who rejected this as a foreignisation of Welsh print culture. Second, in 1795, a preacher from an illegal Protestant denomination which had dissented from the Anglican Church subverted the pro-war message of these liturgies by translating pacifist English satires on them into Welsh and joining them into a larger Welsh TT. He thus intensified the radical message of the source texts (STs), but also reinforced Welsh religious identity outside the British state church. Third, in 1796, an anonymous translator transformed a grand pro-war ST into a short pacifist TT by omission and translation of a small part only. All three cases highlight how the central place of translators in negotiating colonial dominance enabled them to radically rewrite STs to express political opinions and influence their native textual tradition. The colonisation of ethnic groups by centralising states in early modern Europe, therefore, did not necessarily result in hegemonic rule over the politics and culture of the colonised. In Wales, translators into the Welsh language successfully used their position to refute English-language and British hegemony.

Political Domination, Religion and Language in Early Modern Britain

Welsh, a Celtic language spoken in Wales, had developed a written literary standard by the 12th century and was part of the medieval and Renaissance translation cultures that rendered texts from classical languages into European vernaculars (Russell, 1995: 111–113, 131). Wales was incorporated into the emerging British state by King Henry VIII's Acts of Union of 1536 and 1543 (Williams, 1987: 258–275) and thus became what has been called an 'internal colony' (Evans, 1991; Hechter, 1998: 59–112; Williams, 2005).[2] The unequal power relationship between colonial English and colonised Welsh was codified by the Act of 1536. The state language (English), spoken by less than 10% of the Welsh population, was declared 'the natural mother tongue' for the whole of Great Britain, the language of law courts and an essential qualification for the holding of office (Bowen, 1908: 87; Roberts, 1997). As a result of this legislation, the native Welsh ruling class embarked on a process of Anglicisation, with many moving to the rising centre of imperial power, London.

At the same time, this emerging British state sought to replace Catholicism with a Protestant state church, an objective which would be furthered by the use of Welsh, the language spoken by the population. Hence, in 1563 Queen Elizabeth I passed An Act for the Translating of the Bible and the Divine Service into the Welsh Tongue, which decreed that 'the Bible, consisting of the New Testament and the Old, together with the Book of Common Prayer and the Administration of the Sacraments should be translated into the British or Welsh tongue'. It also established that a copy of this Bible should be placed in every church in areas where Welsh was spoken. The dominance of English was ensured by the obligation to place an English Bible and Book of Common Prayer next to the Welsh versions, so that 'such as do not understand the said Language, may by conferring both Tongues together, the sooner attain to the Knowledge of the English Tongue' (Bowen, 1908: 149ff.). The ensuing 1588 translation of the Bible into Welsh (from Hebrew and Latin) 'effectively saved the Welsh language from extinction' (Bassnett, 2011: 98) and led to the development of a translation culture that valued fluency and intelligibility above all else.[3] Though Welsh and English belong to different branches of the Indo-European 'family' (Celtic and Germanic respectively), Welsh-language culture survived as a peripheral part of the dominant English-language state culture, with fluent translations and adaptations from English constituting the larger part of Welsh literary texts until the beginning of the 19th century (Ashton, 1893: 18; Parry, 1953: 226–227). This made the translator a central cultural agent in Wales, who had the power to influence whether and how values from the dominant source culture were introduced into Welsh life. The domesticating approach to translation adopted by Welsh translators aimed at deleting all traces of English culture, thereby committing acts of 'ethnocentric violence' against the dominant English culture and in resistance to it.

By the end of the 18th century, the Anglican Church was a powerful instrument of state hegemony in early modern Britain. It provided the administrative structure of the state through its parish system and disseminated state ideology through English-language sermons, liturgies, hymns, prayers and catechisms. These could be bought and read privately, but, most importantly, every parish priest was obliged to perform them with the congregations in religious services. At times of pestilence and war, additional religious ceremonies of public fasting were decreed by the reigning king or queen, who constituted the head of the state and of the Anglican Church. For all such days of 'fasting, humiliation, and the imploring of divine intercession', official liturgies were published as pamphlets and distributed to parishes (Bartel, 1955). In order to ensure observance of these state church rituals in Wales, translations of such texts into Welsh were produced from at least 1683 (Morris, 1983). These were undertaken by translators employed by the crown and published by the licensed royal printers at the centre of imperial power, in London. Neither the names of the authors of the STs nor the names of the translators were given on the TTs. Both were invisible instruments of state hegemony.

Official Translation and Cultural Subversion

At the outset of the war against the French Republic, George III of England proclaimed an additional public day of fasting for 19 April 1793. A text published and distributed to all parishes, *Form of Prayer to be used in all Churches and Chapels throughout that Part of Great Britain called England, Dominion of Wales and Town of Berwick-upon-Tweed*, urged the population to abstain from food, and instead to attend worship. The official Welsh translation was entitled *Furv Gweddi, i'w Harver o vewn y Rhan o Brydain Vawr à Elwir Lloegyr, Tywysogaeth Cynmru, a Threv Berwic-ar-Dwid*. An anonymous London-based Welshman produced this fluent translation, whose text was laid out in exactly the same format as the English text, and both language versions were published by Eyre and Strahan, 'Printers to the King's Most Excellent Majesty' in London. The Welsh translation, *Furv Gweddi*, employed the Welsh language – a symbol of the cultural Welsh nation – to further British state patriotism against a French enemy. The translator fully rendered the different parts of the *Form of Prayer* into Welsh: the Morning Prayer (Borëawl Weddi), Communion Service (Gwasanaeth y Cymmun) and the Order for Evening Prayer (Y Drevyn am Brydnawnawl Weddi), and the intervening hymns and dialogues between priest and congregation. As is usual in official translation, the translator had little space for creativity, constrained by the fact that the state was patron and employer. Within these limits, however, he demonstrated an eagerness to further the state ideology by a choice of lexis which went beyond the original text and bordered on mis-translation. Where, for instance, in a passage which occurred in the morning and evening prayer, God was asked to 'assist our warfare against an enemy to all Christian Kings, Princes and States', the word 'warfare' was omitted in the TT, and God was instead implored simply to assist 'our effort': 'ein hymdrech yn erbyn gelyn i holl Vreninodd, Tywysogion, a Thaleithiau Cristynogawl' ('our effort against the enemy of all Kings, Princes and Christian States'). By rewriting 'warfare' as the more neutral 'effort', the translator hoped to ensure that a Welsh audience, which he perceived as more intensely religious than the Englishmen among whom he lived, would not perceive this request to God as blasphemous. Throughout, the translator provided a fluent translation into his native colonial language to the best of his ability, thus helping maintain the unequal power relationship between political centre and periphery.

Unnoticed by the state authorities, however, the anonymous translator of this 1793 *Form of Prayer* into *Furv Gweddi* used his paid employment to attempt a change in the Welsh textual tradition by altering its orthography. His identity was eventually revealed through this use of a new orthography for the translation which he himself had devised to correspond with contemporary Enlightenment ideals of rationality and transparency. He was William Owen Pughe (1759–1835), a key member of the Welsh intellectual diaspora in London, which was then developing the tenets of Welsh cultural nationalism (Carr, 2000). As other colonised nations have been shown to do, they collected, published and translated Welsh literary treasures into English, but they also worked on modernising Welsh on the basis of what they perceived to be the principles of the Enlightenment. Pughe (who later wrote a Welsh version of John Milton's *Paradise Lost*) was one of the editors of the first published volumes of medieval Welsh poetry and prose, but his main focus was language reform. In an effort to 'restore the Welsh language to its primitive purity as well as to improve the minds of our countrymen' (Williams, 1942: 132), he postulated a limited number of 223 'elementary words' from which all other lexical items were derived. This, among other changes, included a major reorganisation of the established Welsh orthography to replace the double consonants used in Welsh printed texts, *ch*, *dd*, *ff*, *ng*, *ll* and *rh* with single letters (denoting the sounds $|x|$, $|\eth|$, $|f|$, $|\eta|$, $|\dot{l}|$ and the aspirated alveolar $|r|$). This necessitated in turn the introduction of the grapheme v – unusual in Welsh print – to denote the sound $|v|$, since the consonant f which had fulfilled this function now denoted $|f|$.

Pughe, a Welshman who lived in London, was well aware of the dominance of the British state church, whose parishes provided the administrative structure for Britain. By securing the commission of translating the 1793 *Form of Prayer*, he hoped that his position as royal translator would enable him to use the TT to establish his 'rational' orthography in the Welsh language. His translation, *Furv Gweddi*, was used in every parish church during the mandatory religious service throughout Wales on the official day of fast, 19 April 1793. Reading material was relatively scarce at the time, which is why such translations were kept for years and consulted time and again, prolonging their impact.

The state remained unaware of this attempt to subvert an official publication. Nevertheless, Pughe's attempt to break with 500 years of Welsh printing conventions was ultimately unsuccessful. He had not accounted for the strong feelings aroused by his violation of Welsh cultural norms. The native clergy of Wales, who constituted the larger part of its intelligentsia, were politically pro-British and held a considerable amount of power as employees of the state church. At the same time, however, they exerted considerable cultural influence in maintaining Welsh traditions and were thus able to reject Pughe's reform. As Venuti (1998: 68) suggests, 'translation constructs a domestic representation for a foreign text and culture', but 'it simultaneously constructs a domestic subject, a position of intelligibility that is also an ideological position, informed by the codes and canons, interests and agendas of certain domestic social groups'. The Welsh Bible and Welsh religious publications in the traditional orthography had been at the heart of the canon of Welsh culture since the 16th century. The attempt to change their orthography, their visual representation, was therefore seen as an attack on the linguistic and cultural integrity of this canon (see also Cronin, 1996: 66), which was guarded by the Welsh clergy as the culturally dominant social group. The English letter *v* instead of the Welsh *f*, present even in the first word of the title page *Furv Gweddi,* evoked a hostile reaction from Anglican priests, Welsh schoolmasters and Nonconformist Protestant ministers alike, who overcame their religious disagreements in defence of their common cultural tradition. Reverend John Williams of Llanrwst in north Wales was the first to condemn the translation, on the grounds that it lacked Welsh patriotism:

> The *infamous translation*, as it is stiled [*sic*], of the Prayer for the late <u>Fast</u>, the Clergy of this country attribute to <u>You</u>: and they are indignant, to a high degree, on the occasion. And so am I, who boast as great love to my native language & country, as the best of them. (Morris, 1983: 136–7; original emphasis)

Williams was not attacking the fluency of the translation: what he perceived as 'infamous' was its appearance in a foreignised orthography. Letters by other Welsh intellectuals indicate that the disapproval was general. Henry Parry from Holyhead on the isle of Anglesey, for instance, informed the famous poet and author Walter Davies that:

> William Owen Pughe has broken his shins with the Welsh clergy by his introduction of the new Orthography to the Welsh Language in the Form of Prayer for the General Fast. I am so far of his opinion that necessity first brought the double characters to use; it is, indeed a clumsy contrivance, but since it has been so long sanctioned by custom and habit, it is dangerous to meddle with. (Jenkins, 1908b: 27)

The reply by Davies, a measured man who in general welcomed Pughe's efforts, clarifies the reasons for the rejection of the new orthography. Noting that 'innovations in the Welsh Orthography [were] W^m. Owen's hobby horse of late', he complained that a text printed in this orthography looked 'Cornish, or at least did so when I saw it Sunday last' (Jenkins, 1908b: 27). Cornish, the Celtic language native to the Duchy of Cornwall in south-west England, whose last native speaker was said to have died in 1777, had not benefited from a Bible translation as Welsh had. The few surviving texts in the Cornish language had been 'written down using the contemporary English orthography' (Russell, 1995: 113–114, 222), and thereby the 'specificity' of the language, of which vocabulary and spelling are a part, was severely compromised by English influence. Like early modern Irish and Welsh, Cornish had come under 'intense pressure' (Cronin, 1996: 66) from colonial English, but unlike them it had yielded and disintegrated. Davies's derision at the Cornish appearance of Pughe's texts was a rejection of the foreign appearance of the Welsh translation, suggesting that it resembled the Anglicised ruins of a dead Celtic language.

Despite the negative response, Pughe persisted in using his position as official translator to gain access to the circles which, by editing and publishing new editions of the Bible, greatly influenced Welsh cultural identity. He secured the commission for the translation of the *Form of Prayer* again in 1794, and from 1795 turned to the influential Methodist leader Thomas Charles of Bala, asking him to adopt his orthography in one of several Bible editions then underway. Charles appeared susceptible to his advances, but opposition arose once more against this alien orthography, seen as an affront to Welsh cultural identity. Reverend John Roberts of Tremeirchion (near St Asaph), one of a team of translators from the classical languages into Welsh, campaigned against it because:

> It will do much harm. The orthography of the copy prepared for the press, is very much changed and altered, and makes the language a different dialect from that of the Bible in present use.... The present orthography of the Welsh version of the Bible, has been thought for centuries not only unexceptionable, but a model of purity and correctness, and considered as the established standard of criticism and pure language. Any departure from the national standard will be particularly inconvenient to the public. (Jenkins, 1908a: 556)

It is significant that the change in spelling was perceived by Roberts to be 'inconvenient to the public', creating what Venuti has called 'resistancy' – a 'strange and estranging' appearance of the text in the target culture (Venuti, 2008: 263) – since it challenged the TL norms, in this case the expected orthography (Munday, 2012: 220–221, Figure 9.1). The 'purity' and 'correctness' of what Roberts described as a 'national standard' for his cultural nation, embodied in the Bible as a central artefact of Welsh culture, was under threat from culturally foreign intrusion. Pughe's attempted use of official translation in the service of the state to change the appearance of Welsh translations thus foundered on the cultural nationalism of the Welsh religious intelligentsia, who were stalwart supporters of the British state and its Church, but who rejected an orthography that made printed Welsh texts appear Anglicised, foreign and disintegrated. Foreignisation was in this case perceived as an act of violence against the Welsh textual tradition.

Radical Translation and the Subversion of Dominant Ideology

One of the immediate effects of the French Revolution of 1789 had been the inclusion of socially and ethnically marginal groups into public discourse. From 1793, the war conducted by Britain against the young French Republic witnessed the emergence of an unprecedented wave of anti-war texts from such quarters in the dominant English language. As English artisans and workers began to write and to publish politically radical and anti-war texts, their Welsh counterparts were drawn to these as potential STs for political translations which could be used to subvert British state ideology. This may be described in terms of Steiner's *Wahlverwandschaft* ('elective affinity'), whereby the translator overcomes linguistic and cultural differences by being drawn to the ST 'because he is kindred to it' (Steiner, 1998: 398). Welsh translators recognised their own nascent political radicalism in this new wave of English radical ideology which emerged in the 1790s. The result was a steep rise in political translation from English. Between 1700 and 1789, only five political pamphlets had been translated into Welsh, yet the decade following the revolution of 1789 witnessed the publication of at least 20. Once the war had commenced, English radicals rewrote state Church publications like the *Form of Prayer* into politically radical texts whose purpose was diametrically opposed to that of the official STs. Welsh translators rewrote even more drastically by selecting disparate English texts, translating them into Welsh and reconstructing them in ways that strengthened their very own radical or anti-war message (Davies, 1980; Löffler, 2013; Löffler, 2014: 52–62).

Thomas Evans (1764–1833), a weaver and Unitarian minister who lived and preached far from the imperial metropolis, in the tiny hamlet of Brechfa, near Carmarthen, in south-west Wales, created some of the most innovative and radical Welsh translations in this genre (Davies, 1926: 56–65). Self-taught in English, he corresponded with and translated the works of the foremost English religious radicals of the time, Joseph Priestley and Theophilus Lindsey. One of the first proponents of Unitarianism in Wales – a radical Protestant sect which under the Religious Toleration Act 1689 was illegal in Britain until 1813 – Evans founded the Welsh periodical *The Miscellaneous Repository: Neu Y Drysorfa Gymmysgedig*, whose contents, despite the bilingual title (which shows how recently the concept of the periodical had been borrowed from English culture) was entirely in Welsh (Löffler, 2012: 28–29). Evans translated from English and wrote Welsh texts that were influenced by English models. His texts contributed to creating a new Welsh cultural reality of political radicalism, set in train by the French Revolution (for a series of publications on this subject, see the 'Wales and the French Revolution' series published by University of Wales Press since 2012). Among his most subversive pieces are two series of prayers and hymns that combine a rewriting of *Furv Gweddi* with translations of radical English texts that had subverted the official English liturgy. Evans leaned on the text *Form of Prayer*, its Welsh translation as *Furv Gweddi* of 1793 and 1794, and the politically subversive versions of the *Form of Prayer* published in the satirical London serial *Politics for the People* (1794). He translated and assembled these texts into cultural artefacts that were at times politically more radical than their English counterparts, steering Welsh cultural identity towards an almost republican pacifism, which until then had not existed in Welsh culture.

The first series of these translations appeared in the first number of Evans's *Miscellaneous Repository*, in spring 1795. From the variety of material contained in *Politics for the People*, Evans chose pieces that mocked the official *Form of Prayer* of 1794. He translated 'A prayer for the people who live under despotic governments' (*Politics for the People*, vol. II, no. 5, 1794: 4–6) as 'Gweddi i'w harfer gan y bobl a fyddo yn byw dan lywodraeth greulon drahaus, ar ddydd ympryd' ('A Prayer to be used by those people who live under a cruel and tyrannical government, on a day of fast'). This was followed by a radical hymn from the previous issue of *Politics for the People*, 'An HYMN for the FAST DAY, to be sung by the FRIENDS OF MANKIND' (*Politics for the People*, vol. II, no. 4, 1794: 3–7), which he interpreted more freely by adding at least three new stanzas and calling it 'HYMN i'w chanu ar ddydd ympryd gan gyfeillion dynolryw' ('A HYMN to be sung on the fast day by the friends of mankind'). The sequence closed with 'Gweddi arall i'w harfer gan gyfeillion dynolryw ar ddiwedd addoliad' ('Another prayer to be used by the friends of mankind at the end of worship'), for which no ST has been discovered so far.[4] While Evans relied on Pughe's *Furv Gweddi* for intralingual translation, it is significant that he too rejected Pughe's new orthography, preferring the traditional spelling as part of his bid to write fluent texts acceptable to his target audience.

Evans added to the ideological impact of the English texts by combining them in his translation and by renaming them with clear reference to official fast-day worship. The first prayer had no directions for use in the ST, but in the TT was described as for the *ddydd ympryd* ('day of fast'). Evans translated this text closely, which perhaps enabled him to discover key themes and vocabulary for his own writing. The radical themes for the whole series were established as a lament for the suffering caused by tyrannical wars, a plea to God to assist mankind by removing despots, and in the hope of recovering the natural liberty of man, one of the key themes of the French Revolution. Evans developed political concepts and synonyms until then used in the religious domain only. 'Tyrants' and 'despots' became *treiswyr*, *trawslywodraethwyr*, *gormeswyr* and *gorthrymmydd* ('rapists', 'misgovernors', 'tyrants' and 'oppressor'), for instance. This enabled him and future religious assemblies to discuss the 'misuse of authority' by the hegemonic powers ('[c]amddefnyddio [eu] hawdurdod') (Löffler, 2012: 226–227). The phrase 'misuse of authority' was an addition by Evans which helped transport his translation from the pacifism of the English ST to political radicalism (for a short analysis of the adaptation of the hymn in this series, see Löffler, 2012: 47–49). The closing piece of the translated series most radically challenged the dominant political status quo (from a religious perspective, as is to be expected in early modern Europe). In one key passage, God is called upon to

> attal y llifogydd mawrion o waed dynol ac sydd yn boddi y ddaear wrth ewyllys brenhinoedd CRISTIANOGOL, y tu hwnt i bob esampl yn yr oesoedd mwyaf creulon, barbaraidd, anwybodus a thywyll. Siomma

ddychymmygion pawb o ddifrodwyr gwaedlyd ddynolryw ac sydd yn ymgyssylltu yn erbyn rhydd-did a gwybodaeth, y rhai ydynt wir *synagog satan,* a dychwel eu calonnau, diddymma bob egwyddor o greulondeb gwladol ym mhob dwyfron; fel na byddo creulondeb rhyfel a chelanedd yn aros ond yn unig mewn hanes, fel coffadwriaeth arswydus am ffyrnigrwydd a chreulondeb dyn! (In Löffler, 2012: 234)

stem the great floods of human blood which, beyond any example from the cruellest, darkest, most barbaric and ignorant ages, drown the earth by the will of CHRISTIAN kings. Disappoint the designs of all the bloody despoilers of mankind who join forces against liberty and knowledge, they are the true *assembly of satan*, and turn their hearts, dissolve every rudiment of political cruelty in every bosom; so that the cruelty of war and carnage remain only in history, a terrible memorial of the ferocity and cruelty of man! (Löffler, 2012: 234–235; original emphasis)

To call the Christian kings of Europe the 'true assembly of satan' was not only blasphemous but politically seditious in the late 18th century, and could have earned Evans the death sentence for high treason. It is no surprise that these translations were mentioned in the speech given by Judge George Hardinge when in 1802 Evans was sentenced to two years in prison and to stand in the stocks twice for singing a political song. The severity of the sentence was due to the prosecution's knowledge that Evans had 'altered and corrupted the form of prayer … for the fast day' in 1795, because he was 'disaffected to our Government' (Löffler, 2013: 104–105). By publishing his translation anonymously, Evans had tried his very best to make himself invisible in order to escape political persecution. The impact of Evans's translation was enhanced by its publication as an affordable Welsh periodical distributed by travelling salesmen. Echoing the official *Form of Prayer*, it was also ready to use in pacifist religious services held by the illegal Unitarian denomination on the fast day. Given the attention paid to Evans's subversion of the official *Form of Prayer* at his court case in 1802, it is most likely that he and other Unitarian ministers used this translation to perform anti-war religious services in the Carmarthen area in the second half of the 1790s.

The existence of Evans's translations, then, confirms Venuti's claim that 'the identity-forming power of translation always threatens to embarrass cultural and political institutions because it reveals the shaky foundations of their social authority' (Venuti, 1998: 68). The social and political authority of the British state was challenged by Evans's domesticating approach and resultant fluent translation, which also assisted in the creation of a political vocabulary that enabled further expression of radically new political ideas in a colonised language. Venuti's view that a domesticating approach to translation constitutes an 'act of ethnocentric violence', therefore, cannot be confirmed in this specific case. On the contrary, the wish to produce fluent translations appears to have enabled

Evans to write more sophisticated Welsh in the political domain, and thus had an educational effect.[5]

Subverting the Source Text by Omission and Translation

Most politically radical Welsh texts were heavily religious in the 1790s, but there was one exception: a non-religious pacifist text that was translated from a secular English text of which, however, about 95% had been omitted. In 1795, an anonymous English author had published *An Accurate and Impartial Narrative of the War by an Officer of the Guards in Two Volumes*, which admiringly described the British military campaigns on the continent between 1793 and 1795. This account was over 270 pages long and mainly written in verse. In 1796, a 15-page Welsh prose publication entitled *Dioddefiadau y Byddinoedd Brutanaidd yn y Dychweliad trwy Holland, yn y Blynyddoedd 1794, a 1795* (*The Sufferings of the British Armies on the Return through Holland in the Years 1794 and 1795*) contained the translation of 15 pages from the end of the English text. Rather than acknowledging its English source, this translation pretended to be an anonymous, gripping first-hand account which perhaps may be understood as a pseudo-translation in reverse. Where the author of a pseudo-translation would write an original text but present it as a translation from an exotic or prestigious nonexistent source in order to enhance its literary status (Toury, 1984: 83), this translation was presented as a short, original pamphlet, hiding any connection with its English source. The reasons for this act were that the ideology of the Welsh translation directly challenged the English text (which was supportive of the hegemonic ideology) and that the title and form of the ST may have led to doubts about the legitimacy of the translation by its intended lower-class Welsh audience. The main tool used by the translator to subvert the prevailing state ideology was omission.

The translator discarded nearly 95% of the English text and provided a new title, which began with the word *Dioddefiadau* ('sufferings'), thus creating a cultural artefact whose ideology was diametrically opposed to that of the source. Most of the English text was a versified glorification of the officer's life on the battlefield and in the ballroom, accompanied by detailed prose notes outlining technical details of military campaigns. It had clearly been written for the entertainment of an English upper-class audience. Only its last chapter, 'A Concise Narrative of the Retreat through Holland to Westphalia in the Years 1794, and 1795', which lamented how 'the brilliant conquests of the Allies were ... wrested from their hands in a manner unequalled in the annals of history', was in prose (Anonymous, 1795: vol. II, p. 105). Moreover, only this chapter described the suffering of common troops and civilian populations in the Netherlands and in Belgium. The translator chose only two sections from this last chapter, thereby omitting most of the ST because it did not suit the ideological purpose of condemning the war against France. The impact of the text was enhanced by its publication as a cheap Welsh pamphlet, which changed the socio-ethnic target audience from an English ruling elite to a dominated Welsh group.

Apart from omission, the translator also employed a strategic placement of key words, phrases and passages as a tool in changing the ideological message. The difference in title has already been mentioned. Once the reader opened the book, the Welsh translation began with the word *afiechyd* ('illness'), where the ST had given a poetic description of military uniforms. Most of the translation describes in shocking images the suffering of wounded commoners, simple soldiers and their families, who had joined the entourage of the British army on the continent. Again, the isolated location of these descriptions towards the end of the ST was important. After 240 pages of endless ruminations about balls and military victories, it is questionable whether many English upper-class readers would have proceeded to this very graphic description of how the family of a common sergeant of the 55th Army had frozen to death:

> Near another cart, a little further on the common, we perceived a stout-looking man, and a beautiful young woman with an infant about seven months old at the breast; all three frozen, and dead. The mother had most certainly expired in the act of suckling her child, as with one breast exposed she lay on the drifted snow, the milk to all appearance in a stream, drawn from the nipple by the babe, and instantly congealed. The infant seemed as if its lips had but just been disengaged, and it reposed its little head upon the mother's bosom, with an overflow of milk, frozen as it trickled from the mouth. (Anonymous, 1795: vol. II, p. 123)

> Yn agos i gertwyn arall ychydig ymhellach ar y mynydd, ni a ganfyddem ddyn o olwg nerthol, a benyw iefangc brydferth, a phlentyn bâch ynghylch saith mis oed wrth ei bron. – y tri wedi rhewi i'w marwolaeth. Y fam yn ddiammeu a drengoedd wrth roddi bron i'w phlentyn, o herwydd ei bod a'g un fron yn noeth, wedi gorwedd ar yr eira lluwchiedig, a'r llaeth yn ôl pôb golygiad wedi ei dynnu o'r fron yn ffrwd gan y plentyn, ac wedi ceulo yn union. Yr oedd yn ymddangos nad oedd y plentyn ond newydd ollwng ei afael, ac yr oedd wedi gosod ei ben bâch ar fynwes ei fam, a'r llaeth wedi rhewi fal yr oedd yn dylifo o'i enau; yr oedd yr olwg arnynt yn iraidd ac yn wridiog, megis rhai fyddai'n cysgu'n esmwyth. Ynghylch hanner canllath ymhellach, yr oedd dŷn marw arall. (Anonymous, 1796: 12–13)

The very close and fluent Welsh rendition of the scene, on the other hand, was the centre piece and high point of the 15-page translation. The most shocking paragraph from a marginal chapter took pride of place here. Cheap pamphlets like *Dioddefiadau y Byddinoedd* were read aloud during the knitting or spinning evenings that were characteristic of the Welsh home industries at the time. New to Welsh writing, this deeply disturbing description was presented to listeners and readers whose own territory had not seen war for centuries, and it must have shocked them. The translator had probably been spurred into action by the Supplementary Militia Act of 1796, which demanded the raising of an additional 4457 supplementary militiamen from Wales (Owen, 1997: 27). The British government achieved this number partly by forceful recruitment of Welshmen by press gangs, and by heightened war propaganda in the form of public posters and pamphlets. The translation attempted to raise suspicions against this oppressive military state patriotism. Its impact was confirmed by the problems which military press gangs and state recruiters encountered in the area where it had been published in 1796 and in subsequent years (Howell, 2000: 203–205).

Conclusion

The three cases here analysed demonstrate the power of the translators – positioned as they are between dominant and subordinate (colonial and colonised) cultures – to choose to 'faithfully' reproduce, select, restructure, re-assemble, fabricate or omit (Tymoczko & Gentzler, 2002: xxi; Venuti, 1998: 68). This chapter has explored the complex relationships between a dominant state, a subordinate ethnic nation and politically subversive groups in the 1790s. Significantly, the dominant domesticating translation strategy *into* the subordinate language, Welsh, which produced fluent translations, may be perceived to be supportive of the TL, while the foreignisation of an aspect of the TL was rejected by the target culture. The *Furv Gweddi* produced by official translator William Owen Pughe in an orthography that resembled English was rejected as 'foreignised' by the pro-British but culturally Welsh intelligentsia because it was reminiscent of colonial English. Venuti's suggestion that the dominant domesticating paradigm of translation *always* constitutes ethnic violence, based as it is on his work on 20th-century literature in major European languages (Venuti, 2008: 265–277), cannot be upheld for early-modern translation into a subordinate language. The subversive fluent translations produced by Thomas Evans in the second case study developed radical ST ideology further by selection, reassembly and rewriting, challenging the political powers of Britain and Europe in the process. While Evans's act of translating from English apparently confirms the *culturally* dominant position of the SL, English, it enabled him to create translations which were so fluent that SL and source culture values disappeared into a new Welsh radicalism. The anonymous creator of the non-religious pacifist translation from a pro-war English text in the third case study chose extreme omission and domestication, reducing a long pro-war verse narrative by 95% in order to produce a short Welsh version of starkly anti-war prose which was diametrically opposed to the ST ideology. The translators in the second and third case studies thus 'embarrassed' apparently hegemonic political powers by means of translation.

Following the tradition of Welsh religious writing and translation established in 1588 by means of the translation of the Bible into Welsh, all three translators took a domesticating approach to produce fluent poetry and prose texts that endowed Welsh culture with new themes, concepts and lexical items and aimed at deleting source culture values and SL traces. Two of the three translators chose to remain invisible in order to escape the political persecution meted out to Welsh, English, Scottish and Irish radicals in Britain at the time. While there is no doubt that the legislation of 1536 and 1543 rendered Wales an internal colony of Britain, with English as the politically dominant language, the complex use and cultural effect of translation from English into Welsh denies assumptions of a simple political and cultural hegemony by the dominant power.

Notes

(1) Maria Tymoczko's work (1999) is important in the context of colonisation and de-colonisation of a Celtic country, the Republic of Ireland, but it considers translation from post-colonial Irish into the former colonial language (English) and is therefore not central to this argument.
(2) There is no doubt that Wales has displayed features of a colony in its relation to medieval England and later Britain, especially as regards the power relationship between Welsh and English, but the notion of Wales as a colony or now in a post-colonial situation is debated.
(3) Like Martin Luther, who used *verdeutschen* ('to Germanise') (Bassnett, 2014: 58–59), early-modern Welsh translators routinely used *Cymreigio* ('to Cymricise') instead of to 'translate'.
(4) For the English STs, see *Politics of the People*, volume II, numbers 4 and 5 (1794). For the three Welsh texts and a back-translation into modern English, see Löffler (2012: 226–234).
(5) The educational purpose which lay behind the translation work of some early-modern Welsh authors in the privacy of their manuscripts is not the topic of this study, but is clearly attested in Welsh manuscripts from the period.

References

Anonymous (1793a) *Form of Prayer to be used in all Churches and Chapels throughout that Part of Great Britain called England, Dominion of Wales and Town of Berwick-upon-Tweed*. London: Charles Eyre and Andrew Strahan, Printers to the King's Most Excellent Majesty.
Anonymous (1793b) *Furv Gweddi, i'w Harver o vewn y Rhan o Brydain Vawr à Elwir Lloegyr, Tywysogaeth Cynmru, a Threv Berwic-ar-Dwid*. London: Charles Eyre ac Andrew Strahan, Argrafwyr i Ardderchocav Vawrhydi y Brenin.
Anonymous (1795) *An Accurate and Impartial Narrative of the War by an Officer of the Guards. In Two Volumes. Comprising the Campaigns of 1793, 1794, and the Retreat through Holland to Westphalia, in 1795*. London: Printed for the Author.
Anonymous (1796) *Dioddefiadau y Byddinoedd Brutanaidd yn y Dychweliad trwy Holland, yn y Blynyddoedd 1794, a 1795*. Croesoswallt: Thomas Wood.
Ashton, C. (1893) *Hanes Llenyddiaeth Gymreig, o 1650 A.D. hyd 1850*. Liverpool: I. Foulkes.
Bartel, R. (1955) The story of the public fast days in England. *Anglican Theological Review* 37 (3), 190–200.

Bassnett, S. (2011) The translator as cross-cultural mediator. In K. Malmkjær and K. Windle (eds) *The Oxford Handbook of Translation Studies* (pp. 94–107). Oxford: Oxford University Press.

Bassnett, S. (2014) *Translation Studies* (4th edn). London: Routledge.

Bowen, I. (1908) *The Statutes of Wales*. London: Unwin.

Carr, G. (2000) William Owen Pughe and the London societies. In B. Jarvis (ed.) *A Guide to Welsh Literature c. 1700–1800* (pp. 168–186). Cardiff: University of Wales Press.

Cronin, M. (1996) *Translating Ireland: Translation, Languages, Cultures*. Cork: Cork University Press.

Cronin, M. (2004) Global questions and local visions: A microcosmopolitan perspective. In A. von Rothkirch and D. Williams (eds) *Beyond the Difference: Welsh Literature in Comparative Contexts* (pp. 186–202). Cardiff: University of Wales Press.

Davies, D. (1926) *The Influence of the French Revolution on Welsh Life and Literature*. Carmarthen: W. Morgan & Son.

Davies, H.M. (1980) Morgan John Rhys and James Bicheno: Anti-Christ and the French Revolution in England and Wales. *Bulletin of the Board of Celtic Studies* 29 (1), 111–127.

Davies, S. (2012) O Alice i Alys: Cyfieithu Clasur i'r Gymraeg. *Llên Cymru* 35, 116–146.

Eaton, D.I. (1794) *Politics for the People*. London: Dan Isaac Eaton.

Evans, N. (1991) Internal colonialism? Colonization, economic development and political mobilization in Wales, Scotland and Ireland. In G. Day and G. Rees (eds) *Regions, Nations and European Integration: Remaking the Celtic Periphery* (pp. 235–264). Cardiff: University of Wales Press.

Evans, T. (1795) *The Miscellaneous Repository: Neu, Y Drysorfa Gymmysgedig* 1 (1). Carmarthen: I. Ross.

Hechter, M. (1998) *Internal Colonialism: The Celtic Fringe in British National Development 1536–1966* (2nd edn, with a new introduction and a new appendix by the author). New Brunswick: Transaction Publishers.

Howell, D.W. (2000) *The Rural Poor in Eighteenth-Century Wales*. Cardiff: University of Wales Press.

Jenkins, D.E. (1908a) *The Life of the Rev. Thomas Charles of Bala, Volume II: 1784–1805*. Denbigh: Llewelyn Jenkins.

Jenkins, D.E. (1908b) *The Life of the Rev. Thomas Charles of Bala, Volume III: 1804–1814*. Denbigh: Llewelyn Jenkins.

Löffler, M. (2012) *Welsh Responses to the French Revolution: Press and Public Discourse 1793–1802*. Cardiff: University of Wales Press.

Löffler, M. (2013) The Marseillaise in Wales. In M. Constantine and D. Johnston (eds) *'Footsteps of Liberty and Revolt': Essays on Wales and the French Revolution* (pp. 93–113). Cardiff: University of Wales Press.

Löffler, M. (with Jenkins, B.) (2014) *Political Pamphlets and Sermons from Wales 1790–1806*. Cardiff: University of Wales Press.

Miguélez-Carballeira, M., Price A. and Kaufmann, J. (2016) Introduction. Translation in Wales: History, theory and approaches. *Translation Studies* 9 (2), 125–136.

Morris, O.H. (1983) Ffurfiau gweddi. *National Library of Wales Journal* 23 (2), 130–140. [Despite the title, this article is in English.]

Munday, J. (2012) *Introduction to Translation Studies: Theories and Applications* (2nd edn). Abingdon: Routledge.

Owen, B. (1997) *History of the Welsh Militia and Volunteer Corps 1757–1908: Carmarthenshire, Pembrokeshire and Cardiganshire (Part 1)*. Wrexham: Bridge Books.

Parry, T. (1953) *Hanes Llenyddiaeth Gymraeg hyd 1900*. Cardiff: University of Wales Press.

Roberts, P.R. (1997) Tudor legislation and the political status of 'the British tongue'. In G.H. Jenkins (ed.) *The Welsh Language Before the Industrial Revolution* (pp. 123–152). Cardiff: University of Wales Press.

Russell, P. (1995) *An Introduction to the Celtic Languages*. London: Longman.

Steiner, G. (1998) *After Babel: Aspects of Language and Translation* (3rd edn). London: Oxford University Press.

Toury, G. (1984) Translation, literary translation and pseudotranslation. *Comparative Literature: An Annual Journal* 6, 73–85.

Tymoczko, M. (1999) *Translation in a Postcolonial Context: Early Irish Literature in English Translation*. Manchester: St Jerome.

Tymoczko, M. and Gentzler, E. (2002) *Translation and Power*. Boston, MA: University of Massachusetts Press.

Venuti, L. (1998) *The Scandals of Translation: Towards an Ethics of Difference*. London: Routledge.

Venuti, L. (2008) *The Translator's Invisibility: A History of Translation* (2nd edn). London: Routledge.

Williams, C. (2005) Problematizing Wales: An exploration in historiography and post-coloniality. In J. Aaron and C. Williams (eds) *Postcolonial Wales* (pp. 1–22). Cardiff: University of Wales Press.

Williams, G. (1987) *Recovery, Reorientation and Reformation: Wales c. 1415–1642*. Oxford: Oxford University Press.

Williams, G.J. (1942) Original documents: 4. Letters of Morgan John Rhys to William Owen [-Pughe]. *National Library of Wales Journal* 2 (3–4), 131–141.

6 The Greek–Turkish Population Exchange: Reverberations of a Historical Experience Through Translation

Maria Sidiropoulou and Özlem Berk Albachten

This chapter explores the 1923 population exchange between Greece and Turkey through an analysis of Greek and Turkish translations of Bruce Clark's *Twice a Stranger* (Granta Books, 2006), written some 80 years after the event.[1] We aim to demonstrate that discursive formations and narratives on this historical episode circulating in both countries have significantly shaped the representation of the Anatolian experience in the two target versions. Each translation contains discursive elements which appear both to reinforce and to resist hegemonic political discourses by accentuating locally privileged aspects of the experience. The recollections of the Muslims and Christians who survived the population exchange indeed reverberate in a very similar way through the Greek and Turkish target versions of Clark's source text. Both target versions provide eloquent culture-specific accounts of the population exchange and thus exemplify the different ways in which 'power/knowledge' about a shared past can circulate (Foucault, 1977, 1980). The workings of power and ideology have resulted in politically divergent translation choices, which underscores the potential of translation to shape collective memory and reinforce or resist powerful geopolitical narratives. As pointed out by Bayraktaroğlu and Sifianou (2001: 2), Greece's and Turkey's shared past has resulted in the establishment of profound cultural and emotional ties:

> The relationship between the Turks and the Greeks spreads over some 600 years, when the whole Balkan region was under the Ottoman Empire. From shortly after the Byzantine Empire and the capture of Constantinople by the Ottomans in 1453 until the Greek war of independence

in 1821, the two states lived in the same territory, and under Ottoman sovereignty. Even after the autonomous state of Greece was founded in the 1830s, a considerable number of Greeks preferred to stay on Turkish soil rather than move west to meet their compatriots. Until the exchange of populations in 1922–1923, there were spots of high Greek concentration in various parts of Anatolia […] and high concentrations of Turkish people in certain areas in Greece.

The population exchange of 1923 was intended to please both states, but this settlement was not unproblematic since, owing to the deep bonds between the exchanged communities, '[i]t was a cause of pain as well as a response to pain' (Bayraktaroğlu & Sifianou, 2001: 3). This historical episode has been a productive theme in Turkish and Greek literature, and several texts dealing with the subject have been translated into English and other languages or from Turkish to Greek and vice versa (Berk, 2006). This has resulted in a large pool of data that facilitates the exploration of the ways in which translation shifts reflect and refract the narratives that mediate and construct reality.

In *Twice a Stranger*, the journalist Bruce Clark explores how the 1923 population exchange between Greece and Turkey forged the future of both countries. The back cover of the book reads as follows:

In 1923, after a long war over the future of the Ottoman world, nearly two million citizens of Turkey and Greece were moved across the Aegean – expelled because they belonged to the 'wrong' religion. Bruce Clark's fascinating account of these turbulent events draws on new research in Greece and Turkey, and interviews with surviving refugees who lived through those years, allowing the victims of this large-scale ethnic cleansing to speak for themselves for the first time.

In the book, Clark discusses

how the exchange was negotiated; how the politicians decided who to include and who to exclude […] how the exchange was experienced by ordinary people in various parts of Greece and Turkey, and how the effect of the exchange is still palpable in the environment, the daily life and the self-understanding of those places. (2006: 19)

In his influential analysis of the media as a discursive system, Jean Baudrillard maintains that news media not only reproduce the form and content of ideologically shaped messages but also prefigure dominant patterns of production and consumption. This implies that real-life events are constructed and interpreted through a cultural and ideological lens, which is why they cannot simply be evaluated according to their truth value. Baudrillard goes as far as saying that journalists and publicists '*are manipulators of myth*: they stage an object or event as fiction' (1990: 93;

original emphasis). Bruce Clark himself tellingly acknowledged that his focus on the traumatic experiences of the population exchange was the 'psychological trauma of a separation' in a world where 'cultural identities were rich, complex and ambivalent' (Clark, 2006: 10, 2).

Translators, of course, can also be seen as manipulators of myths, in that they have to interpret the author's choices and make a myriad of conscious or unconscious decisions which then need to be decoded by potential readers. As pointed out by Ernst-August Gutt, this complex chain of meaning, especially concerning its unacknowledged cultural, ideological and political assumptions, has not always been taken into consideration, since 'finding the right way of expressing the content in the receptor language has tended to obscure the problems of the com-municability of the content itself' (Gutt, 2000: 103). Presupposing that the infinite ways of expressing content in a given target language and culture constitute one of the main concerns in translation studies, we can evaluate meaning as a dynamic process that is constantly being constructed and negotiated by authors, translators, readers and, of course, editors and publishers, whose interpretations always remain fragmentary and partial and thus can never be taken for granted. The main goal of this chapter is precisely to explore the ways in which diverse cultural, historical, political and situational factors have impinged on the Greek and Turkish translators' interpretation of the source text, and how meaning has been repackaged for readers (whose own interpretation may well be different from the intended one).

Intercultural Transfer as Simulation and the Contribution of Power

Intercultural communication through translation may be viewed as a type of simulation. For Baudrillard, the simulation of meaning is 'the generation by models of a real without origin or reality', which induces the real to 'coincide with their models of simulation' (Baudrillard, 1994: 1, 2). Baudrillard employs the allegorical example of a territory that is represented by a map to suggest that simulation (e.g. the making of a map) and the real (e.g. the territory simulated by the map) need not be coexistent. Rather, a simulacrum, a copy of copies, can *create* and thus indeed *survive* real – i.e. lived – life and its (symbolic) representations. It is precisely in this sense that Baudrillard's view of history diagnoses a world whose notions of what is real and what is artificially constructed become increasingly blurred, to the point of an annihilation of authenticity, as evident in some of the first lines of his work *Simulacra and Simulation*:

> Today abstraction is no longer that of the map, the double, the mirror, or the concept. Simulation is no longer that of a territory, a referential being, or a substance. It is the generation by models of a real without origin or

reality: a hyperreal. The territory no longer precedes the map, nor does it survive it. It is nevertheless the map that precedes the territory – *precession of simulacra* – that engenders the territory, and if one must return to the fable, today it is the territory whose shreds slowly rot across the extent of the map. It is the real, and not the map, whose vestiges persist here and there in the deserts that are no longer those of the Empire, but ours. *The desert of the real itself.* (Baudrillard, 1994: 1; original emphasis)

John Johnston (1992) discusses the relevance of Baudrillard's ideas with reference to the process of translating. In accounting for the reproduction of *simulated meaning relations* in postmodern times, Johnston poses a question which few translation scholars have attempted to address, asking whether, in the end, not 'every translation is a simulacrum, if we understand this word in two different senses, and according to what the translation may be said to accomplish'. Translators may, firstly, aim at fidelity and accuracy, merely reconstituting 'the target language in its vehicular aspect [...] through reference to the already written, to previously established cultural codings', while, secondly, they may 'deterritorialize the target language in such a way that it can't be recoded and recuperated by appeal to established cultural and spiritual meanings'. In the latter case, the end result diverges from the original but is also resonant with it, 'bringing to fulfilment or pushing along further what the original carried only as a precursor' (Johnston, 1992: 54). Drawing on Johnston's pioneering work, we also contend that the act of translating can be paralleled to a simulation process. At the same time, however, we turn Johnston's arguments towards a new direction by arguing that, like the map, target versions can be seen as simulacra which survive the source text and *precede* it (not chronologically, but rather in terms of access in the target environment). It appears that the two target versions here analysed, as simulacra, are in no way *obvious copies* of the *reality* depicted in the original. Rather, they are blurred representations of this reality, enhancing certain aspects of Bruce Clark's English text as well as resisting the narratives of antagonism and separation which occasionally prevail in the target environments. The analysis of translation shifts in two independently produced target texts, in short, allows an exploration of the ways in which both versions (as simulacra) negotiate and reflect the process of simulating the source text.

Power seems to be a condition for the *operational efficiency* of the simulation, and therefore pragmatic approaches to translation practice (such as functional approaches, relevance theory or politeness theory) could benefit from a more comprehensive understanding of this concept. There is little doubt that power-sensitive approaches to the analysis of translation strategies could help shed light on pragmatically oriented variables such as illocutionary or perlocutionary force, speaker–addressee distance, shifts typical of cultural transfer, the way translators exhibit politeness patterns in performing speech acts of representation, and how hegemonic narratives determine the choices of the translator (Sidiropoulou, 2013). The narrative of suffering highlighted in both target texts, for instance, may be a conscious or unconscious manifestation of a painful collective experience. However, while cultural representations are always transformed in the course of translational recontextualisations, our cognitive mechanisms and abilities act as factors of *attraction* which ensure that the final output resembles the original representation. As Dan Sperber (1996: 108) puts it, the transmissions of mental representations 'tend to be biased in the direction of attractor positions in the space of possibilities'. In other words, the shifts which shape the Anatolian experience in and across the two translated versions may be partly motivated by *interpretive* and *critical* considerations (Martin & Nakayama, 2003), but the limited space of possibilities available to both translators guarantees that both texts share a relevant number of characteristics in spite of their differences.

The Greek Simulation

The knowledge produced by local discursive formations seems to reverberate recognisably in the Greek target version. The Greek translator, Vicky Potamianou, shapes the conceptualisation of the historical experience by foregrounding prevailing assumptions in the target culture. This includes an emphasis on the role of political leadership and highlighting the cultural stereotypes associated with Pontic Greeks. Unlike its English source, the Greek version places more emphasis on human suffering and the uncertain plight faced by the inhabitants of the areas affected by the population exchange. In the first set of examples, the neutral English item *departure* is rendered with the more expressively connoted *uprooting* (ξεριζωμού):

ST1   These memories reflect the prosperity and dynamism and cultural attainments of the Greek community on the eve of its departure; and also... (2006: 110)

TT1   Όλοι όμως θυμούνται την ευημερία, τον δυναμισμό και τα πολιτιστικά επιτεύγματα της ελληνικής κοινότητας τις παραμονές του ξεριζωμού και επίσης... (2007: 139)

BT1   *Everybody remembers the prosperity and dynamism and cultural attainments of the Greek community on the eve of its uprooting and also...*

Another instance of this preference for manipulating a lexical frame in order to foreground expressiveness is the way in which the Greek version employs the sea as a source of metaphors to conceptualise refugee actions. Lexical frames such as *waves* (Κύματα), *flowing* (συνέρρεαν) or *flooded* (κατακλυστεί) evoke the forceful movement of water, which may be associated with the displacement of desperate masses of refugees:

ST2   Some refugees were crowding into the relative safety of the Ottoman capital, which was already filled with homeless Muslim Turks... (2006: 46)

TT2   Κύματα προσφύγων που πίστευαν ότι στην οθωμανική πρωτεύουσα θα ήταν πιο ασφαλείς συνέρρεαν στην Κωνσταντινούπολη η οποία είχε ήδη κατακλυστεί από Τούρκους μουσουλμάνους... (2007: 67)

BT2   *Waves of refugees, who believed that they would be safer in the Ottoman capital, were flowing to Constantinople which had already been flooded by Muslim Turks...*

Expressiveness, achieved through metaphorical transfer, is a feature often preferred in the Greek translation, which appears in stark contrast to the negative politeness typical of English (Brown & Levinson, 1978; Sifianou, 1992). Positive and negative politeness are concepts devised to account for communication style preferences, both locally *on the ground* and in the wider realms of *culturally shaped behaviour*. Positive politeness aims to establish common ground between interlocutors (e.g. by avoiding disagreement and highlighting the speaker's interest or concern for the hearer), while negative politeness refers to the speaker's concern not to make assumptions (e.g. by avoiding direct or pessimistic turns, or by favouring communicative strategies such as apologising and impersonalising) (Sifianou, 1992: 131). Cultures tending towards positive politeness tend to adopt evaluation and expressiveness as a communication style (Sifianou, 1992), as evident in the numerous translation shifts that highlight pain and make suffering explicit.

It should be noted that the Greek text also displays expressiveness in the description of the Muslim community's suffering: the English back-translation 'Muslims who were *exiled*' ('κάποιους μουσουλμάνους που εξορίστηκαν', 2007: 107), for instance, clearly emphasises the suffering of the Muslim community when compared with the ST item 'Muslims who were *departing*' (2006: 84). Overall, positive politeness, a communicative norm of the Greek language, allows for an enhancement of the dramatic overtones of the ideological discourse and accentuates the narrative of suffering. In the Greek version there also seems to be a preference for contravening assumed (or expected) political outcomes that in English are often presented positively. For example, the ST item 'The Turkish demand for the city's *inclusion* had caused Nansen "grave concerns"' (2006: 63) is rendered in the target version as 'The demand of Turkey for *not excluding* Istanbul had caused Nansen "grave concerns"' ('Η απαίτηση της Τουρκίας να μην εξαιρεθεί η Ισταμπούλ είχε προκαλέσει στον Νάνσεν «σοβαρές ανησυχίες»'; 2007: 83). This shift renders the Turkish demand in a more ambiguous and less direct way, heightens the anxiety caused by the request, and hints at a desire on the Greek side for Constantinople to be excluded from the areas which would exchange their populations. There are also several instances where the target text foregrounds, through what may be termed *ideological variance*, the option which would have been preferred or expected by Greek citizens. Preferred conscious or subconscious expectations, therefore, manifest themselves through a kind of *surface negation*, which reveals the narrative perspective of the Greek simulacrum.

The Greek target version seems to give more prominence to spatial considerations in describing the population exchange. The English metaphor 'pocket of the Greek wealth' (2006: 110), which describes the city of Trebizond, is rendered as 'islet of the Greek community' ('νησίδα Ελληνισμού στο άκρο της Ανατολίας'; 2007: 138–139). Since the settlement of nationalist territorial demands was a key issue at the time, geopolitical and spatial awareness is evidently relevant to the representation of this historical episode. At one point, Clark quotes from an interview that does not explicitly refer to the place name Nepien (Νεπιέν), but it must have been mentioned in the interview's original version, because it *is* recovered in the Greek text. The translator, therefore, seems to have consulted the Greek sources used by the author:

ST3   The Turkish army came to the place where we were. (2006: 65)
TT3   Ήρθε ο τουρκικός στρατός στο Νεπιέν, όπου ήμασταν. (2007: 88)
BT3   *The Turkish army came to Nepien, where we were.*

Spatial awareness, arguably a reflection of the nationalist territorial debate surrounding the population exchange, contributes to the representation of the experience by making lost homelands cognitively salient in the collective memory of the Greek target culture. A preference for spatial specificity is manifested in various ways, for instance when the English term *place* (2006: 82) becomes *village* (χωριό, 2007: 105), or *survivors* (2006: 10) is transformed into the more explicit lexical frame *inhabitants* (κατοίκους, 2007: 28), which points to a spatial awareness that ignores the *matter of life and death* binary opposition implied by the lexical item *survivor*. The Greek text also assigns more prominence to the willingness on the part of political leaders to act on behalf of the people they represent, which results in a more powerful portrayal of political figures than in Bruce Clark's English text. The profile and relevance of Prime Minister Eleftherios Venizelos, for instance, is clearly reinforced in the Greek simulacrum, when the ST item 'a politician with a *better than average* sense of the international mood' becomes the TT item 'a *genius* politician with full awareness of the international mood' (Σαν ευφυής πολιτικός με πλήρη συναίσθηση της διεθνούς συγκυρίας). Such an ideologically charged shift responds to (subconscious) expectations of how esteemed political leaders ought to be portrayed:

ST4   Venizelos was not only advocating draconian measures; as a politician with a better than average sense of the international mood, he had clear ideas about easing the presentational difficulties that a forced eviction of Muslims would bring. (2006: 55)

TT4   Ο Βενιζέλος δεν ήταν μόνο υπέρ των δρακόντειων μέτρων. Σαν ευφυής πολιτικός με πλήρη συναίσθηση της διεθνούς συγκυρίας έβλεπε καθαρά τα επικοινωνιακά προβλήματα που θα προκαλούσε μία αναγκαστική απέλαση μουσουλμάνων από την Ελλάδα. (2007: 76)

BT4   *Venizelos was not only advocating draconian measures. As a genius politician with full awareness of the international mood, he saw clearly the communicational problems the compulsory eviction of Muslims from Greece would cause.*

Shifts which positively depict Eleftherios Venizelos are frequent in the Greek translation, which tends to enhance the image of political authorities – even in the case of Turkish leaders. The translator is aware of the impact that Turkish Prime Minister Mustafa Kemal had on the political scene, and this is why he becomes a frequent point of reference. In the example below, the English phrase 'Turkish *nationalist writ*' becomes '*Kemalist regime*' (κεμαλικό καθεστώς) in the TT, and the phrase 'imposing his authority on a fractious coalition' becomes 'to lead a problematic coalition' (να ηγηθεί ενός προβληματικού συνασπισμού), which carries much more positive connotations. The Greek translation stresses Mustafa Kemal's leading responsibility in the coalition and reasserts his role as an international statesman:

ST5   How, then, did the 'Oriental mind' respond? In Allied-occupied Istanbul, where the Turkish nationalist writ did not yet run, Nansen had difficulty at first in finding negotiating partners who spoke for the Ankara government. Mustafa Kemal himself had no interest in holding face to face negotiations; he was far too busy dealing with the aftermath of victory and imposing his authority on a fractious coalition. (2006: 57)

TT5   Ποια λοιπόν ήταν η αντίδραση του «ανατολίτικου νου»; Στην κατεχόμενη από τους Συμμάχους Κωνσταντινούπολη, όπου το κεμαλικό καθεστώς δεν είχε ακόμα ισχυροποιηθεί, ο Νάνσεν αρχικά δεν [sic] αντιμετώπιζε δυσκολίες να βρει συνομιλητές που εκπροσωπούσαν την Άγκυρα. Ο ίδιος ο Κεμάλ δεν είχε καιρό για κουβέντες καθώς ήταν πολύ απασχολημένος με την εμπέδωση της νίκης του και την προσπάθεια να ηγηθεί ενός προβληματικού συνασπισμού. (2007: 77)

BT5   *What was then the reaction of the 'Oriental mind'? In Allied-occupied Constantinople, where the Kemalist regime was not yet dominant, Nansen originally had [sic] no difficulty finding interlocutors representing Ankara. Kemal himself had no time for negotiations because he was busy with consolidating his victory and with his attempt to lead a problematic coalition.*

This translation pattern in the Greek version seems to echo a preference found in translated press articles. Kaniklidou's (2012) research demonstrates that press translations often adjust the public representation of political leaders (e.g. of Barack Obama) to favour locally preferred principles of political conduct, a pattern that results in more vigorously active and positively inclined political actors in translated discourse.

Another salient feature of the Greek target version is a certain nostalgic attitude and an affirmative acknowledgement of intercultural affinities across the Aegean, through the introduction of Turkish borrowings. It is worth noting that this strategy appears in agreement with the author's goal of highlighting the 'rich, complex and ambivalent' (Clark, 2006: 5) cultural identities within this geographical area. Interestingly, the Greek translation recovers Turkish loanwords used by Greek interviewees which were standardised in *Twice a Stranger* as it would have been difficult to portray in English typical dialectal features associated with Asia Minor. This again seems to demonstrate that the translator had access to the research materials gathered by Clark in order to write *Twice a Stranger*. In the Greek translation, for instance, the ST item *mayor* (2006: 65) is not translated into the standard Greek item δήμαρχος, but into μουδούρης (2007: 88; from Turkish *müdür*), which was probably used in the original interview. In the same vein, the Greek translation often disregards the standard Greek term for *estate* (κτήμα) in favour of the Turkish borrowing *tsifliki* (*çiftlik* in Turkish), which is an emotionally loaded term that carries connotations of wealth and ownership. Turkish borrowings in the Greek translation are numerous; they are usually low-tenor options with an expressive function and they are instrumental in conveying emotiveness. The Greek version of Bruce Clark's work appears to attempt to emphasise the positive associations that these lexical items activate in the mind of Greek readers, revealing in the process the cultural affinities between Greece and Turkey. The Greek text similarly reinforces nostalgic evocations, when for instance the pessimistic expectation 'relatively *unsullied* memories' shifts into 'relatively *happy* memories' (σχετικά ευτυχισμένες αναμνήσεις):

ST6   ... there is no group that retains such fond and relatively unsullied memories of the homeland as the Cappadocians; and there is no part of Anatolia where Greek visitors, especially those who originate from the region, are made so welcome. (2006: 45)

TT6   ... δεν υπάρχει ομάδα που να διατηρεί ζωντανές και σχετικά ευτυχισμένες αναμνήσεις περοσσότερο από τους Καππαδόκες, ούτε περιοχλη στη Μικρασία που να δέχεται τόσο θερμά τους Έλληνες επισκέπτες ιδίως εκείνους που έχουν τις ρίζες τους εκεί. (2007: 115)

BT6   ... *there is no group that retains such fond and relatively happy memories of the homeland as the Cappadocians; and there is no part of Anatolia where Greek visitors, especially those who have their roots in the region, are made so welcome.*

Overall, the Greek translation seems to verify Bruce Clark's claim that, despite the Greek–Turkish nationalist divide, positive memories of coexistence survived:

Yet *mingled with the memories of terror and betrayal, feelings and recollections persisted which somehow transcended the Greek–Turkish divide;*

personal friendships, commercial partnerships, a sense of common participation in a single world, constituted by landscape, language, music, food and all the trivia of everyday life. (2006: 10; emphasis added)

The population exchange was a traumatic event, and traumas need to be healed. In the Greek text, the conscious or unconscious attempt to overcome painful experiences results in the accentuation of spatial awareness, a slightly more nostalgic narrative, an attempt to highlight cultural affinities through the use of borrowings, and an acknowledgement of the suffering on both sides. This translated simulacrum also entails an increased sense of self-respect (evidenced by the favourable representation of Eleftherios Venizelos), due regard for the political other (the favourable representation of Mustafa Kemal), as well as humorous overtones, particularly in the depictions of Pontic Greeks. The comparison between Clark's English text and its Greek version shows that translation choices regarding the representation of Pontic Greeks in their new homeland concur with local stereotypes, which describe them as 'being lively, irascible, flexible, creative and stubborn' (Clark, 2006: 75). The English depiction 'a *resourceful* Pontic farmer' (2006: 81), for instance, is rendered into Greek as 'a *stubborn* Pontic farmer' ('ένας *πεισματάρης* Πόντιος αγρότης', 2007: 104). The simulacrum, therefore, offers a politically and culturally 'correct' representation of the Anatolian experience that complements the painful collective memories of the atrocities committed during the population exchange as experienced by the locals.

The Turkish Simulation

As a result of the workings of power and the narratives circulating in both cultural environments, the Greek and Turkish versions overlap in certain shift types, while they vary at other points. It should be noted that the Turkish translator, Müfide Pekin, comes from a family which moved from Crete to Izmir as a result of the exchange, which might explain some of the strategies employed in the Turkish simulation. To begin with, the Turkish translation also conceptualises the disaster by highlighting the perspective of human suffering. This is manifested in the fact that, on the back cover, the Turkish publication adds a new paragraph which highlights the tragic aspect of the experience:

TT7   Zorunlu nüfus mübadelesi devletler hukuku ve diplomasi tarihi bağlamının dışında bir de insanlık tarihi açısından okunmalı. Bruce Clark, *İki Kere Yabancı* kitabında bu trajik olaya insan açısından bakıyor. (2008: back cover)

BT7   *The forced population exchange should be read not only within the context of international law and diplomatic history, but also from the point of view of human history. Bruce Clark, in his book* Twice a Stranger, *looks at this tragic event from the human perspective.*

A sensation of personal involvement and the issues at stake for both communities is heightened in back-translated options such as 'the struggle to share Anatolia' ('Anadolu'yu paylaşım mücadelesi', 2008: 11), which renders the English item 'the contest for Anatolia' (2006: 10). The Turkish version of Bruce Clark's book enhances its expressiveness by stressing the brutality and senselessness of certain aspects of the population exchange. There are eloquent conceptual representations of war atrocities when English expressions like *x killed y* (2006: 10) are occasionally rendered as *x massacred y* (katletti, 2008: 11), with the semantics of *massacre* obviously implying indiscriminate slaughter, whereas *killing* describes a more purposeful and selective action. Quite in contrast to the source text, both translated versions exhibit a sharp spatial awareness, which may be due to the translators' sociocultural and spatial proximity as well as psychological involvement with the events narrated, but which may also reflect the anxieties caused by the territorial negotiations taking place at the time of the population exchange. In the following examples, the translator recovers the relevant place names, and as a result specific locations in Asia Minor become cognitively salient:

ST8   In mid-September, the Turkish army occupied the town, consolidating the phenomenal success which began in August with the rout of the Greek army from an inland fastness where it had camped for a miserable year after narrowly failing to capture Ankara, the Turkish nationalists' headquarters, in the early autumn of 1921. (2006: 22)

TT8   Türk ordusu Ağustos'ta başlattığı taarruzla Yunan ordusunu Anadolu içlerinde bozguna uğratmış, Yunan ordusunu önünde bir yıldır ümitsizce beklediği ama bir türlü ele geçiremediği Türk kurtuluş savaşının karargâhı Ankara önlerinden batıya doğru sürerek kazandığı olağanüstü zaferini, 1921 Eylül'ünün başlarında Ayvalık'a girerek perçinlemişti. (2008: 24)

BT8   *The Turkish army routed the Greek army in inland Anatolia after the raid started in August and, by entering Ayvalık at the beginning of September of 1921, they consolidated the phenomenal victory of driving the Greek army towards the West from the outskirts of Ankara, the headquarters of the Turkish War of Independence, where the Greek army had desperately waited for a year after narrowly failing to capture it.*

Both target versions seem to offer an empowered and more overtly legitimised representation of political leaders (see examples 4 and 5 above). In the following example, Mustafa Kemal's authority is enhanced in the Turkish text by omitting the adjective *military*, a shift which widens the scope of the noun *triumph* (*zafer*) and, perhaps more importantly, avoids the bellicose connotations of the English text:

ST9   So in autumn 1922, after Kemal's military triumph, this idea reemerged in a far more drastic form. (2006: 54)

TT9   Böylece, 1922 sonbaharında, Mustafa Kemal'in zaferini takiben, mübadele fikri çok daha yakıcı bir biçimde yeniden gündeme gelecekti. (2008: 61)

BT9   *So in autumn 1922, after Mustafa Kemal's triumph, this idea of the population exchange would re-emerge in a far more drastic form.*

The representation of Mustafa Kemal is also positively enhanced in example 10, which omits the potentially denigrating word *masters* and specifies that he was acting specifically on behalf of the sultan and not just an undefined political body:

ST10   In 1919, when Mustafa Kemal sailed into the port, sent by his Ottoman masters on a mission to pacify the region… (2006: 73)

TT10   1919'da Osmanlı padişahı tarafından asayişi sağlamak için gönderilen Mustafa Kemal, Samsun'a ayak bastığında… (2008: 83)

BT10   *In 1919, when Mustafa Kemal, who had been sent by the Ottoman sultan to restore order, set foot in Samsun…*

As is the case with the Greek rendition, the Turkish text also presents political figures in accordance with narratives of leadership circulating in the target environment.

Interestingly, the Turkish translation seems to draw attention to the legal aspects of the exchange as a strategy for stressing the persuasive force of the argument. This can be observed in the addition of a reference to the official treaty – Convention Concerning the Exchange of Greek and Turkish Populations – which clearly demonstrates the legitimising intention of the Turkish text:

ST11   Orthodox Christians were deported from Turkey to Greece, Muslims from Greece to Turkey. (2006: front flap)

TT11   30 Ocak 1923'te imzalanan 'Yunan ve Türk Halklarının Mübadelesine İlişkin Sözleşme ve Protokol' gereğince Yunanistan'da yerleşik Müslümanlar Türkiye'ye, Türkiye'de yerleşik Ortodoks Rumlar Yunanistan'a gönderildi. (2008: back cover)

BT11   *According to the Convention Concerning the Exchange of Greek and Turkish Populations, signed on 30 January 1923, Muslims settled in Greece were deported to Turkey, Orthodox Greeks settled in Turkey were deported to Greece.*

The concern for activating this legal frame is also evident in the judicial preference 'must be given the right' ('geri dönme hakkı verilmesi') as opposed to the rather sober English expression 'must be allowed':

ST12   Both in Bosnia, with a degree of success, and in Kosovo, with rather less success, peace makers have insisted that everybody who was violently uprooted must be allowed to return. (2006: xiv)

TT12   Bir yere kadar başarıyla Bosna'da, daha az başarılı olarak da Kosova'da, barışın mimarları yerlerinden vahşice sökülüp atılan herkese geri dönme hakkı verilmesi konusunda direndiler. (2008: xvii)

BT12   *Both in Bosnia, with a degree of success, and in Kosovo, with rather less*
success, peace makers have insisted that everybody who was violently
uprooted must be given the right to return.

These shifts demonstrate that the Turkish simulacrum also focuses on legitimising solutions by the application of legal terminology.

Another characteristic of the Turkish translation with respect to the legal lexical frame is its tendency to present politically sanctioned decisions as consolidated and fixed. Thus, the phrase *virtual separation* (a matter of essence) becomes *complete separation* (tam manasıyla birbirlerinden ayrılmaları) (a matter of degree), which suggests that the solution is coherent, binding and permanent:

ST13   This and other nearby mountains were the scene, in the early 1920s, of some of the fiercest and most proudly remembered clashes in the decade of war which led to the virtual separation of the Turks from the Greeks. (2006: 66)

TT13   Bu ve yakınındaki diğer dağlar 1920'lerin başlarında Türklerle Yunanlıların tam manasıyla birbirlerinden ayrılmalarıyla sonuçlanan savaşta, gururla hatırlanan en kanlı çarpışmaların yaşandığı yer. (2008: 76)

BT13   *This and other nearby mountains were the scene, in the early 1920s, of some of the bloodiest and most proudly remembered clashes of the war which led to the complete separation of the Turks from the Greeks.*

In a similar move, the English phrase *broadly agreed* (2006: 74), used to describe the outcome of international negotiations, becomes *completely agreed* (tamamen anlaşıyorlardı; 2008: 86), with the target version implying full accord. Another example that presents narrative identities as consolidated and unified is manifested through the back-translated phrase 'other Turkish citizens' ('diğer Türk vatandaşlarından'; 2008: 37), which renders the English expression 'other citizens of Turkey'. The plurality and diversity implied in the English sentence is absent in the Turkish rendition.

Political awareness is also reflected in the avoidance of nationalistic overtones or in the assumption, also present in the Greek version, that religious differences did not constitute a problem. This is reflected in the following example, where the Turkish text omits the modifier of the lexical item *Christian minorities*:

ST14   This was because Mustafa Kemal, the new leader of the Turkish nation, insisted firmly that Christian minorities had no place in the republic he proposed to build. (2006: 46)

TT14   Yeni Türkiye devletinin lideri Mustafa Kemal, kurulacak cumhuriyette azınlıkların yeri olmadığı konusunda ısrarlıydı. (2008: 52)

BT14   *Mustafa Kemal, the new leader of the Turkish state, insisted firmly that minorities had no place in the republic that was going to be built.*

There are also examples which eschew references to nationalism, when for instance the English item 'the Turkish nationalists' headquarters' (2006: 22) becomes 'headquarters of the Turkish War of Independence' ('Türk kurtuluş savaşının karargâhı'; 2008: 24). In addition, the collocation denoting the *phenomenal success* of the Turkish over the Greek army is shifted into the phrase *phenomenal victory* (*olağanüstü zaferini*; see example 8 above), which celebrates the event by activating the conflict frame and by adding militaristic overtones to the Turkish text.

Overall, the Turkish simulacrum of the population exchange displays strategies shared by the Greek text, but also exhibits a geopolitically specific representation of the historical ordeal. Discursive formations in the target environment clearly produce new knowledge and assumptions about what is regarded as politically correct, and this can be traced in the shifts affecting the two translated simulacra, both of which seem to adapt the representation of the historical event to the projected needs and expectations of their potential reading public.

Translation as Simulation and the Contribution of Power

The above types of shift seem to show that both target versions foreground the historical experience of human suffering by exploiting semantic variations in terms of textual expressiveness and evaluativeness. This shared intention of framing the translated narratives through discourses of affliction is also expressed through the cover images of both target publications (Figure 6.1), which underscores the emotional significance of this disaster in the collective memory of the Greek and Turkish populations.

Courtesy of Granta Books   Courtesy of Potamos Publishers   Courtesy of İstanbul Bilgi Üniversitesi Yayınları

Figure 6.1 Cover pictures of the British, Greek and Turkish publications

The Greek and Turkish publishers chose similar cover images, both of which are notably more dramatic than the original. The presence of what looks like a peasant woman in travelling clothes carrying a baby in her arms is significantly more evocative than the ST's image, which does not enlighten potential readers about the suffering and the social status of the depicted characters. By and large, the types of shift observed in both translated simulacra exhibit a conformity to normative schemata induced by dominant target culture narratives and by geopolitical constellations of power. Translation shifts in the two versions, therefore, suggest that local power struggles have an important role to play in the shaping of human experience and knowledge. They do, however, also present a number of differences: the Greek version seems to favour a feeling of nostalgia for the lost homeland, whereas the Turkish version appears primarily concerned with activating a legal frame as a strategy of political legitimisation. A comparative summary of presumed discursive strategies demonstrates significant divergences in the way locally preferred narratives shine through in the two target texts, as shown in Table 6.1.

Table 6.1 Presence (+) or absence (–) of eight discourse strategies in the two target texts

	Discourse strategy	Greek (2007)	Turkish (2008)
1	Conceptualising the disaster (evaluation + expressiveness)	+	+
2	Political awareness	+	+
3	Spatial awareness	+	+
4	Empowered political leaders	+	+
5	Turkish loan items and a 'good old days' narrative	+	–
6	The representation of Pontic Greeks	+	–
7	Activating the legal frame	–	+
8	Solutions integrated and fixed	–	+

When seen from the broad vantage point of a Baudrillardian simulacrum, target texts reflect the process of simulating a source text. Out of the three levels of simulated reality, namely an 'obvious copy of reality', 'a copy so good that it blurs the boundaries between reality and representation' and a third-level simulation 'which produces a reality of its own without being based upon any particular bit of the real world' (Lane, 2000: 30), translation shifts have the power to engender the second and third types of simulation, blurring the boundaries between source and target versions and thus producing a new reality. A significant factor that seems to affect the simulation process is institutional power, which is reflected in the reinforcement of the legal framework in the Turkish target text. The simulacra precede the *reality* of the source text, in that readers read the simulacra first and are unlikely to have access to the *real*; thus, the simulacrum survives and takes precedence over the real in their consciousness. Despite frequent claims to the contrary, translation processes do not function according to the logic of transparent representation. Interpretations of the source text are in fact a copy for which there is no original, since they are always affected by a surplus of meaning, which disrupts and unsettles the source text. The text emerging from the translation process is presented as a copy of the 'truth', but this conceals the diversified nature of any conception of truth, since translations cannot offer any direct access to the source text, which in turn cannot offer any direct access to an original experience. As John Johnston points out, 'in a reversal of the relationship between "original" and "imitation", the translations propose themselves as the "origin" of a new set of meanings' (1992: 49). The belief in a primary, original reference, therefore, is displaced by the genesis of a simulacrum, the shifts of which constitute the substance of the translated text.

The multiperspective translation processes here analysed show that both target texts constitute the mirror image of the host culture, because the translators – consciously or unconsciously – complete the unavoidable gaps and omissions in Bruce Clark's text according to the codes available in their respective cultures, and the agendas of publishing industries, the translatorial habitus, and so on. The representation of political leaders, the enhancement of spatial awareness, the emphasis on cultural affinities, the legal frame narrative and the humorous overtones included in the representation of Pontic Greeks blur the boundaries between original and representation by supplementing the text with new and shared knowledge(s) that participate in the construction of, and at the same time conform to, the needs and expectations of the respective target audiences. Often disguised as 'faithful' copies, translations acquire total integrity and become what is considered the real, but this perspective ignores that what guarantees the success of the process is not solely the original, but the demarcated and demarcating differences between the source and target texts. The two translations of *Twice a Stranger* are in no way 'obvious' copies of the 'reality' depicted in the original. Rather, they are blurred representations of this reality, enhancing the values of solidarity, consensus and tenacity, and resisting the narratives of antagonism and separation occasionally assumed of Greece and Turkey. Specific geopolitical narratives (Baker, 2006) circulating in the target environments seem relatively clearly to condition the translational representations of the Anatolian experience of 1923. Different simulacra may foreground different representations of the same historical event not only because of differing historical experiences and collective memories, but also because the *discursive formations* (Foucault, 1977, 1980) and the knowledge they produce and eventually may sustain shape and are at the same time shaped by dominant narratives reverberating in the respective environments.

Discursive strategies require different layers of addressee involvement (emotional, ideological, etc.) that produce knowledge by reinforcing or contesting local discourses, which is why the constructivist potential of narratives should not be underestimated. Shifts with strong constructivist potential are a result of the power differentials between and among text producers and readers. Discourse participants construct meaning through representational and symbolic systems that are subject to power relations, while the power axis between authors and readers regulates the dissemination of knowledge in the target environment. The Greek and Turkish simulacra pursue a predominantly expressive/informative function with a strong ethical resonance, because target readers most likely still remember the historical event and in some cases may have been directly affected by it, granting them some kind of power over the producers of the simulacra. This became clear when the translation strategies used in the Greek translation of Bruce Clark's text were contrasted with the strategies used in the Greek translation of an academic political text (Sidiropoulou, 2013). The network of power relations that weighed upon the academic text differed, in that its predominant function was informative, its topic did not seem to have an ethical resonance, and its potential for exercising institutional power was much lower, while the power ultimately remained with the political scientist who produced the text. The Greek- and Turkish-speaking audiences for Clark's English text, on the other hand, can tell whether the representation of the experience is compatible with their personal experience and thus in agreement with the narratives disseminated in the respective cultural environment.

Translation as simulation provides opportunities for reprocessing experiences and consolidating narratives about the self and the other in fast-moving globalising societies. This makes the simulacrum survive the real as it consolidates narratives (e.g. the shared shifts) or helps to resist them (e.g. the distinct shifts). The shifts in the Greek and the Turkish simulacra show that some interpretative and critical considerations are shared (Martin & Nakayama, 2003): both versions are concerned with highlighting the consequences of the disaster, empowering the profile of political leaders, and exhibiting heightened political and spatial awareness. What is clear is that differences in the two simulacra derive from *attractor positions in the space of possibilities* (Sperber, 1996: 108): on the one hand, they seem to resist some of the homogenising narratives circulating in this particular geopolitical landscape, for instance in the case of the accounts that offer a conflictive perspective of the relationship between the two states; yet, on the other hand, they also conform to some other narratives which seem to be shared. The power of the translator, situated within the wider power network surrounding any translation (e.g. publishers, editors, etc.), seems to provide opportunities for reshaping the most controversial aspects of a historical experience and collective memory in order to achieve a consensual resolution to a potentially conflictive state of affairs.

Note

(1) This chapter is part of a collaborative project between translation scholars from Greece and Turkey, which explores dominant representations of the population exchange across the two sides of the Aegean. The relationship between Turks and Greeks and the 1923 exchange has attracted the attention of researchers in various disciplines and academic communities and has resulted in several cooperative projects between universities across the Aegean, as manifested by various publications (e.g. Bayraktaroğlu & Sifianou, 2001; Sifianou & Bayraktaroğlu, 2012) and conferences.

Acknowledgement

Maria Sidiropoulou would like to thank the Special Account Research Fund (ELKE) of the National and Kapodistrian University of Athens for funding this research.

References

Baker, M. (2006) *Translation and Conflict*. London: Routledge.
Bayraktaroğlu, A. and Sifianou, M. (eds) (2001) *Linguistic Politeness Across Boundaries: The Case of Greek and Turkish*. Amsterdam: John Benjamins.
Baudrillard, J. (1990) Figures of the transpolitical. In P. Foss and J. Pefanis (eds and trans) *Revenge of the Crystal: Selected Writings on the Modern Object and Its Destiny, 1968–1983* (pp. 163–198). London: Pluto Press.
Baudrillard, J. (1994) *Simulacra and Simulation* (S.F. Glaser, trans.). Ann Arbor, MI: University of Michigan Press.
Berk, Ö. (2006) Reconstruction of the Greek–Turkish population exchange in recent literary works. Paper presented at the conference Rethinking the Past: Experimental Histories in the Arts, 28–29 July, University of Technology Sydney, Australia.
Brown, P. and Levinson, S. (1978) *Politeness: Some Universals in Language Usage*. Cambridge: Cambridge University Press (1987).
Foucault, M. (1977) *Power, Knowledge and Ethics*, in Αλήθεια και εξουσία, Μισέλ Φουκό, Εξουσία, Γνώση και Ηθική, Ζήσης Σαρικας μεταφρ (pp. 11–37). Αθήνα: Ύψιλον (1987).
Foucault, M. (1980) *Power/Knowledge: Selected Interviews and Other Writings, 1972–1977* (C. Gordon, ed.). New York: Pantheon Books.
Gutt, E.-A. (2000) *Translation and Relevance: Cognition and Context*. London: Routledge.
Johnston, J. (1992) Translation as simulacrum. In L. Venuti (ed.) *Rethinking Translation: Discourse, Subjectivity, Ideology* (pp. 42–56). London: Routledge.
Kaniklidou, T. (2012) English–Greek news creating narratives: A translation perspective. PhD thesis, Department of English, National and Kapodistrian University of Athens.
Lane, R.J. (2000) *Jean Baudrillard*. London: Routledge.
Martin, J.N. and Nakayama, T. (2003) *Intercultural Communication in Contexts*. Boston, MA: McGraw Hill.
Sidiropoulou, M. (2013) Representation through translation: Shared maps of pragmatic meaning and the constructionist paradigm. *Journal of Pragmatics* 53 (3), 96–108.
Sifianou, M. (1992) *Politeness Phenomena in England and Greece*. Oxford: Clarendon.
Sifianou, M. and Bayraktaroğlu, A. (2012) 'Face' stereotyping and claims of power: The Greeks and Turks in interaction. In C.B. Paulston, S.F. Kiesling and E.S. Rangel (eds) *The Handbook of Intercultural Discourse and Communication* (pp. 292–312). Oxford: Wiley-Blackwell.
Sperber, D. (1996) *Explaining Culture: A Naturalistic Approach*. Oxford: Blackwell.

Texts

Clark, B. (2006) *Twice a Stranger*. London: Granta Books.

Clark, B. (2007) Δυό φορές ξένος (Βίκη Ποταμιάνου, trans). Αθήνα: Ποταμός.

Clark, B. (2008) *İki Kere Yabancı*. (M. Pekin, trans). Istanbul: Bilgi Üniversitesi Yayınları.

7 Translation Choices as Sites of State Power: Gender and Habitus in Bestsellers in Franco's Spain

Cristina Gómez Castro

Power and Habitual (Self-)Manipulation

> Translation in all its forms is frequently the site of a variety of power plays between the actors involved. Some of these are quite deliberate manipulations of the original for a wide variety of reasons, ranging from the desire to save money to the desire to control behaviour, from the desire to follow perceived norms to the desire for cultural hegemony. (Fawcett, 1995: 177)

The Manipulation School's claim that any translation is inherently manipulative prefigured the current interest in the social factors that affect translation processes (Hermans, 1985). Subsequently, the cultural turn of the 1990s changed the focus of attention to a wide range of questions with ideological significance that attempt to examine the role that translation plays in the historical and political arena (Bassnett & Lefevere, 1998). The conceptual boundaries of translation Studies appeared to shift again in the early 2000s, from the cultural turn to what could legitimately be regarded as a power turn, inspiring scholars to increasingly focus on questions of sociocultural identity and agency in order to explore the role of translators and other related agents from a sociological perspective (cf. Gentzler & Tymoczko, 2002). Drawing on the long-standing interest of translation studies in questions of power and ideology, this chapter aims to explore the ways in which gender was represented in bestselling novels published in Spain under Franco's political regime (1939–1978).[1] Directly associated with economic interests, bestsellers offer a significant vantage point from which to observe the power games at stake in any national publishing sector. The representation of women under Franco's regime, perceived as 'the axis of social morality', was one of the most tempting targets of (self-)censorship ('el eje de la moralidad social'; Ortiz Heras,

2006: 2; unless otherwise stated, the translations into English of Spanish quotations are mine). The following analysis of the textual interventions exercised by different agencies (mainly censors and translators) aims to bring to light the position of translation 'in the dialectic of power, the ongoing process of political discourse, and strategies for social change' (Gentzler & Tymoczko, 2002: xviii).

Deliberate and unconscious (extra)textual alterations that bear ideological consequences are part and parcel of publishing processes and of any form of literary activity (McLaughlin & Muñoz-Basols, 2016). Concepts such as patronage, that is, 'the powers (persons, institutions) that can further or hinder the reading, writing and rewriting of litera-ture' (Lefevere, 1992: 14), remind us of the significance of the immediate power networks affecting literary translation activity, which in turn are embedded in less immediately perceptible political and literary power structures of a given culture. Ideological domination or patronage in the field of translation is, however, clearly detectable in the authoritarian cultural policies established under fascist regimes in Italy and Germany during the first half of the 20th century, and in Spain until the mid-1970s. Under these authoritarian regimes, the cultural sphere was dominated by state mechanisms of control in order to ensure ideological uniformity (cf. Rundle, 2010; Sturge, 2004). Literary translation fields curtailed by censor-ship can be described as sites of struggle, where each agent (translators, publishers, censors, etc.) tries to make the most of their specific capital in the competition for power and resources (cf. Gómez Castro, 2008). The establishment of authoritarian control mechanisms by fascist regimes had a severe impact on the respective field of translation, and attachments to specific literary practices, especially in the commercial publishing sector, may bear on literary output even years after the authoritarian power base had been removed (cf. Cornellà-Detrell, 2013).

The relationship between translation and censorship can be described as twofold (St-Pierre, 1993: 67):

> Translation can be a means of avoiding censorship (by publishing the work in a foreign tongue, or by attributing the ideas expressed to a foreign author), but it can also be an occasion to suppress elements of an original text, whether in the name of 'taste', or of the 'genius of the language' – the justification for such expressions will vary according to context.

In target cultures dominated by authoritarian politics, suspicion of foreign influences tends to be the norm. Here, censorship acts as a coercive and modifying force that renders translations culturally, ideologically and politically acceptable by erasing any allegedly offensive or threatening content. State censorship, therefore, engenders a negative environment for the activity of translation, with government bodies attempting to exert control on imported and exported cultural materials. Spain under Franco is a prime example of state-sponsored patronage, since, over a period of almost 40 years, all cultural expressions were subject to the ideological and political requirements of the regime. From the beginning, cultural agents working in such an environment were conscious of the social and political conditions in which they had to conduct their work. As a result, more and more native Spanish authors admitted their increasing recourse to self-censorship in order to get their works published – and translators did the same, either on their own initiative or because of the pressures exerted by publishing houses. During the dictatorship years, this practice gradually evolved from dominant official power to internalised self-censorship, which may indeed be seen as the ultimate form of efficient state control. Once writers and translators began to internalise the cultural, ideological and political requirements of the authoritarian state, it became difficult to break with a habitus formed through repressive policies of mind control, a situation that led poet and publisher José Luis Cano to claim, shortly before the end of Franco's rule, that 'it would be hard, when there is freedom of expression in the country, to write without the censoring blinkers' ('va a costar trabajo, cuando haya libertad en el país, escribir sin las anteojeras censoriales'; in Beneyto, 1975: 130).

Visible and Invisible Constraints

In order to understand how repressive cultural policies may lead to the gradual naturalisation of self-censoring behaviours on the part of literary mediators, it is worthwhile fleshing out the working philosophy of official patronage. State censorship during the Franco years was a coercive ideological mechanism that aimed at maintaining political dominance and preserving a conception of morality that had been imposed by the Catholic Church at the end of the Spanish Civil War (1936–1939) (Linder Molin, 2011). Official control was mainly through two press laws. The first was issued in 1938 and had a severe impact on Spanish culture, as it forced publishers to submit all manuscripts to the censorship office in Madrid prior to publication, which caused significant delays, or financial losses if the text was deemed unpublishable. It was superseded in 1966 by the less restrictive Law of Press and Printing, as a result of a sudden economic boom and owing to the need to present the country in a more positive light on the international scene (Linder, 2004: 159). The new legislation was designed to accelerate the production and distribution of printed materials, with official control resting on two main procedures: voluntary pre-publication censorship (*consulta voluntaria*), which could result in a positive or negative report about the book under review; and direct submission (*depósito*) of the printed work to the Ministry of Information and Tourism, which did not require a censor's report. It was, indeed, possible to publish a book without the regime's explicit permission, but with an important caveat: any text not subject to pre-publication censorship was always potentially liable to sudden withdrawal from national circulation, so if an already distributed publication was deemed to be counter to the public good, this decision could result in significant economic losses for the publisher. Another new and important legislative mechanism was the so-called *silencio administrativo*, namely official silence regarding publishing matters. By legally declaring silence, the authorities did not explicitly approve a given book and its content, but merely abstained from blocking its commercial distribution. In practice, as a result of this new legislation, publishing houses now encountered 'a tougher state of affairs in economic terms, as full print runs of books which met with administrative silence during voluntary consultation could be sequestered' (Linder Molin, 2011: 177). In actual fact, the main outcome of the apparently less repressive Law of Press and Printing from 1966 was to move the red pencil from the hands of the censors to the publishers and from the publishers to the writers and translators, thus ensuring that self-censorship would become part and parcel of writing, editing and translating; indeed, it would become an acquired habitus for literary practitioners.

In Francoist Spain, most literary practitioners confessed to exerting self-censorship on their own texts, and the power of official censorship meant that 'many writers became their own censors' ('convertir a muchos escritores en censores de sí mismos'; Beneyto, 1975: 158). It should also be noted that the new and apparently 'generous' 1966 Law of Press and Printing also brought about the establishment of the Registro de Empresas Importadoras de Publicaciones Extranjeras (Register for Firms Importing Foreign Publications), an agency created with the aim of supervising the activity of the publishing houses which decided to import foreign works (cf. Rojas Clarós, 2013). From that moment on, the owner of any importing company could be liable to heavy penalties if an imported work was considered to be unacceptable. As a result, the new system led to the establishment of highly specialised contractual arrangements which tried to safeguard the interests of publishers, to the extent that contracts often stipulated that the translator would get paid only if the text was allowed to be published (Cisquella *et al.*, 1977: 138). Self-censorship, thus, became widespread among writers and translators, who strove to conform to official discourses, ideological expectations and commercial pressures in order to gain approval for their work. The techniques they adopted sprang out of what Bourdieu (1990: 66) calls *illusio*, the belief that the 'game' social actors within the field collectively agree to play is worth playing, and included 'all the imaginable forms of elimination, distortion, downgrading, misadjustment, infidelity' that one could think of (Santaemilia, 2008: 224). The practice of excising specific instances of unacceptable utterances was 'subtler and less aggressive' (Santaemilia, 2008: 245) than the banning of a whole text. Common targets of this censorial practice were all literary expressions of female nudity, sexually suggestive dialogues and any reference to allegedly immoral behaviour on the part of women. Self-censorship in cross-cultural communication constitutes a practice that is 'limited to translators who censor their own translations to conform to society's expectations' (Merkle, 2010: 19) yet, crucially, this cultural practice may evolve over time from a conscious decision-making process into a subliminal affect that quasi-determines literary output. Consequently, we may consider self-censorship, especially in the context of a highly repressive literary field, as an invisible habitualised constraint and a normative reflex.

Bestsellers in the Repressive Literary Field

The national literary field was in crisis after the end of the Spanish Civil War in 1939, mainly due to a lack of printing equipment as well as to political repression, which led many publishers to emigrate to South America. This was the case, for example, with the companies Grijalbo (Mexico) and Losada (Argentina), two highly successful publishing houses established by Republican expatriates who were forced into exile (Cornellà-Detrell, 2015: 40). The ones who remained in the country had to rely on the importation of foreign works that could help them fill the literary gaps in the national polysystem. This resulted in translations becoming an important and long-standing cultural catalyst within the Spanish literary field, until social and economic improvements allowed national literary production to flourish, from the end of the 1960s onwards (cf. Amorós *et al.*, 1987). Nonetheless, during the 1970s, towards the end of the regime, the percentage of translations remained very high and continued to yield substantial profits. As John Milton (2000: 177) points out, 'it may often be cheaper to recycle an already existing translation than to commission a new translation', so it is not surprising that many publishing houses moved into the habit of reprinting existing translated texts and of including them in popular anthologies. Incidentally, this occurred to a large extent within the realms of horror and science fiction novels, two genres with a considerable impact on the nation's literary production. It was thanks to the 'cloning' of this kind of literature that Spanish authors started to become increasingly popular, as the imitation of foreign styles led them to the centre of the literary field in a process of 'habituation and establishment of those models into the native Spanish textual system(s)' ('aclimatación y fijación de dichos modelos a el(los) sistema(s) textual(es) nativo(s) español(es)'; Rabadán, 2001: 36; see also Gómez Castro, 2013).

The concept of the North American bestseller emerged during this period, its international dissemination largely resting on television advertising and publicity campaigns, techniques of book promotion that significantly contributed to the genre's overseas success (cf. Carrero Eras, 1977). The selection of new foreign materials for the Spanish domestic literary market was based mainly on economic criteria, similar to what had happened in the German literary field under the Nazi regime, where 'within the narrow bounds set by censorship processes, anything saleable was exploited' (Sturge, 2004: 59). Any literary work with mass appeal yet not necessarily great artistic value has the potential to become a bestseller, a literary product mainly defined by commercial success. Following Vila-Sanjuán (2004: 459), a bestseller can be defined as 'a literary subgenre with its own identity, characterised by entertaining novels written without any literary pretension but with the clear aim of making the reader have a pleasant time and catch his or her attention from the very beginning' ('un subgénero literario con entidad propia al que pertenecerían un amplio segmento de novelas de entretenimiento, escritas sin pretensiones literarias pero con la intención clara de hacer pasar un buen rato al lector y atrapar su atención desde el primer momento').

The specific characteristics of the bestselling novels that circulated in the Spanish market during the last years of Franco's dictatorship needed to be retained in translation so as to ensure the reproduction of the conditions that prompted their economic success. For Jean-Marc Gouanvic (2005: 163), an acceptable work of translation '(re)produces in the target text the capacity of a work of fiction to provoke the adherence of a reader to the source work of fiction'. This process requires the preservation of the source text's *illusio* (Bourdieu, 1990), which in turn 'is closely linked to the dynamics of a field, existing only in the action of agents equipped with the habitus and symbolic capital acquired in that field' (Gouanvic, 2005: 164). The structural characteristics prevalent in bestsellers at the time were indebted to traditional literary techniques common until the end of the 19th century, such as plots mainly based on a clear narrative focus and a selection of characters whose discourse is often represented in the form of dialogue (Yui, 1997: 170). A swift understanding of the plot is ensured through linear narrative progression and the exclusion of elements that could hinder the reader's understanding; in addition, this type of literary fiction needs to be entertaining, enjoyable and ideally offer a happy ending (López Molina, 1997: 100). In these stories, 'larger than life' characters (Zuckerman, 1996: 30) frequently perform extraordinary actions or recover from the most adverse circumstances, and their adventures tend to take place in exotic or at least 'interesting' settings (Vila-Sanjuán, 2004: 461). The escapist tendencies of readers appear to dictate narrative structure, choice of location, characters and storyline, since, of course, 'common day scenarios with no glamour [do] not sell' ('lo cotidiano y exento de glamour no vende'; Servén Díez, 2006: 51).

Many bestsellers are set in the United States, with storylines that echo their characters' search for the proverbial American Dream, for freedom, wealth and success in the land of boundless opportunities. Bestselling fiction drawing on the North American way of life was successful both in its source culture and in the repressive Spanish context under censorship. This is mainly because the translations tended to reproduce the fictional discourse developed within a given source text (cf. Venuti, 1998), in an effort to also maintain what Gouanvic (2005: 163) describes as 'resemblance in difference'.

Bestsellers are a clear example of a genre where the target text tries to maintain the major literary characteristics of the source text in an effort to ensure the interest of the reader in the same way that the source text managed to do in its original context. In spite of this, the censorship was conducted through the official channels of state control, while the self-censorship exercised especially by practising translators had a significant impact on the representation of gender in translated Spanish fiction at the time.

Gender and the Politics of the Masculine State

Spain remained a deeply Catholic country under Franco's authoritarian regime. Political and cultural repression resulted in the strict observance of sexual and religious morality through all channels of official and public discourse (Abellán, 1980: 88). Apart from the systemic protection of good morals as a central pillar of governance, the state clamped down on any controversies that could endanger the (spiritual) essence of the imagined community (cf. Anderson, 1991). The image and role of women and the question of gender need to be considered as vital elements for any analysis of translational politics, in terms of contextual, poetological and linguistic constraints. Linder (2004: 157) has rightly described the imposed moral and political order in Francoist Spain as a 'typically fervent version of male patriarchy within the institutions of marriage and the family', implying of course that those who held power in society and politics were male, with females tending to remain at the mercy of a state that was run by a male elite. As a result, two opposing gender realities coexisted in a cultural context where women had to be morally impeccable but men could indulge in extramarital affairs.

From the regime's very beginnings, the administration closely monitored the image and role of women in all cultural spheres, and the censors' reports show that gender was one of the most scrupulously surveilled areas in the translational field (for an extensive survey of official censorship files between 1970 and 1978, see Gómez Castro, 2009). Any instances of morally reprehensible female conduct were excised or altered, as were those instances that clashed with the ideals of the good mother or the virtuous wife.

The publication of censored North American bestsellers in Spanish translation stimulated the introduction of a new, subversive moral code and inspired a gradual change in the public representation of gender, and the same occurred in terms of cinematic representations of womanhood and femininity (Gutiérrez Lanza, 2011: 318). From the late 1960s onwards, the transformation of traditional values, especially in relation to sexual morals, became more noticeable, because the fascist regime's '"corrective" measures of public morality and religiosity that had been in force since the end of the Civil War had not really taken root among the people' (Gutiérrez Lanza, 2002: 151). Qualitative changes in aesthetic and moral judgement had started at a slow pace, yet quickly gained momentum towards the end of the regime, not least because of the wider ideological impact of (largely student-led) Western liberalisation movements.

The relationship between censorship and the representation of gender can be readily glimpsed when analysing the portrayal of women in foreign source texts and their Spanish translations. It can reasonably be claimed that official censorship and self-censorship gave rise to a number of strategic translational options that were systematically applied within a national literary field governed by totalitarian political values. While the authorities strove to maintain the political status quo, publishers and translators, consciously or unconsciously, strove to circumvent cultural repression with similar techniques yet divergent ideological objectives. Under liberal political regimes, the translator's voice may float to the surface in differing shades, tones and nuances (Hermans, 1996), but translational mediations under totalitarian conditions conceal it, as a consequence of the sheer might of institutional coercion and strategic acts of self-censorhip on the part of the agents in the translational field. Never-theless, a revolutionary subcultural tide bound to overcome traditional gender roles and sexual morals swept through the Western world of the late 1960s and 1970s, representing an incendiary change in public attitude that would not stop at the gates of a backward-looking fascist state. The translation of American bestsellers in Francoist Spain, therefore, provides valuable insights into the official reaction to increasingly liberal represen-tations of gender and sexuality, as well as into the evolving and shifting patterns of literary expression and translational mediation.

Gender-Induced Translation Choices in Bestsellers

North American bestsellers could be submitted to the censorship office either in their source language or in the translated form. Most commonly, censors would receive a translated version of a specific novel, with its most controversial aspects likely to have been already expurgated by the translator or other agents, mindful of the novel's potential to be banned from circulation. It is not difficult to find examples of both non-official and official *gender filtering* carried out by those involved in the translation process and/or the censorship authorities. This exemplifies the close links between internal self-censorship and state coercion during the transla-tion process. The following translation examples, which demonstrate the interaction of authoritarian control with the subjective intuitions of self-censorship, are taken from three North American bestsellers. Among the main translation techniques used to deal with controversial and poten-tially objectionable topics are *modification* and *elision*.

Strategic modification

Modification strategies may generally include 'any kind of textual alteration either formal or semantic' ('cualquier tipo de alteración textual de tipo formal o semántica'; Bandín Fuertes, 2007: 201; see also Chesterman, 1997: 92). In order to achieve a more nuanced description of translational decision-making, we can distinguish the two sub-strategies: *moderation* and *commutation*.

The concept of moderation was introduced by Merino (1986: 287; revisited by Valero Garcés, 2007: 160) as an analytical tool to pinpoint the connotative modification of a given source expression. Moderation could be accomplished by various means and differing degrees of textual manipulation. A translator's resort to euphemisms, for example, would frequently serve to anticipate and block an unfavourable interpretation of the text on the part of the authorities. Mario Puzo's bestselling novel *The Godfather* (1969) exemplifies this strategy very well: it was first submitted in English to government censors, who highlighted numerous passages with explicit sexual content and asked to see the Spanish translation of the book; yet, even though the Barcelona-based publisher, Grijalbo, and the translator, Angel Arnau, were able to work from the censored English text, the authorities demanded further amendments upon the submission of the finished translation, requesting the moderation and excision of additional erotic passages (censorship file 13192-70). Hence, only upon further moderation was the Spanish title, *El padrino*, allowed circulation within the literary field. The readers of both the English original text and its Spanish version are presented with a hierarchically gendered world that pushes women into the narrative background, where their only concern is to look after the family, to look attractive and – against the backdrop of the sexually liberalised atmosphere of the late 1960s – to be ready for an occasional erotic encounter. Whereas the female members of Don Corleone's family are subordinated to the male hierarchy, as demanded by the moral codes of the mob, the men are devoted both to the family's business and to the family itself, as fittingly and ominously stated by one of the novel's male characters, Michael Corleone: 'Don't ever take sides ... against the family' (Puzo, 1969: 243). While the women are fully conscious of their subordinated social position and largely comply with the role models of the good wife and mother – gender stereotypes, of course, that were promulgated by the Spanish regime – some are depicted in a way that was deemed excessively liberal and thus contradicting the ideological requirements of strict Catholicism, as in the case of Johnny Fontane's second wife, 'his former movie co star [who] is a nymphomaniac' and who 'proves not to be a one woman man [*sic*] and sleeps with as many men as she wishes too' (Daginawalla, 2013: 5). An obvious example of translational moderation relates to a conversation between the aforementioned crooner Johnny Fontane, Vito Corleone's godson, and Sharon Moore, a young and aspiring actress who auditions for a small part in a Hollywood movie, where she professes that she would never think of making love with just anyone, because 'It's just that I have to be turned on to do it with a guy, you know what I mean?' (Puzo, 1969: 158). In the back-translated censored version, this became 'The truth is that I need to feel something to give myself to a man' ('La verdad es que debo sentir algo, para entregarme a un hombre'; Puzo, 1970: 164). The erotic connotations of 'to be turned on' are erased in the Spanish target text, transmuting this female character into a more acceptable kind of woman, who acquiesces to sexual advances only when feeling in love. Similarly, where the maid of Don Corleone's daughter attempts to refute the stereotype that depicts women from Las Vegas as being sex-obsessed, stating that 'I'm not really a swinger like most of the girls here in Vegas' (Puzo, 1969: 308), the back-translated Spanish version simply reads 'I'm afraid I am somewhat different from girls in Vegas' ('Me temo que soy algo diferente de las chicas de Las Vegas'; Puzo, 1970: 309). Originating from Las Vegas, the maid is seen as a pleasure-seeker because of her affair with Sonny Corleone. She has the audacity to sleep with him during his sister's wedding, so the expression was moderated in order to offer a more gentle image of women from a city usually associated with licentiousness.

The modification strategy of commutation requires that 'the original information remains secret and the information provided is completely different from the original' ('la información original permanece en secreto y se comunica una información totalmente diferente de la original'; Vilches, 1989: 31; revisited by Gutiérrez Lanza, 2000, in a study of censorship and cinema in Francoist Spain). The commutation technique was a convenient self-censorship device, allowing the translation agents to screen the source text for objectionable content and to modify potentially offensive passages. This strategy can be well illustrated by recourse to Irwin Shaw's *Rich Man, Poor Man*, from 1969. The book reflects on critical social issues within North American society from the end of World War II up to the end of the 1960s, by centring on the fortunes and misfortunes of the German-American Jordache family. Upon initial examination by Spain's official censors, the English original received an 'official silence', which meant that its explicit sexual language and pornographic scenes were not officially approved yet its commercial distribution was not blocked (censorship file 8762-72). The subsequent Spanish translation, *Hombre rico, hombre pobre*, translated by J. Ferrer Aleu and published in 1972 by Plaza & Janés, in Barcelona, contains numerous watered-down versions of passages referring to sex, prostitution, divorce or contraception. For example, where in the original the Jordaches' daughter, Gretchen, is told by a man that 'You were going to go down there and get laid' (Shaw, 1969: 55), the Spanish translation has him stating that she was 'going there to get raped' ('Usted iba allí para que la violasen'; Shaw, 1972: 65). So, while the English-language narrative depicts the girl as actively looking for sex, the Spanish version spins a misogynous tale of victimisation which blames Gretchen for her own potential rape. Elsewhere, Gretchen lasciviously proclaims 'I'm horny and unlaid and disappointed' (Shaw, 1969: 346); rather than sexually aroused and unsatisfied, she is merely 'angry and disappointed' in the Spanish translation ('Estoy cabreada y defraudada'; Shaw, 1972: 379). In these examples, self-censorship in conjunction with the translation strategy of commutation have effected drastic changes in propositional content that result in psychologically skewed representations of the novel's female characters.

Strategic elision

North American bestsellers geared for circulation on the Spanish market under Franco's regime were also subject to stringent strategies of elision. Unlike moderation and commutation strategies, whose main aim is to divert the attention of the reader from a potentially controversial topic to a less problematic one, elision consists of simply deleting the problematic content, with no need for rewording (this is termed 'omission' by Chesterman, 1997: 109–110). This text-altering technique, as with all the translation strategies highlighted here, could be carried out by government officials, by translators or editors. Most of the time, however, non-governmental agents such as translators or editors would themselves omit parts of a given source text in order to forestall any potential confrontation with official censorship. Harold Robbins's novel *The Betsy* (1971) serves as a good example of the employment of this coercive procedure. Harold Robbins remains one of the most prolific and most widely published authors of all time, and his novels have fast-paced storylines and all the ingredients of sex, money, power and violence that readers around the world were (and still are) craving. Just like Robbins's exhilarating and bawdy depictions of American life in the 20th century, the publication history of *The Betsy* in Spain was nothing short of eventful. It entered the official book control system through a Spanish translation from Argentina entitled *Betsy*. The translation had been carried out by Raquel Albornoz, who recently acknowledged that she had not dared to self-censor the text, attributing any possible changes to the official authorities in her country for the simple reason that, at the time, Argentina itself was reeling under a repressive dictatorial regime with its very own censorial mechanisms (personal communications, January 2005 and May 2006). Nonetheless, in Spain this translation was deemed by two official censors to be pornographic and unpublishable, as the implementation of cuts would have affected too many passages and would have rendered the storyline incomprehensible. Yet, within the following three months the book's fortunes changed in dramatic fashion, from being regarded as dangerous and reprehensible – and thus forcing the publisher, Luis de Caralt, to abandon any publishing plans – to being introduced on the Spanish market. It has become a well established idea in research on Francoist cultural repression that 'censorship was not passively "suffered" by Spaniards; they developed strategies to counter its effects' (Labanyi, 1996: 213), and one of these strategies was the resubmission of a book under a different title and cover. Translated by Domingo Manfredi Cano, yet with all pornographic and controversial scenes expurgated or modified, *Los ejecutivos* (*The Executives*) eventually managed to bypass official inspection. Unaware of the new title's true identity, the censors allowed this cornerstone of North American mass literature to enter into the Spanish literary system through official channels. In a bold move that might be termed literary camouflage – in fact, a readjustment to the *illusio* (Bourdieu, 1990) in the repressive translational field – Luis de Caralt managed to secure publication of a commercially promising work (censorship file 1349-73). The novel revolves around an automobile tycoon and his love life, and the storyline routinely hinges on passages that depict 'in graphic detail the frenzied copulation between the elderly head of a car dynasty and his young daughter-in-law' (Wilson, 2011: 27). Just like in many other North American bestsellers at the time, the female characters in *Los ejecutivos* are at ease with any kind of sexual proposal, a circumstance which had to be softened in the second translation before its resubmission to the authorities. Any hints at readiness for casual sex were not tolerated; unsurprisingly, source text passages with graphic sexual content such as 'Her legs were open too. Her pantyhose were soaked' (Robbins, 1971: 103) were deleted before the novel's official submission. Additionally, repressive legislation such as the ban on the sale of contraceptives (which was lifted only in 1978) played a role in self-censoring strategies, as evident in the preemptive elision of the sentence 'I brought everything to the Riviera with me except my B.C. pills' (Robbins, 1971: 376).

The end of the regime in 1978 brought about a change in official policies and public attitudes towards sex and morality, and this gradually became reflected in the patterns of writing and translation techniques in the national literary field, including an increasing 'permissiveness threshold' ('umbral de permisividad'), as highlighted by Gutiérrez Lanza (2000: 176).

Power Plays or 'the Game of the Possible'

In an early contribution to the historical understanding of Francoist censorship, Janet Pérez (1984) employs the phrase 'the game of the possible' to discuss the various techniques of dissent available for coming to terms with the restrictions of cultural oppression. Pérez's notion reminds us of the Bourdieusian prerogative to situate the fortunes of translation within sociological parameters, within fields of conflict where people have to struggle for capital while acquiring a specific *feel* for the social game. Official censorship became part of the *illusio*, the *raison d'être* of cultural agents in an extremely conservative country like Franco's Spain. Translational agents participated within a literary field that became structured around self-censoring dispositions, which gradually became integrated into the literary field's *illusio*. Literary activities, on the whole, are 'subjected to guidelines or practices sometimes predetermined which represent, to a greater or lesser degree, an instrument of social control' ('sujeta a pautas o prácticas muchas veces predeterminadas que representan, en mayor o menor grado, un instrumento de control social'; Carbonell i Cortés, 1999: 216). This is why in cultural fields of intense state intervention a specific transindividual habitus – a predilection towards instinctual self-censorship – becomes a decisive element of the *modus operandi* of intercultural agents. From the 1980s onwards, translators and editors began to yield to the market demands of a system that became increasingly defined through capitalist values. The new interdependencies of slowly globalising national markets and cultural tastes had an impact on Spanish cross-cultural mediation, the consequence being that 'the moral tolerance threshold was gradually being raised' (Gutiérrez Lanza, 2011: 318). This transformed a sociocultural field where, until then, the dynamics of literary gender representation had been strongly opposed to the rights, freedoms and interests of female citizens. Maintaining the image of women as upholders of the nation's morality (Linder, 2004: 157) had been an element of crucial significance for the authoritarian state, and proved, unquestionably, one of the principal ideological concerns in a very conservative literary field characterised by repressive translation practices.

Note

(1) The work presented in this article derives from research undertaken in the field of translation, censorship and gender in Spain as part of the TRACE project, currently funded by the Spanish Ministry of Science and Innovation (FFI2012-39012C04-04).

References

Primary sources

Puzo, M. (1969) *The Godfather*. New York: G.P. Putnam's Sons.
Puzo, M. (1970) *El padrino* (A. Arnau, trans.). Barcelona: Grijalbo.
Robbins, H. (1971) *The Betsy*. New York: Trident Press.
Robbins, H. (1974) *Los ejecutivos* (D. Manfredi Cano, trans.). Barcelona: Luis de Caralt.
Shaw, I. (1969) *Rich Man, Poor Man*. New York: Delacorte Press (1970).
Shaw, I. (1972) *Hombre rico, hombre pobre* (J. Ferrer Aleu, trans.). Barcelona: Plaza & Janés.

Archivo General de la Administración (Alcalá de Henares)

Betsy. Censorship file no. 1349-73.
El padrino. Censorship file no. 13192-70
Hombre rico, hombre pobre. Censorship file no. 8762-72.
La familia/El ejecutivo. Censorship file no. 5514-73.

Secondary sources

Abellán, M. (1980) *Censura y creación literaria en España (1939–1976)*. Barcelona: Península.

Amorós, A., *et al.* (1987) *Letras españolas 1976–1986*. Madrid: Castalia.

Anderson, B. (1991) *Imagined Communities: Reflections on the Origin and Spread of Nationalism*. London: Verso.

Bandín Fuertes, E. (2007) Traducción, recepción y censura de teatro clásico Inglés en la España de Franco. Estudio descriptivo comparativo del corpus TRACEtci (1939–1985). Unpublished PhD thesis, Universidad de León.

Bassnett, S. and Lefevere, A. (1998) *Constructing Cultures: Essays on Literary Translation*. Clevedon: Multilingual Matters.

Beneyto, A. (1975) *Censura y política en los escritores españoles*. Barcelona: Euros.

Bourdieu, P. (1990) *The Logic of Practice* (R. Nice, trans.). Stanford, CA: Stanford University Press.

Carbonell i Cortés, O. (1999) *Traducción y cultura: De la ideología al texto*. Salamanca: Colegio de España.

Carrero Eras, P. (1977) Notas para una sociología de la cultura literaria en España desde 1939. *Revista Española de Opinión Pública* 47, 91–121.

Chesterman, A. (1997) *Memes of Translation*. Amsterdam: John Benjamins.

Cisquella, G., Erviti, J.L. and Sorolla, J.A. (1977) *Diez años de represión cultural. La censura de libros durante la Ley de Prensa (1966–76)*. Barcelona: Editorial Anagrama.

Cornellà-Detrell, J. (2013) The afterlife of Francoist cultural policies: Censorship and translation in the Catalan and Spanish literary market. *Hispanic Research Journal* 14 (2), 129–143.

Cornellà-Detrell, J. (2015) La obra de James Baldwin ante la censura franquista: El contrabando de libros, la conexión latinoamericana y la evolución del sector editorial peninsular. *Represura* 1, 32–60.

Daginawalla, Z. (2013) Gender roles in *The Godfather*. Working paper published in Academia.edu, at http://www.academia.edu/9775398/Feminist_Analysis_of_The_Godfather, accessed 6 June 2016

Fawcett, P. (1995) Translation and power play. *The Translator* 1 (2), 177–192.

Gentzler, E. and Tymoczko, M. (eds) (2002) Introduction. In E. Gentzler and M. Tymoczko (eds) *Translation and Power* (pp. xi–xxviii). Boston, MA: University of Massachusetts Press.

Gómez Castro, C. (2008) Translation and censorship in Franco's Spain: Negotiation as a pathway for authorization. In C. O'Sullivan (ed.) *Proceedings of the 7th Annual Portsmouth Translation Conference* (pp. 63–76). Portsmouth: University of Portsmouth.

Gómez Castro, C. (2009) Traducción y censura de textos narrativos Inglés–Español en la España Franquista y de transición: TRACEni (1970–1978). Unpublished PhD thesis, Universidad de León.

Gómez Castro, C. (2013) The reception of anthologies of science fiction and horror and terror tales in the last years of Francoist Spain: Censoring aliens and monsters. In T. Seruya, M. Lin Moniz, D. Delabastita and A. Assis Rosa (eds) *Translation in Anthologies and Collections (19th and 20th Centuries)* (pp. 205–216). Amsterdam: John Benjamins.

Gouanvic, J.-M. (2005) A Bourdieusian theory of translation, or the coincidence of practical instances: Field, 'habitus', capital and 'illusio'. *The Translator* 11 (2), 147–166.

Gutiérrez Lanza, C. (2000) *Traducción y censura de textos cinematográficos en la España de Franco: Doblaje y subtitulado inglés–español (1951–1975). Catálogo COITE (1951–1975)*. León: Universidad de León.

Gutiérrez Lanza, C. (2002) Spanish film translation and cultural patronage: The filtering and manipulation of imported material during Franco's dictatorship. In E. Gentzler and M. Tymoczko (eds) *Translation and Power* (pp. 141–159). Boston, MA: University of Massachusetts Press.

Gutiérrez Lanza, C. (2011) Censors and censorship boards in Franco's Spain (1950s–1960s): An overview based on the TRACE cinema catalogue. In D. Asimakoulas and M. Rogers (eds) *Translation and Opposition* (pp. 305–320). Bristol: Multilingual Matters.

Hermans, T. (ed.) (1985) *The Manipulation of Literature. Studies in Literary Translation*. London: Croom Helm.

Hermans, T. (1996) The translator's voice in translated narrative. *Target* 8 (1), 23–48.

Labanyi, J. (1996) Censorship or the fear of mass culture. In H. Graham and J. Labanyi (eds) *Spanish Cultural Studies: An Introduction. The Struggle for Modernity* (pp. 207–214). New York: Oxford University Press.

Lefevere, A. (1992) *Translation, Rewriting and the Manipulation of Literary Fame*. London: Routledge.

Linder, D. (2004) The censorship of sex: A study of Raymond Chandler's *The Big Sleep* in Franco's Spain. *TTR: Traduction, Terminologie, Rédaction* 17 (1), 155–182.

Linder Molin, D. (2011) *The American Detective Novel in Translation: The Translations of Raymond Chandler's Novels into Spanish*. Salamanca: Ediciones Universidad de Salamanca.

López Molina, L. (1997) Análisis de *La piel del tambor* desde las 'teorías y prácticas' del best-séller. In J.M. López de Abiada and J. Peñate Rivero (eds) *Éxito de ventas y calidad literaria. Incursiones en las teorías y prácticas del best-séller* (pp. 95–104). Madrid: Verbum.

McLaughlin, M. and Muñoz-Bassols, J. (2016) Introduction. 'Ideology, Censorship and Translation Across Genres: Past and Present', special issue, *Perspectives – Studies in Translatology* 24 (1), 1–6.

Merino, R. (1986) Estudio crítico de la traducción de obras de teatro Inglés contemporáneo al Castellano. Unpublished degree dissertation, Universidad del Pais Vasco/EHU.

Merkle, D. (2010) Censorship. In Y. Gambier and L. van Doorslaer (eds) *Handbook of Translation Studies* (pp. 18–21). Amsterdam: John Benjamins.

Milton, J. (2000) The translation of mass fiction. In A. Beeby, D. Ensinger and M. Presas (eds) *Investigating Translation* (pp. 171–179). Amsterdam: John Benjamins.

Ortiz Heras, M. (2006) Mujer y dictadura Franquista. *Aposta: Revista de Ciencias Sociales* 28, 1–26.

Pérez, J. (1984) The game of the possible. Francoist censorship and techniques of dissent. *Review of Contemporary Fiction* 4 (3), 22–30.

Rabadán, R. (2001) Las cadenas intertextuales inglés–español: Traducciones y otras transferencias (inter)semióticas. In E. Pajares, R. Merino and J.M. Santamaría (eds) *Trasvases culturales: Literatura, cine, traducción 3* (pp. 29–41). Vitoria-Gasteiz: UPV/EHU.

Rojas Clarós, F. (2013) *Dirigismo cultural y disidencia editorial en España (1962–1973)*. Alicante: Universidad de Alicante.

Rundle, C. (2010) *Publishing Translations in Fascist Italy*. Berlin: Peter Lang.

Santaemilia, J. (2008) The translation of sex-related language: The danger(s) of self-censorship(s). *TTR: Traduction, Terminologie, Rédaction* 21 (2), 221–252.

Servén Díez, C. (2006) Lectura de masas: El best-seller. In D. Noguera Guirao (ed.) *Lecciones de literatura* (pp. 43–56). Madrid: Ediciones de la Universidad Autónoma.

St-Pierre, P. (1993) Translation as a discourse of history. *TTR: Traduction, Terminologie, Rédaction* 6 (1), 61–82.

Sturge, K. (2004) *The Alien Within: Translation into German During the Nazi Regime*. München: Iudicium.

Valero Garcés, C. (2007) *Modelo de evaluación de obras literarias traducidas:* The Scarlet Letter/La letra escarlata *de Nathaniel Hawthorne*. Bern: Peter Lang.

Venuti, L. (1998) *The Scandals of Translation*. London: Routledge.

Vila-Sanjuán, S. (2004) *Pasando página: Autores y editores en la España democrática*. Barcelona: Círculo de Lectores.

Vilches, L. (1989) *Manipulación de la información televisiva*. Barcelona: Paidós.

Wilson, A. (2011) *Harold Robbins: The Man Who Invented Sex*. London: Bloomsbury.

Yui, J.A. (1997) De best-séllers y otros demonios. In J.M. López de Abiada and J. Peñate Rivero (eds) *Éxito de ventas y calidad literaria: Incursiones en las teorías y prácticas del best-séller* (pp. 169–183). Madrid: Verbum.

Zuckerman, A. (1996) *Cómo escribir un nestseller: Las técnicas del éxito literario* (J.M. Pomares, trans.). Barcelona: Grijalbo Mondadori.

Part 3

Media Translation in the Global Digital Economy

8 Translation and Mass Communication in the Age of Globalisation

José Lambert

Introduction to an Updated Version of Some Old Musings

It is not without some irony that I write this short introduction to the English version of a paper which I first published in 1989 under the title 'La traduction, les langues et la communication de masse' in the journal *Target*. The evidence that scholars in translation studies also need to read translations is one of the paradoxes of the discipline. Maybe it is less the translation that is needed than a kind of warning: several of the shifts in *translation culture* that were analysed in my 1989 article still belong to unexplored provinces of our discipline and they remain a significant challenge, particularly from the perspective of academic interdisciplinarity. In 1989, translation studies did not make use of the concept of *globalisation*, which gradually came to the fore in Pierre Bourdieu's (1979) sociology, from where a critical exploration of the international circulation of discourses was initially launched. With a certain delay, the arts and humanities would eventually realise that globalisation was not just about the economy. Only at the dawn of the new century did the exploration of the translation component in the age of globalisation take off. Several outstanding publications (e.g. Cronin, 2003; also Bielsa & Hughes, 2009) started to explore *the links between translation and the globalised world*, and the new state of the art in translation studies was finally about to recognise globalisation as one of the key concepts in the field. And this is exactly why the republication a 1989 article, translated and revised, makes sense. Notwithstanding the many new and fascinating publications on translation, many research projects worldwide are still struggling to identify and understand the profound changes in translation culture brought about by globalisation processes. The article was necessary in its original context because translation studies was still blind to many of the questions I was addressing, and hence several aggressive statements at the beginning of the text: 'Therefore, it is time … ', 'All relationships … need to be reformulated', and so on.

127

Since the end of the 20th century, technology has evolved rapidly and a number of major publications have been devoted to *the new world of translated communication* (e.g. Gambier & Gottlieb, 2001; Sin-Wai, 2015). It is not at all clear, however, whether the awareness of several crucial shifts in communication has truly spread within translation studies. New technologies have heavily impacted on the translation component of modern communication as well as the societies that generate and adopt the new communication systems: *new communities of practice* are appearing everywhere. In spite of this, it is hard to deny that many publications on the links between two or more given societies – nations, cultures, languages and so on – still reflect a static world. The difficulty is not that traditional translation culture has suddenly disappeared, but that many researchers are not sufficiently aware of *the multifarious world-view components in translation cultures*. One basic issue has become the question of what kind of communication societies are making use of and, in turn, what kind of translation culture they are adopting. Crucially, in many contemporary situations the idea of *target orientedness* needs to be clarified in new conceptual arrangements and terminological labels. Are translations phenomena of one culture only? Are translations the result of given needs (on behalf of given 'target' cultures)? And where exactly do they come from? Since at least the end of the 20th century, translations are distributed *multilaterally* from particularly strong centres in waves that generate the need for specific commodities, and therefore it is essential to reconsider this practice within multilateral environments and with respect to the capitalist distribution of all kinds of (symbolic) goods. The consequences of such a redefinition of the concept of translation, which began when we started linking it with the notion of *norms* – the sociological turn in translation studies is much older than the 21st century – cannot be underestimated. According to one of the classics of translation theory, translation is supposed to be a *decision-making process* (Levý, 1967). The problem is, who exactly decides? There are clear indications that multilateral translations (and the international generation of translation needs) are no privilege of the last two centuries: how would we have known about religions and about legislation (for instance the Code Napoléon) without the multilateral planning and production of translations? There can be no doubt about the need for new and large-scale research projects on translation phenomena focusing on such ideas.

As a final note, I would like to add that it was not possible to reformulate the statements from the 1989 text without some updating, particularly as several arguments may have lost (part of) their relevance. The 'revision' of the original paper has consisted of refining a number of ideas and adding references to a few publications from the intervening years.

Translation and Mass Communication

It has become a truism to state that translation is part of communication. The idea that mass communication is a key sector for translation appears to be equally self-evident, and something which at first sight requires little explanation. Therefore, it is time that the discipline of translation studies, which makes much of the links between culture and translation, analyses all the phenomena involved in mass communication, understood as the globalised domain of social discourse. The aim of this article is therefore to briefly outline the boundaries of a field of research that would appear to be of primary interest both for the study of translation and for the study of communication, if not for the humanities more generally. In fact, it would be no exaggeration to claim that the relevance of the research models that have been developed since the 1960s will depend in part on their effectiveness in addressing the issue of the mass media. The links between mass communication and translation are a result of:

- the intensification of globalised communications compared with traditional communication networks;
- the supranational and multinational nature of the sources of dissemination, and their concentration in a limited number of centres, from where dissemination takes place in multiple directions;
- the continual acceleration due to the use of new technologies;
- the establishment of new communication models and new 'genres', giving rise to a new hierarchy of artistic, journalistic and other genres (genres are closely linked to a hierarchy of values and tend to reflect changes in norms and models).

Despite the obvious links, mass media specialists have generally overlooked the question of translation; translation scholars, on the contrary, have paid increasing attention to this phenomenon (see the works by Yves Gambier, Anthony Pym, Henrik Gottlieb, Michael Cronin, etc.). Mass communication is characterised by a multiplicity of receivers, irrespective of linguistic, political or other borders, and by a reduction in the number of senders. This has several consequences, such as the homogenisation of messages, which of course is nothing new, because traditional communications, in the process of being supplanted by mass media, have also gone through a kind of homogenisation process. Mass communication has gradually become monopolised by international/multinational players, resulting in a huge number of messages originating from a small number of senders. This process leads to the proliferation of messages in different languages and modes of communication which adapt to the needs of the receiving setting. Obviously, one particular outcome of this is a marked multiplication of the number of translations.

There is a tendency for the initial communication to become monopolised by players who are increasingly difficult to localise geographically.

Such a global situation redefines the relationships between the 'source system' and the 'target system'. In addition, a completely new and almost inevitably multilingual system of communication networks has developed which systematically distributes messages across the world's cultures and frequently disregards or challenges traditional national barriers (e.g. the importing of American films into France often includes French-speaking Belgium; the importing of American films into the Netherlands often includes Dutch-speaking Belgium). All relationships involving cultural export and import, therefore, need to be reformulated, no doubt including Toury's much-disputed idea that 'translation is a fact of one system only'. The proliferation of 'intermediaries', particularly when messages are multiplied by means of translation, confirms the camouflaging strategies that seek to create conformity between globalised messages and local messages, or to conceal the monopolies on the sender side (Lamizet, 1983: 10; Gambier & Gottlieb, 2001). Until recently, this process of multiplication has been largely ignored, no doubt because communication specialists have accepted that these are simply technical processes.

If the question of translation is still gaining prominence at the beginning of the 21st century, it is because mass communication (first and foremost through the internet, but also in the form of texts, software, video games, songs, films, television programmes, video recordings, etc.) is increasingly being organised on an international rather than a local or national scale. A well known economic fact illustrates the extent to which the mass media have redrawn the global power landscape: a large proportion of global communications (press agencies, cinema, television, songs, etc.) is dominated by multinationals, which implies a *de facto* weakening of regional, national and even supranational structures.

The Distribution of Globalisation Discourse

The growing globalisation of communication is inevitably leading to the redrawing of the world map of languages (de Swaan, 2001; Lambert, 1991) and the loosening of bonds between people, languages and nations established by European Romanticism. Particularly thanks to the internet, television, cinema and advertising, the globalised paradigm has found its way into the majority of households throughout the world. As a result, there are very few societies that can still regard themselves as 'monolingual' – although in reality this has always been an ideal – even if the discourse presented by speakers and the media is in one and the same language. The origin of this discourse is often partly or entirely foreign, but in order to function as an 'honest' text, public discourse must conform to the monolingual model, and therefore tends to camouflage all traces of its origins. At present, the 'native' tongue is still managing to hold its own, albeit with concessions to the imported discourse. Even in so-called bilingual societies, the fact that a message has the characteristics of a translated message is often reason enough to make it appear compromised or even suspect. There is little doubt, therefore, that the multiplication of translations has an ambiguous function: it can be both a protectionist tool and a practice which destabilises monolingual traditions. This ambiguity is in fact a characteristic of all imports (Lambert, 1980, 1986). By imposing the principle of translation on the various member states, the European Union is, at the same time, both protecting their 'native' linguistic traditions and calling them into question. The constantly evolving linguistic map of the EU illustrates both the fragmentation and the uniformisation of politico-linguistic units: all the official languages of the member states are recognised, and documents are official only if they are available in all the different languages. This remains a relatively new situation, not only because it promotes the mobility of a proportion – however limited – of European citizens, but also and especially because it makes the linguistic practices of member states subject to rules which establish the use of multiple European languages by the official bodies of each country. Outside the EU, however, those same states have no difficulty in accepting the traditional hierarchical relationships between languages: for example, Angela Merkel and Nicolas Sarkozy speak very good English, but in interviews and press conferences always express themselves in German and French respectively.

Languages and Their Interactions

Monolingual models of analysis, whether those of the dominant discourse in society or those of linguistics, are in fact the result of a vast simplification, of an essentialist, static view of the phenomenon of language. When we call monolingualism into question, we are questioning both the internal coherence of a spoken and written language within a defined cultural context and its coherence *vis-à-vis* other languages. Linguists have long shown that languages are most definitely not homogeneous or closed systems. In a broad sense, 'multilingualism' needs to be understood as the coexistence of different linguistic practices within a language and the interaction between different languages across societies. From a strictly logical point of view, the simple fact that languages are standardised presupposes the existence of the opposite: a non-standardised language. While dominant groups tend to seek to standardise linguistic attitudes and practices, it is important to acknowledge that this tendency always goes hand in hand with its opposite, namely a drive towards de-standardisation. Among the inevitable phenomena involved in the way languages function, the interference between them – especially through translation – is one of the most important aspects that determine the evolution of tongues and consequently their continual redefinition. Nevertheless, the dominant views on the subject of language, even among scholars, continued until recently to be based primarily on their standard usage, despite the criticisms of this model that have been made from sociolinguistics and sociology (Bourdieu, 1982; Gardner-Chloros *et al.*, 2000; Lippi-Green, 1997).

From the perspective of translation studies, there are good reasons to widen the concept of 'translation' insofar as translations are not necessarily texts which tend to be clearly identified as such. Often, in fact, they are not even *whole texts*, since all languages continuously borrow words, structures, expressions and so on from other languages. No language is entirely without contacts; all of them have privileged relationships with certain tongues while maintaining links with others, and the assimilation of foreign elements also seems to follow regular patterns, defined at least in part by cultural circumstances and power relations (de Swaan, 2001; Weinreich, 1953). Hegemony and domination have always played an important part in these relationships as regards lending and borrowing. It is nothing new to distinguish between true loan translations or calques (e.g. *fair play* in French) and words which are borrowed but altered in some way (*mass media*, *mass-média* and *masse-média*), which we could see as translations in a broader sense. To date, however, no attempt has been made to link such phenomena to the strategies followed by translators: are they a fact of the language, the culture, or the work of the translator? Loan words and translations of this kind are of course eventually lost from view and completely assimilated, so that what one might call the 'archaeological character' of languages exists but is of interest – to a greater or lesser extent – only to specialists.

In the wake of globalising communications, the new relationships between languages are clearly having an impact on linguistic interactions, and it would not be unreasonable to posit that discourses and linguistic elements chosen to be imported and translated follow the fluctuations of global trends. Despite the multiple parallels that exist between linguistic borrowings and translations, we have no theoretical framework that allows us to draw a clear distinction between non-autonomous micro-structural units shared between languages and entire texts. In this respect, the notion of *languages in contact* deserves to be rewritten from a perspective that focuses on the *circulation of discourses*. In a way, the considerable broadening of the concept of 'translation' is analogous to the extension of the concept of 'text' in the field of cultural semiotics (in the debates around the notion of cultural translation, many walls between disciplines tend to survive, for example between translation studies, cultural studies, anthropology...).

Additionally, it is also of vital importance to broaden this concept of translation in the opposite direction, since *no translation results entirely from translation, in the sense that non-translation is part of the translation process*. It was in comparative stylistics (Vinay & Darbelnet, 1958) where the concept of 'non-translation' was first created and defined as one of the processes of translation. It has become clear from the analyses of the interactions on all levels between 'source' and 'target' cultures that non-translation is not a strictly linguistic process, but may occur at any level of the translating activity as a result of tensions between different systems. The presence of translation in the non-translated language, and the presence of non-translation in the translated messages, allows us to define the boundaries between 'translation' and 'language' more flexibly. These questions would be of secondary importance if the evolution of globalised communications were not continuously affecting linguistic and cultural exchanges in a completely new way. Specifically, in order to gain a better purchase on the way communication functions within and across cultures, it is paramount to study the compatibilities and incompatibilities between languages as well as the compatibilities and incompatibilities between translations and their 'original' languages.

The paradox of the presence of translations within language and the fact that non-translations are present in translation becomes a structural opposition within every language, depending on the extent to which it is either more closed or more open to neighbouring systems (see Even-Zohar, 1978). It has become clear from a large number of studies that priorities, and consequently strategies, in the area of translation do vary, depending on cultural factors, to the extent that translations become true barometers of cultural, linguistic and other relationships. Insofar as relationships between languages have changed drastically, it is urgent to develop tools to identify the new and transformative systemic strategies and tendencies that are continuously evolving within present-day languages and societies. Let us consider the following rule as a hypothesis: there is a close correlation between strategies of micro-structural assimilation (vocabulary, proper names, etc.) and strategies of macro-structural assimilation (textual corpora, including hypertexts, genres, techniques such as dubbing/subtitling), which means that some languages and cultures can be shown to be more open than others, and that the variations in their permeability suggest profound changes in the language/culture in question. In a nutshell, we take the view that translation is both an active agent in and a symptom of linguistic and cultural exchanges.

The End of a Myth: Monolingual Cultures

Multilingualism has always entailed the risk of *heterogeneity* – and not just linguistically – within a territory or territories, and this is why the powers that be, and consequently our own traditional views, have ignored heterogeneous tendencies and promoted linguistic *homogeneity*. In spite of this, presenting an image of most societies and institutions as monolingual involves severely distorting real individual and collective practices. Homogeneity is always relative; it corresponds to an ideal, never to a reality. Linguistic standardisation is never achieved totally, and it is important to determine for every culture what form it takes and how it is evolving. As has already been discussed, linguistic importation – particularly through translations – plays a key role in these processes of interference, but its scope varies and fluctuates, depending on the situation.

It must be stressed that translation is not, and never has been, the sole solution to the 'problem' of multilingualism. *It seems impossible to understand the function of translations without taking into account the many other solutions that exist, including non-translation.* Structurally, translation represents just one of the possible options available when dealing with multilingualism. It is the result of a selection process, just as any individual translation is itself the result of options that have been chosen in response to the problem of translation in general. Put simply, all present-day societies are forced to come up with a solution to the 'problem' of languages and thus also to the 'problem' of translations. Of course, the norms and models that are adopted within different societies are subject to the influence of the community and, in particular, its institutions (Brisset, 1986; Simon, 1989; Toury, 1978). Even unique linguistic and translation practices must necessarily be situated against the general background of the canonical practices of a particular time and place. This is one of the consequences of the concept of 'norms': all individual conventional practices exist in a relationship with other practices in one way or another; political institutions, of course, have the highest likelihood of shaping them.

Some of the solutions that have been used throughout history to deal with multilingualism include:

- the most radical option – genocide, or the destruction of a language community, if not of the community itself;
- adoption of one of the community's languages as a common language;
- adoption of a neutral language as a common language (Esperanto, etc.);
- the recognition of two (or more) common languages;
- a distinction between passive ('receiving') and active ('sending') practices in a language, or the 'alternate' coexistence of two (or more) languages;
- the 'democratisation' of languages as a principle, implying the necessary and complete translation of all messages into the other language(s).

According to certain theories of translation, it all comes down to questions of prestige and power: the question of languages and communication is primarily a political question. In any case, it is not possible to determine whether one solution is more successful than the others, as demonstrated by the fact that societies may frequently change their strategy. It is also quite common for several of the solutions set out above to be combined. There are even reasons to support the view that the most rational and economical solution, though not the easiest in ecological and political terms, is to reduce the number of languages to just one. One of the major factors determining a preference for one of the options above (or for other arrangements) is the relative strength or weakness of the linguistic groups within the multilingual community – to put it bluntly, the (available) resources and positions within the power struggle. The development of French as a cultural language over centuries, for instance, has had a major influence on the linguistic perceptions of Belgian, Swiss and Canadian citizens, just as the economic prestige of English has influenced the linguistic preferences of populations throughout Africa. In crude economic terms, it might seem more rational to promote homogenisation, but it might well be more profitable and less problematic to adopt the 'client's' language.

Globalisation takes place in conjunction with the development of mass communication technology, which inevitably promotes new forms of institutionalisation. Multilingualism, which compromises the (relative) linguistic homogeneity of a territory, spreads in a wide range of divergent ways, either according to the commercial needs of multinationals, the federal model found in certain states, each with their own specific features, or even according to the more complex formula of code-mixing, used in some cosmopolitan families in western Europe and elsewhere. Translation is only one of the possible formulas, and also presents a number of options. In any event, the extension of multilingualism does by definition represent a threat to traditional institutions. Insofar as contemporary multilingualism is often linked to a single international language (and this process of international standardisation is by no means the first in history), established cultural systems find themselves exposed to erosion and needing to review their communication principles and practices, based on the importance of the imported discourses. Multilingualism inevitably puts pressure on communication relationships in today's societies: insofar as multilingualism has become an option for many citizens, at least as a passive practice – for example at the cinema and when listening to songs – it calls into question traditional ideas about the stability and autonomy of societies. Researchers have a duty to examine the nature of potential conflicts and what is at stake.

It is almost inevitable that the conflict between native and foreign discourses will give rise to moral debates and protectionist measures in the economic, linguistic or political spheres. It was to some extent predictable that 'la querelle du franglais' (the quarrel about 'franglais' during the 1970s; see Etiemble, 1973) would break out, and that this would happen in a society that had fought more consistently than any other for the linguistic integrity of its territory. It is also symptomatic that other societies in western Europe did not feel the need to plunge into similar quarrels in the 1980s. Even France, following a shift in its own linguistic policy (Bruguière, 1978; Vermes & Boutet, 1987), ultimately ceased to view this issue as controversial. The coexistence of languages within France and within Europe has become a fact. While in the past most states tended to ignore this reality, political and other institutions are now being forced to come to terms with the situation.

In our current multilingual societies, translation occupies a privileged place among and above the other solutions. This is particularly evident in the strategies being followed by the EU, but also in new strategies being adopted by commercial organisations worldwide. The secret of translations, in contrast to the other options, is that they are able to remain hidden: at first sight, the international discourse is indistinguishable from the native discourse. Once it is subject to a number of well defined techniques and strategies, translation makes it possible to hide, to a greater or lesser degree, the differences inherent in languages and, consequently, in globalised communication. No one knows this better than the retailer or advertising agent who, in a very high percentage of cases, when selling products in the global marketplace needs to address potential customers in their own language.

The Pitfalls of Multilingualism

Supposing that all languages could be made equivalent and all the possible ways of dealing with multilingualism were equally effective, we would still have to recognise that linguistic communication (or the selection of linguistic resources) never takes place under ideal circumstances. All mixed-language societies demand that their members abide by certain norms at the expense of others, because linguistic exchanges do not take place independent of history and established positions (Bourdieu, 1982). All the options will, though, in a mixed society, require a specific sub-group to sacrifice certain everyday social practices. Only a radically new situation (the creation of a new nation, an invasion, an internal revolution, a mass exodus, the sudden rise of a new economy, the use of new communication technologies) can successfully induce people to change their linguistic behaviours.

Despite the apparently democratic formulas underpinning language policies, the idealistic – or perhaps hypocritical? – nature of the political choices that have been made regarding translation is more than evident. Equality between languages, like equality between any social group, is a utopian ideal. Even if such a democratic situation was imaginable, it would end up giving way to an increasingly hierarchical structure in which socio-economic relationships would have particular influence. Sociological views of language and theories of translation agree in recognising the links between languages on the one hand and prestige and power on the other. Inequality between languages is a global phenomenon spurred by new forms of mass communication. Nevertheless, it should be stressed that even if translation is becoming a ubiquitous practice, it will not manage to restore the pre-Babelian equality between languages. This has been confirmed by a very diverse range of studies on the cultural functions of translations, particularly those that recognise the impact of global cultural relationships on the links between 'target' and 'source' systems.

The observation that the globalisation of communication will lead to a redefinition of the relationships between languages and consequently of the world map of linguistic systems is not new. It is clear enough that English has become far and away the favourite international language of mass communication, which will result in profound changes in communication patterns and also, and even more importantly, in the value systems linked to them.

Insofar as traditional discourses on translation essentially deal with the – relatively common – cases in which a translation is identified as such, it has so far not been observed that a huge number of messages – primarily translations – are distorting the linguistic homogeneity of territories, particularly in advertising and journalism, but also in numerous other fields. Within translation studies, translations are still largely interpreted as bilateral operations between two national languages and two nations. The fragments of text scattered through everyday discourse are not noticed by many linguists and historians of translation, who do not recognise that, quoting Rimbaud, 'Je est un autre' ('I is another'). Modern societies are constantly quoting other societies, but they are doing so without realising it. Psychoanalysis, sociology and other disciplines ask questions about the origins and effect of our discourses in order to discover what guides and shapes them, with the primary aim of reaching better definitions of the principles underlying human behaviour. This is precisely what the analysis of translation seeks to do, by looking at the hidden layers of globalised communications.

It is by no means my intention to suggest that this hidden discourse and its interactions with other discourses are negative. Some societies are not concerned about this at all, while others find it a worrying issue, depending on their particular value systems. Research will determine precisely how the international and the 'local' (regional, national?) levels act upon each other, and only in-depth observation of specific cultural situations can guarantee solid results – see for instance Cronin's (2012) concept of 'politics of microspection'. It is thus not certain whether globalised discourse will win out everywhere, nor that it will do so in the same way each time. Depending on their value system, societies are uncertain about which way to go: homogenisation (but if so, in whose name?) or heterogeneity?

It would be going too far to describe the dissemination of globalisation discourse in terms of 'infiltration': this would wrongly suggest that these strategies are all intentional and are designed exclusively as an attempt at colonisation. Although it is clear that many aspects of globalisation do in fact respond to deliberate strategies – the case of advertising is one example of this – we have no reason to presume *a priori* that international institutions are pursuing a wholly conscious strategy in relation to translation. Nevertheless, it still has important effects which are so ubiquitous that they cannot be ignored.

Translation Strategies and Mass Communication

It is important to determine whether (and the ways in which) the various options that are available during the translation process are based on conscious or unconscious choices. How is mass communication assimilated in different cultures? The possible options are situated between two extremes which have hitherto been vaguely referred to as 'homogeneous' (or international) and 'heterogeneous' (more or less local, regional or national). Translation specialists have developed models which make it possible to describe such options and apply them to the new situation created by mass communication in order to gain a better understanding of how societies define themselves in relation to globalisation discourse.

All translations, it has been argued, are the result of choices which are situated between two extremes labelled as (predominantly) 'adequate' and (predominantly) 'acceptable', depending on the tendency to give priority to the 'source system' or the 'target system' (Toury, 1978, 1980). Bilingual publications are a good illustration of the first option, while the translation of advertisement texts (especially in pseudo-translations) generally relies on strategies which focus on acceptability. The majority of translations can be situated somewhere between these two extremes and, according to systemic theories, there is a clear relationship between the way in which these strategies are distributed across cultures and their function or position (Even-Zohar, 1978; Hermans, 1999). Systemic theories posit that the way in which cultures or certain sub-groups within those cultures assimilate foreign texts reflects deeply ingrained values in the receiving context, especially normative views about discourse. Until evidence emerges to the contrary, the same reasoning applies to translation in the broad sense and to non-translation.

Institutional forms of bilingualism claim to place two languages on a strictly equal footing and seek to erase the distinction between the 'model' and the 'translation'. Institutional bilingualism or multilingualism is clearly limited to a small number of countries, and is generally subject to fluctuations or tensions (in relation to Canada, see Delisle, 1987). In many cultures, for instance, bilingualism and multilingualism seem redundant as soon as they affect aspects of everyday life, such as canned foods, beauty products, instruction manuals or other consumer products. While the new (or the old?) Europe of the EU, which has given a completely new impetus to multilingual documents, prefers the status quo to novel strategies, globalised commercial communication is developing completely different communication principles. It is all the more symptomatic that, at the same time and in the same countries, the majority of the messages emanating from multinational institutions opt for an obvious monolingualism – often by means of translation – in a way that tends to obscure the foreign origins of the discourse. The exceptions prove the rule. To give another example, in officially monolingual countries, cinema and television most often rely on dubbing technology and the public ends up seeing as quite natural cowboys speaking Chinese or Sherlock Holmes expressing himself in German. Subtitling, which presents a dual discourse and clearly denotes which one is the 'original', like bilingual publications, is used mainly in multilingual and/or peripheral cultures.

Choices are never made exclusively on the basis of linguistic customs: rather, they refer to collective value systems and economic decisions which transcend the question of languages and 'correct speaking'. They therefore leave multiple traces in the language and in different models of communication. The gradual replacement of literary and intellectual journals in western Europe by multicoloured magazines printed on glossy paper and filled with advertisements, for instance, goes hand in hand with the systematic importation of articles borrowed from North American magazines, and thus also with their translations (which are of course well camouflaged, even in bilingual countries). The systematic recycling of texts from major American, British and German publications is officially acknowledged by the magazines in question for reasons of 'copyright', but readers do not notice it because the marks indicating that something has been borrowed, generally hidden away in a corner of the cover, are likely to be noticed only by insiders.

Large-scale multinational distribution, principally based on a single 'source' language, runs parallel to new communication technologies and the development of new models of communication. A new kind of standardisation has emerged that bears the stamp of multinational institutions and reaffirms the weakening of local or national institutions. Globalisation, however, is not yet leading to the total dissipation of the traditional distinctions between different cultures, which are still dominated by national political elites. Nevertheless, this phenomenon makes it possible to detect the gradual creation of a new world map of communication, languages and – no doubt – power.

Case Studies: Subtitles, 'New Text'

One of the sectors which best illustrates the idea that mass communication in translation is reformulating the conventional principles of texts and genres, both with and against the grain of established practices, is the area of audiovisual communication, which involves dubbing or subtitling. In order to illustrate the points made in the first part of this article, this section will focus on subtitling. The aim is to discuss the principles associated with this translation technique, briefly to review the cultural position of subtitles in western Europe and, along the way, to provide a working model for the analysis of subtitles in different cultural fields. It should be noted that, in the past 25 years or so, several attempts have been made that go beyond merely technical aspects (Delabastita, 1989; Diaz-Cintas & Baños Piñero, 2015), demonstrating that it is indeed not only technological constraints that create the differences and similarities between subtitling and 'normal' translation.

Subtitles do not seem to be winning in the struggle against dubbing, except in the most clearly multilingual cultures, which in many cases are also – perhaps not by chance – peripheral. It is not possible for countries such as Belgium or the Netherlands simply to adopt the models used in countries that are dominant in terms of intellectual output. It should be pointed out that French-speaking Belgium, by moving away from dubbing completely, has shown itself to be unfaithful to the French model, except for the many television programmes borrowed directly from France. In French-speaking Belgium it even happens – and this is symptomatic – that subtitles are modelled on those from the Dutch-speaking part, a region which has rarely been taken as a model in cultural matters (cf. Baumgarten & Cornellà-Detrell, this volume: 18–19).

Subtitles are far more than simply a technological process; they also result in a conventional text or genre which draws its principles from various textual traditions, according to priorities that vary from time to time and place to place (Lambert, 1990). In short, translation by subtitles, like all translation, is governed by conventions, norms and standards, and the overall process can be described with the help of equivalence models. This also makes it possible to detect the well known tensions between the 'target' system and the 'source' system, and even the interferences that exist between them.

One of the first conventions involves 'double communication'. Sophisticated empirical surveys have shown that the 'viewer' of subtitles reads, looks and listens all at the same time, to the point that he or she creates specific habits. Viewers used to dubbing in monolingual cultures, on the other hand, first and foremost perceive the presence of a text at the bottom of the screen as an obstruction (on the perception of subtitles, see d'Ydewalle & De Bruycker, 2007). Translators, for their part, tend to anticipate these habits: (1) by basing their work on both written and audiovisual sources; and (2) by selecting in (verbal) communication the elements which – depending on their aims – warrant inclusion. In subtitles, as in any other translation, non-translation is thus omnipresent and significant. We should furthermore note that subtitles confirm the ambiguous nature of translations, in the sense that the product (in this case the film or televised programme) is always shaped by other models borrowed from the receiving culture.

The selection of elements to be translated follows conventional norms: dialogues between the main characters, for example, take precedence over background noises. When interpreting – usually fictitious – dialogues, subtitlers have difficulty freeing themselves from literary conventions. Even though cinema and television have quite systematically aimed to do away with the 'artifices' of literary language and to promote a deliberately oral language, subtitles are marked by an obvious conflict between linguistic registers. One of the well known devices in novels, namely the tendency to individualise characters through their language by making it local, regional, and so on, is systematically sacrificed by the subtitler in favour of other objectives, so the subtitler is looking for standardisation rather than idiosyncrasy. The opposition between the narrator's language and that of the characters is thus often blunted, highlighting the centrality of the standard written language. Situations like this are even more noticeable in peripheral language areas – which are by definition less standardised – since subtitlers need gradually to create their own norms. The subtitlers employed by national television stations, which have an officially sanctioned socio-cultural mission, bear a heavy responsibility, because the language of television is used in public education networks. Subtitled mass communication has been a powerful agent in redefining the conventions and norms of language (Baetens Beardsmore, 1984). The conventional language of subtitles assumes didactic and moral objectives rather than artistic and mimetic ones, which is precisely the opposite of what happens in the majority of dialogues in novels. This is particularly evident when it comes to expressions which are too regional, too oral, or obscene. This cautious stance is a result of the confrontation between written and oral models. Since the subtitler often makes use of the script, a 'list of dialogues' or the text which has been adapted, it is not difficult to see when the spoken model is followed and when priority is being given to the written model. In fact, it is often easier for the script than for the subtitles to escape 'literary' and moral constraints. When looking for available models to deal with new messages that evade classification, translators tend to sacrifice orality, and thus non-canonical language, in favour of the known precepts of written dialogues and therefore established traditions; they almost never base their work exclusively on the (oral) 'source' text. In any case, these two forms of mass communication – subtitling and translation – appear to be a laboratory for both languages and texts, a crossroads not only between established and new 'genres', but also between international and national discourses. One question that must be asked about any corpus of subtitles is therefore how they are positioned in relation to other genres, both written and audiovisual, both national and international.

A Field of Research

Dubbing, translations of video-recordings, video-games and other 'genres' such as non-linear hypertext illustrate the ambiguities of a discourse which is searching for new paths. The impact of the new public language is also evidently influencing the style of traditional literature, just as the mass literature of yesterday (the crime novel is one example) also succeeded in influencing canonical literature. Therefore, a new series of powerful, globalised communication circuits clearly have a good chance of influencing and perhaps also structuring and defining the hierarchy of communication in general.

Not only textual strategies but also translation strategies deserve to be considered in their relationship to the various types of text. Research has revealed parallelisms with translations of novels, advertising texts and serials. The entire set of contexts surrounding any discourse has been newly configured as a result of globalisation, giving translations a key position in the thick of the battle between conventions and homogenising tendencies. Every individual translation and every individual discourse finds itself in a well defined situation in relation to the new standards which are developing, and researchers will need appropriate tools to discern the changes taking place both now and in the future.

References

Baetens Beardsmore, H. (ed.) (1984) 'Language and Television', special issue, *International Journal of the Sociology of Language* 48.

Bielsa, E. and Hughes, C. (eds) (2009) *Globalization, Political Violence and Translation*. Basingstoke: Palgrave Macmillan.

Bourdieu, P. (1979) *La Distinction: Critique Sociale du Jugement*. Paris: Eds de Minuit.

Bourdieu, P. (1982) *Ce que Parler Veut Dire: L'Economie des Échanges Linguistiques*. Paris: Fayard.

Brisset, A. (1986) Institution théâtrale au Québec et problèmes théoriques de traduction. In M. Lemire (ed.) *L'Institution Littéraire* (pp. 76–85). Québec: Institut Québécois de Recherche sur la Culture.

Bruguière, M. (1978) *Pitié pour Babel: Un Essai sur les Langues*. Paris: Nathan.

Cronin, M. (2003) *Translation and Globalization*. London: Routledge.

Cronin, M. (2012) *The Expanding World: Towards a Politics of Microspection*. Winchester: Zero Books.

Delabastita, D. (1989) Translation and mass-communication: Film and T.V. translation as evidence of cultural dynamics. *Babel* 35 (4), 193–218.

Delisle, J. (in collaboration with C. Gallant and P. Horguelin) (1987) *La Traduction au Canada, 1534–1984*. Ottawa: University of Ottawa Press.

de Swaan, A. (2001) *Words of the World: The Global Language System*. Cambridge: Polity Press.

Diaz-Cintas, J. and Baños Piñero, R. (2015) *Audiovisual Translation in a Global Context. Mapping an Ever-Changing Landscape*. London: Palgrave Macmillan.

d'Ydewalle, G. and De Bruycker, W. (2007) Eye movements of children and adults while reading television subtitles. *European Psychologist: The Journal for Psychology in Europe* 12, 196–205.

Etiemble, R. (1973) *Parlez-vous franglais?* Paris: Gallimard.

Even-Zohar, I. (1978) *Papers in Historical Poetics*. Tel-Aviv: Tel-Aviv University.

Gambier, Y. and Gottlieb, H. (2001) Multimedia, multilingua: Multiple challenges. In Y. Gambier and H. Gottlieb (eds) *(Multi)Media Translation: Concepts, Practices and Research* (pp. viii–xx). Amsterdam: John Benjamins.

Gardner-Chloros, P., Charles, R. and Cheshire, J. (2000) Parallel patterns? A comparison of monolingual speech and bilingual codeswitching discourse. *Journal of Pragmatics* 32, 1305–1341.

Hermans, T. (1999) *Translation in Systems: Descriptive and System-Oriented Approaches Explained*. Manchester: St Jerome.

Lambert, J. (1980) Production, tradition et importation: Une clef pour la description de la littérature et de la littérature en traduction. *Revue Canadienne de Littérature Comparée* 7 (2), 246–252.

Lambert, J. (1986) Les relations littéraires internationales comme problème de réception. *Œuvres et Critiques* 11 (2), 173–189. Also in J. Riesz *et al.* (eds) *Festschrift für Henry H.H. Remak. Sensus Communis* (pp. 49–63). Tübingen: Gunter Narr.

Lambert, J. (1990) Le sous-titrage et la question des traductions. Rapport sur une enquête. In R. Arntz and G. Thome (eds) *Übersetzungswissenschaft. Ergebnisse und Perspektiven* (pp. 228–238). Tübingen: Narr.

Lambert, J. (1991) In quest of literary world maps. In H. Kittel and A. Paul Frank (eds) *Interculturality and the Historical Study of Literary Translations* (pp. 133–144). Berlin: Schmidt. Also in D. Delabastita, L. D'hulst and R. Meylaerts (eds) (2006) *Functional Approaches to Culture and Translation – Selected Papers by José Lambert* (pp. 63–74). Amsterdam: John Benjamins.

Lamizet, B. (1983) La sémiotique et les communications de masse. *International Journal of the Sociology of Language* 40, 9–28.

Levý, J. (1967) Translation as a decision process. In *To Honor Roman Jakobson: Essays on the Occasion of His Seventieth Birthday* (vol. 2, pp. 1171–1182). The Hague: Mouton.

Lippi-Green, R. (1997) *English with an Accent: Language, Ideology and Discrimination in the United States*. London: Routledge.

Simon, S. (1989) *L'Inscription Sociale de la Traduction au Québec*. Québec: Office de la langue française.

Sin-Wai, C. (ed.) (2015) *The Routledge Encyclopedia of Translation Technology*. London: Routledge.

Toury, G. (1978) The nature and role of norms in literary translation. In J.S. Holmes, J. Lambert and R. van den Broeck (eds) *Literature and Translation: New Perspectives in Literary Studies* (pp. 83–100). Leuven: ACCO.

Toury, G. (1980) *In Search of a Theory of Translation*. Tel-Aviv: Tel-Aviv University.

Vermes, G. and Boutet, J. (1987) *France, Pays Multilingue*. Paris: L'Harmattan.

Vinay, J.-P. and Darbelnet, J. (1958) *Stylistique Comparée du Français et de L'Anglais*. Paris: Didier.

Weinreich, U. (1953) *Languages in Contact: Findings and Problems*. New York: Publications of the Linguistic Circle of New York.

9 Power Complexity in Translated Political Discourse

Christina Schäffner

Introducing the Concept of Power

Translation and interpreting are situated practices. The production, dissemination and reception of translations involve agents who are members of social groups and who act in particular sociocultural and sociopolitical contexts. This social embeddedness inevitably brings power to the fore, as a few examples will show.

The first example is an extract from an article in the news magazine *Spiegel International* (12 August 2013: 50–51) which reports about a book entitled *Against All Enemies*, published in 2013. In this book, author Jeffrey M. Carney writes about his work as an informer for the East German secret service (the Stasi) while he was employed as a US Air Force intelligence specialist. In the *Spiegel* article, we read:

> The many blacked-out passages suggest that the book itself is largely free of lies and falsifications. The US Air Force and the NSA [National Security Agency] spent about a year examining the book, and there were many passages that they felt should remain secret to this day, which they redacted. Still, what the censors left untouched offers a thrilling look into everyday life on the invisible front of East–West espionage. (http://www.spiegel.de/international/germany/american-stasi-agent-describes-his-experiences-in-new-book-a-916374.html, accessed 18 July 2015)

The way this book came into being involved censorship, which is a very clear form of the exercise of power. In this case, a specific institution, through its individual representatives, decided what could and what could not be published, and what information could or could not be made available to the home audience. Books on a topic like this one are surely of interest to a wider audience beyond the borders of the United States, which raises questions such as: If a translation of this book were to be commissioned, would the fact that the original book was censored be indicated? Who would decide on the translation and the form of publication? Would additional censorship be applied?

The second example is a short news item published in the weekly magazine *The Economist* (17 August 2013: 8) reporting on initiatives in the UK to protect Afghan interpreters:

> Campaigners handed a petition to Downing Street calling for all Afghan interpreters who worked for the British army to be allowed to settle in Britain. Only those who were on staff in December, when Britain announced a drawdown of forces, are being allowed to resettle. It is feared that those who are left behind will be targeted by the Taliban.

These Afghan interpreters had been working in extreme conflict situations. They were recruited locally, and probably very few of them had received professional training in interpreting. They fulfilled their duties under dangerous conditions, but when they were no longer needed they faced serious challenges due to the changing priorities of the British Army and the perceptions that local people had of their role. Although the article speaks of 'campaigners' in a rather unspecified way, this is an example of social groups trying to exert pressure on the government to take action and/or introduce rules to change the current situation. The passive structure 'being allowed' reflects the asymmetric power relationships: the Afghan interpreters are subordinate and at the receiving end, while those with power are not explicitly referred to, but can be inferred contextually via the reference to Downing Street.

The third example concerns the legal context and the interplay between European Union and UK policies and practices. In autumn 2013, the EU directive on the right to interpreting and translation in criminal proceedings (2010/64/EU) came into force. It aims to guarantee the right to a fair trial and the right to defence for all persons, whether suspects or witnesses, who do not speak or understand the language of the procedure. Implementing this right involves translations of documents such as warrants, charges and judgements, and the provision of interpreting services during the proceedings, and also for communicating with legal counsel. The directive also specifies that EU member states have to ensure that appropriately qualified translators and interpreters are employed. At the time of writing, the directive had not yet been implemented in the UK, but quality issues had been the topic of an ongoing debate in England and Wales since the Ministry of Justice (MoJ) signed a Framework Agreement with Capita Translation and Interpreting (formerly Applied Language Solutions) in 2011. This language service provider has been the sole provider of interpreters since then, but there is evidence that this Framework Agreement had led to miscarriage of justice, as well as reduced incomes for interpreters. Following complaints by courts about poor services, an inquiry into the situation was conducted by the Justice Committee of the House of Commons, which noted a lack of transparency and public accountability in the MoJ's reporting of performance in response to this investigation. The umbrella group Professional Interpreters for Justice (PI4J) has kept dossiers of evidence to record concrete examples of complaints and has been conducting a campaign to reverse the outsourcing of translation and interpreting services (see http://www.linguistlounge.org, accessed 5 July 2018). Translators and interpreters are worried about the practices of Capita Translation and Interpreting, which show disregard of professional standards; in addition, the MoJ's resistance to all forms of pressure raises questions as to the UK's ability to ensure the rights laid down in the EU directive.

These three examples illustrate instances of institutional censorship, pressure and resistance which are linked to power. This concept, however, needs to be reflected on in more depth; in each case, we need to ask questions such as: Whose power is at stake? Power to do what? In relation to whom? Is power exercised or resisted explicitly or implicitly? And how is all this relevant to translation and interpreting?

Power as a Key Concept in Translation Studies

With the development of translation studies as a discipline in its own right, the definition of translation changed. Initially, in the 1960s and 1970s, translation was defined and analysed primarily as a linguistic process involving a 'transfer' of meaning to achieve equivalence between source text and target text. Following various 'turns' in the discipline (Snell-Hornby, 2006), translation is now considered a socially situated and socially regulated practice. This focus on social aspects and the agents involved in these practices has made 'power' a key concept in the field. However, there are also differences in the use of 'power' in different theoretical approaches and models. For example, functionalist approaches such as Skopos theory (Nord, 1997; Vermeer, 1996) place the translator as a professional expert on a par with the other actors involved in the transcultural interaction, such as clients, commissioners and subject specialists. In these approaches, translators are empowered to act professionally due to their expertise as translators and their competence to produce texts which are appropriate for the specified purpose and the target audience (e.g. Hönig, 1997). This characterisation as competent experts is wider than the traditional view of translators as invisible transcoders of messages who are subservient to the authority of the source text and/or the author of the source text. By producing texts for others, translators as experts act in the interest of others, though they are not expected to pursue their own communicative agenda in this transcultural interaction (see Holz-Mänttäri, 1984).

In contrast to the functionalist perspective, approaches inspired by cultural studies have argued for a more proactive and committed role of translators, who in this way become visible and engaged interventionists (e.g. Venuti, 1995). In their volume *Translation and Power*, Gentzler and Tymoczko (2002: xvii) reflect on culturally accepted meanings of the word 'power' as defined in the *Oxford English Dictionary*, and the definitions they list include the following:

- the ability to do or effect something [...] to act upon a person or thing;
- might, vigour, energy;
- possession of control or command over others; dominion, rule; government, domination [...] influence, authority;
- legal ability, capacity, or authority to act.

All these definitions imply a social relationship which can be established between individual people, but more often relationships are established between social groups, involving hierarchy, domination and – more or less willingly – subordination. In some cases, the legal authority to act can be inscribed in specific documents, such as constitutions, statutes and regulations. If we understand translation and interpreting as social activities which take place in social contexts and which involve at least two languages and cultures, then we will have to take into account that these social contexts are marked by power relations between dominant and dominated languages, and dominant and dominated cultures. Deciding which texts from which language(s) and culture(s) are translated for consumption in the receiving culture is a matter of power, as already envisaged in Toury's category of preliminary norms (Toury, 1995) and Lefevere's concept of patronage (Lefevere, 2004). Post-structuralist and post-colonial research into translation has provided rich data to illustrate how translation and translators contribute to maintaining or changing power relations between cultures.

In the wake of the 'cultural turn', not only the (hidden) agendas of social and institutional powers behind translations moved to the centre of research, but also the capacity of individual translators to take authority for their decisions, as Gentzler and Tymoczko (2002: xviii) argue:

> translators must make choices, selecting aspects or parts of a text to transpose and emphasize. Such choices in turn serve to create representations of their source texts, representations that are also partial. This partiality [...] is a necessary condition of the act. It is also an aspect that makes the act of translation partisan: engaged and committed, either implicitly or explicitly. [...] Such representations and commitments are apparent from analyses of translators' choices [...] also demonstrable in paratextual material. [...] the partial nature of translations is what makes them also an exercise of power.

They conclude that 'the 'cultural turn' in translation studies has become the 'power turn' (Gentzler & Tymoczko, 2002: xvi), with Gentzler adding that by basing their work on post-structural or post-colonial theories, '[s]ome translators feel so empowered that they deliberately subvert traditional allegiances of translation, interjecting their own worldviews and politics into their work. Thus, one aspect of the "power turn" in translation studies involves the assertion of power by translators themselves' (Gentzler, 2002: 197).

The question that arises, however, is: if we conceive of translation as a social practice, to what extent and in which ways can individual translators actually assert power? If we agree that translators and interpreters perform in social contexts which are also subject to the intervention (contribution, input, constraint) of various other agents, then the respective power of each agent should also be investigated. Not surprisingly, then, the recent 'sociological turn' in translation studies (e.g. Wolf & Fukari, 2007) has highlighted the role of the various agents in the translational field (not just translators, but also authors, clients, commissioners, editors, revisors, publishing houses, distributors and academics, among others). All these agents have interests and power positions owing to their capital in the field (Bourdieu, 1991) and thus have a role to play in deciding which texts get translated (or not) into which language(s), by whom, and how the resulting translations are disseminated. Giving due attention to the social contexts of translation and all agents involved requires investigating issues of power in its full complexity. In the following sections, I reflect on this complexity with reference to interpreter-mediated political interviews and press conferences, revisiting from a different perspective examples I have discussed in previous publications (Schäffner, 2012a, 2012b, 2015).

Power and Translation in and for Politics

There is no denying that political ideas and arguments cross linguistic, cultural, sociopolitical and ideological boundaries as a result of translation and/or interpreting. Translation and interpreting are essential to the functioning of international and supranational organisations, such as the United Nations and the European Union. They are equally relevant for diplomacy, business, cultural exchange and so on at a bilateral level, and of course also for solving communication needs within multilingual societies. Political and critical discourse analysis (e.g. Chilton, 2004) has investigated 'the ways power is enacted, expressed, described, concealed, or legitimated by text and talk in the social context' (van Dijk, 2008: 27). Translation studies research is equally interested in analysing if and how discursive actions and structures that are linked to power (can) change in the process of translation and interpreting. At the macro-level, censorship is an explicit and most direct way of exercising power through controlling others' access to information and also the use of language.

In other cases of political discourse, translators or interpreters may be given more freedom to act, but translation and interpreting are generally embedded in institutional practices, which are in turn determined by institutional policies and ideologies. The analysis of these complex conditions poses methodological problems concerning the data of analysis. The most readily available materials are publicly accessible translated texts and transcripts of political speeches, interviews or press conferences, for instance on the websites of national governments. These texts, however, have normally undergone various stages of revision, proofreading and checking. It is not always possible for a researcher to have access to earlier draft translations or to a version which openly displays the intervention of a revisor, or even a censor. That is, in these translations as products, the respective interventions of the various agents and their (potential) power are not directly obvious. There are few instances where researchers can investigate which decisions were taken by whom. For example, the Spanish TRACE research project (*TRAducciones Censuradas;* CEnsored TRAnslations) has explored censorship practices during Franco's regime, benefiting from access to records held in archives. Such a combination of various sources – namely source texts and target texts, censors' comments, correspondence and so on – has made it possible to identify the processes and agents involved in decision-making and the reasoning behind particular decisions (e.g. Gutiérrez-Lanza, 2000; Merino & Rabadán, 2002).

The texts analysed in the TRACE project belong to the genres of fiction, theatre and film. In the domain of politics, due to the nature of policy-making, access to archives and correspondence is more difficult. It is often only retrospectively that politically sensitive documents are made available to researchers, or that interpreters who worked for top politicians write about their work (e.g. Kusterer, 1995; Schmidt, 1952) and, in any case, in such personal memoirs, interpreters are cautious not to reveal sensitive issues. Archives of mass media are another valuable source waiting for investigation. A recent example is a research project devoted to the analysis of the BBC Monitoring Service's transcripts collection, which includes a vast body of transcripts of monitored radio broadcasts from around the world during World War II and the Cold War (see http://gtr.rcuk.ac.uk/project/4C7CAAF7-60D6-4F02-87B9-102B42DE4CB9, accessed 18 July 2015).

This BBC example highlights the close link between politics and the media, which play a significant part in mediating between the social domains of politics and the public. The fields of politics and journalism often overlap, as in the case of political interviews or press conferences. These are discursive practices which bring representatives from the fields of politics and journalism together, and when these encounters are mediated by an interpreter they can be considered triadic exchanges (Mason, 2001). Transcripts of press conferences and interviews held by politicians are frequently made available on government websites or on websites of the relevant media. Newspapers, however, normally include only extracts, often incorporated in news reports or comments. These processes of recontextualisation transform the text, which, again, makes it difficult for a researcher to find out which of the agents involved had the decisive word in the text's final published version. However, discursive events such as political interviews and press conferences are also frequently transmitted live on radio, television or the internet, or made available as audio- or video-recordings for future use. This access to the immediacy of the discursive event gives researchers wider opportunities to observe the interaction of all, or at least several, agents involved in the triadic exchange – but only up to a point, since in these transmissions the interpreters tend to be mostly invisible. But despite these limits, observing processes of interpreter-mediated interaction and comparing them to the transcripts provides the researcher with more data than a product analysis alone would bring. In the next section, I will illustrate this with reference to a political interview.

Interpreter-Mediated Political Interview: Whose Words? Whose Voice? Whose Power?

The example is a TV interview aired on 1 December 2010 which the well-known CNN talk-show host Larry King conducted with the then Russian Prime Minister, Vladimir Putin (for an analysis of follow-ups in this interview see Schäffner, 2015). The interview was conducted via satellite, with King situated in the CNN studio in Washington and Putin in a room in Moscow, in front of a TV set. Simultaneous interpreting between Russian and English was provided. A video-recording of this CNN interview is available on YouTube (at https://www.youtube.com/watch?v=YNSoOM4Nq6g, accessed 5 July 2018). A short TV news report for Russia Today which includes extracts of the interview can also be accessed on YouTube (https://www.youtube.com/watch?v=xHhI9DC6x8k, accessed 18 July 2015). In this case, the male interpreter who is rendering Putin's words into English is a different one from the male interpreter originally used for the CNN interview. He is also speaking very fluently and with hardly any noticeable accent, in contrast to the strong Russian accent of the initial interpreter.

The complete interview can be accessed from the archive of the Russian government's website, which includes transcripts in both Russian and English and a video in Russian only (English transcript at http://archive.government.ru/eng/docs/13147/; video transcript at http://archive.government.ru/eng/docs/13147/video.html, both accessed 18 July 2015). In this video, we hear Putin's words in Russian and interpreting of King's questions into Russian. Again, a different interpreter is used, this time a woman who is interpreting fluently and speaking with only a slight Russian accent. This interview was also uploaded to YouTube later (on 18 December 2011), as a version where everything is audible in Russian only, and with English subtitles added throughout (https://www.youtube.com/

watch?v=CWiOfek5qi8, accessed 18 July 2015). The subtitles, however, differ from the text of the transcript. The references to the interview provided on this page take us to the Russian and English transcripts on the official Russian website; therefore it can be assumed that this video was uploaded by the Russian government.

The transcript on the CNN website (which is preceded by the statement 'This is a rush transcript. This copy may not be in its final form and may be updated') is a record of the complete interaction (http://transcripts. cnn.com/TRANSCRIPTS/1012/01/lkl.01.html, accessed 18 July 2015). My analysis will focus on the following extract:

KING: Will you – will – will you go to Zurich to make a personal appeal?
PUTIN: Well, I've been reflecting on that. […] I've been enjoying –
KING: All right, we'll be right back…
PUTIN: – the sport through all my life. I love soccer.
KING: All right, let me get a break on time. We'll be right back with more of the prime minister following this.
(COMMERCIAL BREAK)
KING: Something, Mr. Prime Minister, I don't think you've ever been asked. We have quite a dispute about it in America. What is the Russian policy toward gays and lesbians in your military?
PUTIN: Well, I'd like to finalize my statement regarding whether I go to Zurich or not.
KING: OK.
PUTIN: I think it would be better for me not to be there prior to these elections – […] Now, as regards to the attitude toward gays and lesbians, well, you know […]

To begin with, there is an obvious struggle regarding who controls the interaction. In terms of social roles, Putin is in a more powerful position than the journalist King. In terms of interactional roles, however, each of the interlocutors tries to be in control (on positioning in dialogue, see Weizman, 2008). As we can see in the extract above, after the commercial break King immediately introduces a totally different topic. Putin, however, returns to the prior topic, using a meta-communicative comment ('I'd like to finalize my statement') to signal explicitly his speaking right. At the same time, he is re-establishing the authority of his political position by not immediately accepting the new topic (although he does take it up later). Putin obviously felt he had been denied his interactional role as an interviewee by being cut short and, indeed, interrupting a politician in the middle of his answer can be seen as face threatening. By reclaiming his right to speak, Putin asserted his superior position, which was accepted by King ('OK'). What is most interesting in this example, however, is that both speakers' power is subordinate to the power of the media institution. CNN, one of the world's largest news organisations, depends on income from companies and private sponsors. Ensuring the screening of commercial breaks with a previously agreed duration is more important than letting people finish a conversation (there were actually several such commercial breaks during this interview). The economic policy of the news channel thus determined the timing of the interview, which neither the journalist nor the politician were allowed to ignore.

On Putin's official website, this extract is presented as follows in the English version (the Russian one is identical in structure and content):

Larry King: Will you go to Zurich to make a personal appeal?
Vladimir Putin: You know, that's something I thought about, of course. But I think that now, when FIFA members are coming under such pointed attacks and attempts to disgrace them, they need the space to make an objective decision without any external pressure. As you know, I've been keen on sport all my life, and I love football but I don't think I should appear there before the vote lest my presence be regarded as an attempt to exert some kind of pressure on the decision-making process.
Larry King: Something, Mr Prime Minister, I don't think you've ever been asked. We have quite a dispute about it in America. What is the Russian policy towards gays and lesbians in your military?
Vladimir Putin: I've tried to answer similar questions before. [...]

In this transcript, Putin's answer is presented as one long and coherent turn, the language is more formal (e.g. 'pointed attacks', 'lest my presence', 'exert some kind of pressure'), and there is no reference to commercial breaks. The video-recording, which is accessible from the website, is one long smooth question–answer interaction, thus revealing an editing process which also reflects the power of the institution. In contrast to the economic and commercial values which are relevant to the media institution, however, the values for the political institution of the Russian government are of an ideological nature. The re-recording of Putin's answers with another interpreter is embedded into these ideologically determined aims and contributes to the presentation of Putin as a powerful politician who is the main agent in managing the interaction.

Although the interview was mediated by an interpreter, the interpreter's role, or indeed, power, was denied. The actual words uttered by the initial interpreter in the live interview are accessible only in the CNN transcript. The first reactions to the interview on a CNN blog included critical comments on the interpreter's performance (delivery, voice quality, misinterpretations). It was impossible to find out who had commissioned the assignment, where the interpreter was physically positioned and what briefing he had been given to prepare for the job. The fact that the text was revised for the transcript on the Russian websites and that a re-recording was done with a different interpreter are evidence that the Russian political and media institutions are interested in political messages coming across clearly, coherently and smoothly. Moreover, the fact that in the new video Putin is not interrupted also shows that his power cannot be contested.

And of course, not to show the interview live on Russian TV was also a politically motivated decision.

So what does this example tell us about power, and about the power of the individual interpreter? The first interpreter's performance can be seen only in the transcript of the CNN live interview (and in the YouTube video). As said above, the interpreter at the live interview had been criticised for inaccurate renderings. It is doubtful that these were deliberate decisions taken by the interpreter because he wanted to pursue his own (ideological) agenda. It is much more likely that the situational circumstances (insufficient preparation time, inadequate access to the interlocutors) explain the far from effective performance – although these are speculations which are impossible to confirm. The analysis of the live interview, however, also shows that the power of the primary interlocutors in respect of interaction management is subordinate to the institutional power of the media institution, which in turn is subject to the economic power of its business sponsors. Changing the text in the transcript and re-recording the interview are practices which, in this specific case, happened only in the context of Russian institutions, both the government and the mass media (Russia Today as a Russian TV network with an English-language news broadcast). Catering for the perception of Putin and his policies in the outside world seems to have been the overarching aim which motivated these practices. Readers of the transcripts and/or viewers of the interview would not be aware of these processes and of power relations behind these decisions, nor would they know who were the agents engaged in amending transcripts, providing subtitles and re-recording the interpreter's rendering. In short: in the final publicly accessible products, that is, the transcripts and the video-recordings provided by the Russian institutions, the power behind them is hidden.

Re-recording interviews and changing the interpreter are, however, frequent practices not always related to matters of ideology. This can be illustrated with an interview which the BBC journalist Gavin Esler conducted with the German Chancellor Angela Merkel for BBC *Newsnight* in May 2012. Asked how the interview had been arranged and who had commissioned the interpreter, he replied:

> The Kanzleramt provided Frau Merkel with a translator (or rather an interpreter) – although she speaks perfect English, and I speak some German. We used the interpreter's words as a guide but I thought we could have a better translation which we organised separately in London. This translation was voiced by an actor. (Email, 12 May 2012)

The interpreting, therefore, had been replaced by a voice-over. Again, the processes behind the final product are hidden and invisible to the viewer. But what and whose power is at stake here? And is it indeed power or rather discourse features and institutional practices which such investigation can bring to light? I would like to explore this issue further with reference to interpreter-mediated press conferences.

Interpreter-Mediated Press Conferences and Aspects of Power

At a joint press conference held by the German Chancellor Angela Merkel and the then French President Nicolas Sarkozy on 16 August 2011 in Paris, the following extract from Sarkozy's turn was interpreted into German as follows:

Sarkozy: La première de ces propositions consiste à instaurer dans la zone euro un véritable gouvernement économique de la zone euro. Ce gouvernement économique sera constitué du Conseil des chefs d›Etat et de gouvernement. [Literally: The first one of these proposals is to establish a real economic government of the euro zone. This economic government will consist of the heads of state and government.]
(http://www.ambafrance-uk.org/Conference-de-presse-conjointe-de,19498, accessed 18 July 2015)

Sarkozy: Der erste dieser Vorschläge besteht darin, eine wirtschaftspolitische Steuerung der Eurozone vorzusehen. Diese Wirtschaftsregierung besteht aus den Staats- und Regierungschefs.
[Literally: The first one of these proposals envisages an economic management of the euro zone. This economic government consists of the heads of state and government.]
(http://www.bundesregierung.de/ContentArchiv/DE/Archiv17/ Mitschrift/Pressekonferenzen/2011/08/2011-08-16-pk-merkel-sarkozy-paris.html, accessed 18 July 2015)

What is noticeable here is that the interpreter used two different renderings into German for one and the same French word. Does this indicate any exercise of the interpreter's power? At the time of the press conference, there was quite a political debate concerning the degree of integration and coordination of economic policies within the euro zone. This political controversy was also reflected in the general discourse and the use of the relatively new terms 'governance (of the euro area)' in English texts, 'gouvernance (de la zone Euro)' in French and the somewhat clumsy *wirtschaftspolitische Steuerung* in German. The formulation *gouvernement* économique, however, was in use as well before EU leaders settled on *governance* and *gouvernance*, respectively, for official documents. Among German politicians, there was some unease about using the more immediate equivalent *Wirtschaftsregierung* ('economic government'), and they argued that what was needed for the euro zone was not a government with power and structures, but rather some agreed form of regulation and checking.

At a press briefing of the German government held on 15 August 2011, the eve of the joint press conference, the government spokesman, Steffen

Seibert, informed the journalists present of the Sarkozy–Merkel summit and the topics to be discussed. The transcript of this press briefing quotes Seibert as follows:

> [...] Es geht darum, gemeinsame Vorschläge zur Stärkung der <u>wirtschafts-politischen Steuerung der Eurozone</u> zu erarbeiten. [...]
> [Literally: The task is to draft joint proposals for strengthening the economic management of the euro-zone [...]]

In response to a question – whether speaking of *wirtschaftspolitische Steuerung* meant that working towards a common financial policy would explicitly be ruled out – Seibert replied:

> Wenn Sie so wollen, geht es, um dieses Wort „Governance', das immer in der Luft schwebt, einmal einigermaßen sinnvoll ins Deutsche zu übersetzen, darum, eine weitergehende wirtschafts- und finanzpolitische Steuerung, eine Verbesserung der wirtschaftspolitischen Steuerung zu finden.
> [Literally: If you like, and to find a somewhat meaningful German translation for the word 'governance' that is always floating in the air, the task is to find a more extensive economic and financial management, an improvement of the economic management.]
> (http://archiv.bundesregierung.de/ContentArchiv/DE/Archiv17/Mitschrift/Pressekonferenzen/2011/08/2011-08-15-regpk.html, accessed 18 July 2015)

This extract can also be watched on YouTube (https://www.youtube.com/watch?v=SoW2MXY-WoA, accessed 18 July 2015). The wording of the oral statement is slightly different from the transcript, which had undergone some syntactic and stylistic revision, as is common practice with the German government (see Schäffner, 2012a, 2012b).

Sarkozy's use of *gouvernement économique* at the press conference can also be seen as a reflection of the still ongoing terminological debate rather than as an attempt to engage in a terminological power struggle. So, how can we explain the interpreter's strategies, if they can be explained at all? I would like to argue that there was no deeper political motive behind his choice of two different renderings (*wirtschaftspolitische Steuerung* and *Wirtschaftsregierung*) in close vicinity. A more likely explanation is that the interpreter was aware of the debates about terminology and of the use of *wirtschaftspolitische Steuerung* in official German documents. But did he, as an employee of the language service department of the German government, deliberately want to contribute to the German government's attempts to make *wirtschaftspolitische Steuerung* the accepted term? Did he feel obliged to 'obey' the power of his employer? Or did he realise immediately that Sarkozy had used *gouvernement économique* and not *gouvernance économique*, which made him opt for *Wirtschaftsregierung* for the second occurrence? And did he do this in order to be closer to the actual word used by the French president, or in order to signal to the audience that the terminological differences reflect differences in political opinion? But would the audience have realised this, since *wirtschaftspolitische Steuerung* had been used before? The interpreter did not use any meta-communicative formulation (such as 'sorry' or another form of self-correction) to signal to the audience that he should have used *Wirtschaftsregierung* in both cases if he had wanted to be 'loyal' to the actual words of the French president. Gentzler and Tymoczko (2002: xviii) argued that 'paratextual materials' (e.g. translator's notes, prefaces) are important sources for researchers which help to identify the engagement and commitment of translators in addition to the linguistic choices identifiable in the texts. In the case of interpreting, self-corrections or meta-communicative comments might be considered to fulfil similar functions as paratexts, although much more detailed research would need to be done in order to find out whether this is indeed a viable option.

Interpreters who work at such a high level of political encounters normally accompany politicians over a longer period of time and are thus closely involved in the negotiations. In other words, they are part of the discourse or, more precisely, part of the wider discourse around a specific political issue, and they are thus familiar not only with the terminology but also with the wider context of the negotiations. We find such subtle indications of this in specifications or additions in interpreters' renderings, as can be seen with the addition of 'a lunch' in the first of the extracts below (taken from a joint press conference by David Cameron and Angela Merkel held on 27 February 2014 in London) and the addition of 'on the phone' in the second extract (taken from a joint press conference by David Cameron and Angela Merkel held on 7 January 2015 in London):

Bundeskanzlerin Merkel: [...] Wir haben heute hier natürlich noch einmal
   vertieft über die Frage gesprochen, wie wir uns Europa in den nächsten
   Jahren vorstellen.
   [Literally: [...] We have talked here today once again in depth about the
   question how we envisage Europe in the coming years.]
   (http://www.bundesregierung.de/Content/DE/Mitschrift/Presse
   konferenzen/2014/02/2014-02-27-pk-merkel-cameron.html, accessed 18
   July 2015)
Merkel: [...] and obviously we had the opportunity of a lunch to further
   deepen certain issues.
   (https://www.gov.uk/government/speeches/david-cameron-and-angela-
   merkel-press-conference-february-2014, accessed 18 July 2015)

Bundeskanzlerin Merkel: [...] Ich glaube, es war ein sehr bewegender
   Moment, heute gemeinsam mit dem französischen Präsidenten, mit
   François Hollande, zu sprechen [...]
   [Literally: I think it was a very moving moment to speak today together
   with the French President, with Francois Hollande [...]]

(http://www.bundesregierung.de/Content/DE/Mitschrift/Presse
konferenzen/2015/01/2015-01-08-pk-merkel-cameron.html, accessed 18
July 2015)

Merkel: [...] I think it was a very moving moment when we were able to
address – both of us – the French President Francois Hollande on the
phone, [...].

(https://www.gov.uk/government/speeches/david-cameron-and-angela-
merkel-press-conference, accessed 18 July 2015)

Such additions indicate the interpreter's knowledge of the wider communicative context rather than any attempt to demonstrate their own
power. Additions, omissions and changes in an interpreter's rendition can
be caused by multiple factors, such as time constraints, physical positioning of the interlocutors, stress, as well as by knowledge of the wider context
(as mentioned above) and of course also personal agendas. In the context
of translation of political discourse, the institutional practices and underlying values play an important part in decision-making. As I have shown
elsewhere with reference to metaphors (Schäffner, 2014), there are differences between translations produced by newspapers and those produced
by translation departments of governments. The German government's
translation department operates a very thorough system of checking and
revision; translators make systematic use of previously translated texts
and they are supported by a terminology section. These procedures ensure
consistency in their renderings. Translations for the media, however, need
to be done quickly. Their main goal is to be as understandable as possible
to the broadest international audience, and for that reason the journalists
who function as translators usually survey the English press to follow their
usage. These established practices are also linked to power, but in a more
complex way.

Conclusion

The main question this chapter reflects on is whether translators and
interpreters enjoy a certain degree of scope for exercising their own power
and commitment when they are working with political discourse. As
research in translation studies has shown, there are indeed cases where
translators and/or interpreters deliberately and actively promote specific
political agendas of social groups they themselves closely identify with or,
alternatively, resist the spread of specific political interests (e.g. Boéri &
Maier, 2010; Inghilleri & Harding, 2010).

In the examples chosen for illustration above, the interpreters (and less
so the translators) seem to have been working in contexts which did not
provide any scope for activism and the exercise of power. I would like to
argue, therefore, that post-structuralist claims that power is ubiquitous
should be relativised. If we understand power in the sense of functionalist

approaches, as the empowerment of translators and interpreters so they can act professionally as experts in their own right, then this expertise also includes a critical reflection on the purpose of the task, the context, the interlocutors and their own positioning with respect to the task at hand. At international press conferences and in the case of interviews, interpreters perform in a public and mediatised arena alongside politicians, even if they are not always visible to the audience (but on how a politician constrained the interpreter's performance, see Baker, 1997). In contrast, translators working in translation departments of national or supranational institutions benefit from internal practices (such as revision and proofreading) which are aimed at quality and consistency, but in the final products their individual work usually cannot be identified, as their names are not normally provided (see also Schäffner *et al.*, 2014).

All these cases of socially situated practices involve various agents who operate in specific and complex settings. Researching power in respect of translation and/or interpreting thus cannot ignore the complexity of these settings and underlying values. When members of staff make syntactic and stylistic amendments to transcripts of press conferences before making them publicly available on a website, when revisors check translations produced within specific institutions for terminological consistency, are these examples of the power of staff members and revisors, or just normal practices and job duties? Where can we draw the line? If translators and interpreters who work for political institutions represent the interests of this institution, does this make them subservient and self-effacing?

It is true that translators and interpreters do make choices, and such linguistic choices are visible in the products, that is, the translated texts or the interpreted output. It is equally true that whenever there are choices, there is power. However, not each instance of choice may be an example of a translator's or interpreter's individual power. Various factors may have influenced a particular choice, ranging from the deliberate intention to resist normative usage or the terminology preferred (or even prescribed) by an institution to inappropriate renderings or omissions caused by less than optimal working conditions such as time pressure (on multiple causality, see Brownlie, 2003). Moreover, texts which are accessible to the public have undergone additional transformations for various reasons, not all of them of an ideological nature or performed in order to impose the power of one agent or one political group. The texts thus reflect a plurality of voices and are the result of more or less open negotiations of agents.

There is no denying that translators and interpreters are social agents and, as such, they are actively engaged in and shape the interaction: the cultural and sociological turns in translation studies have raised our awareness of this. The notion of power can indeed be central to our research in this respect, although we also need to be careful not to speak of power too quickly. Translation and interpreting are social acts which occur in sociocultural and sociopolitical contexts. These contexts as well as the wider social structures may impose constraints on translator and interpreter agency, with such constraints being due to ideology, situational settings, client and/or audience expectations, genre conventions and so on.

If we want to investigate 'power-driven translation practices' (Fischer & Jensen, 2012: 11), we thus need to bear in mind that power manifests itself in a multidimensional way within these very practices which involve dynamic struggles between different stakeholders. In the texts resulting from such practices, however, these struggles are normally no longer directly obvious and the complexity of power is hidden. In order for translation studies scholars to shed light on the multidimensional way in which power is manifested in both the practices and the texts, we would need to investigate the complexity of these practices and the role of all the agents involved.

References

Baker, M. (1997) Non-cognitive constraints and interpreter strategies in political interviews. In K. Simms (ed.) *Translating Sensitive Texts: Linguistic Aspects* (pp. 111–129). Amsterdam: Rodopi.

Boéri, J. and Maier, C. (2010) *Compromiso Social y Traducción/Interpretación. Translation/Interpreting and Social Activism*. Granada: Ecos.

Bourdieu, P. (1991) *Language and Symbolic Power*. Cambridge: Polity Press.

Brownlie, S. (2003) Investigating explanations of translational phenomena: A case for multiple causality. *Target* 15 (1), 111–152.

Chilton, P. (2004) *Analysing Political Discourse: Theory and Practice*. London: Routledge.

Fischer, B. and Jensen, M.N. (eds) (2012) *Translation and the Reconfiguration of Power Relations: Revisiting Role and Context of Translation and Interpreting*. Münster: LIT-Verlag.

Gentzler, E. (2002) Translation, poststructuralism, and power. In E. Gentzler and M. Tymoczko (eds) *Translation and Power* (pp. 195–218). Boston, MA: University of Massachusetts Press.

Gentzler, E. and Tymoczko, M. (eds) (2002) Introduction. In E. Gentzler and M. Tymoczko (eds) *Translation and Power* (pp. xi–xxviii). Boston, MA: University of Massachusetts Press.

Gutiérrez-Lanza, C. (2000) *Traducción y Censura de Textos Cinematográficos en la España de Franco: Doblaje y Subtitulado Inglés–Español (1951–1975)*. León: Universidad de León.

Holz-Mänttäri, J. (1984) *Translatorisches Handeln: Theorie und Methode*. Helsinki: Suomalainen Tiedeakatemia.

Hönig, H.G. (1997) Positions, power and practice. Functionalist approaches and translation quality assessment. *Current Issues in Language and Society* 4 (1), 6–34.

Inghilleri, M. and Harding, S.-A. (eds) (2010) 'Translation and Violent Conflict', special issue, *The Translator* 16 (2).

Kusterer, H. (1995) *Der Kanzler und der General*. Stuttgart: Neske.

Lefevere, A. (2004) Mother Courage's cucumbers: Text, system and refraction in a theory of literature. In L. Venuti (ed.) *The Translation Studies Reader* (2nd edn) (pp. 239–255). London: Routledge.

Mason, I. (ed.) (2001) *Triadic Exchanges: Studies in Dialogue Interpreting*. Manchester: St Jerome.

Merino, R. and Rabadán, R. (2002) Censored translations in Franco's Spain: The TRACE project – theatre and fiction (English–Spanish). *TTR: Traduction, Terminologie, Rédaction* 15 (2), 125–152.

Nord, C. (1997) *Translating as a Purposeful Activity: Functionalist Approaches Explained.* Manchester: St Jerome.

Schäffner, C. (2012a) Unknown agents in translated political discourse. *Target* 24 (1), 103–125.

Schäffner, C. (2012b) Press conferences and recontextualisation. In I. Alonso Araguás, J. Baigorri Jalón and H. Campbell (eds) *Ensayos sobre Traducción Jurídica e Institucional / Essays on Legal and Institutional Translation* (pp. 69–83). Granada: Editorial Comares.

Schäffner, C. (2014) Umbrellas and firewalls: Metaphors in debating the financial crisis from the perspective of translation studies. In D.R. Miller and E. Monti (eds) *Tradurre Figure / Translating Figurative Language* (pp. 69–84). Bologna: Centro di Studi Linguistico-Culturali (CeSLiC).

Schäffner, C. (2015) Follow-ups in interpreter-mediated interviews and press conferences. In E. Weizman and A. Fetzer (eds) *Follow-Ups in Political Discourse: Explorations Across Contexts and Discourse Domains* (pp. 205–230). Amsterdam: John Benjamins.

Schäffner, C., Tcaciuc, S. and Tesseur, W. (2014) Translation practices in political institutions: A comparison of national, supranational, and non-governmental organisation. *Perspectives: Studies in Translatology* 22 (4), 493–510.

Schmidt, P. (1952) *Statist auf diplomatischer Bühne 1923–45. Erlebnisse des Chefdolmetschers im Auswärtigen Amt mit den Staatsmännern Europas.* Bonn: Athenäum.

Snell-Hornby, M. (2006) *The Turns of Translation Studies: New Paradigms or Shifting Viewpoints?* Amsterdam: John Benjamins.

Toury, G. (1995) *Descriptive Translation Studies and Beyond.* Amsterdam: John Benjamins.

van Dijk, T.A. (2008) *Discourse and Power.* Basingstoke: Palgrave Macmillan.

Venuti, L. (1995) *The Translator's Invisibility.* London: Routledge.

Vermeer, H.J. (1996) *A Skopos Theory of Translation (Some Arguments For and Against).* Heidelberg: TEXTconTEXT.

Weizman, E. (2008) *Positioning in Media Dialogue.* Amsterdam: John Benjamins.

Wolf, M. and Fukari, A. (eds) (2007) *Constructing a Sociology of Translation.* Amsterdam: John Benjamins.

10 Proximisation Amidst Liquidity: Osama bin Laden's Death Translated

M. Cristina Caimotto

Translation and the Discursive Construction of Identity

On 1 May 2011, Barack Obama gave a speech to announce Osama bin Laden's death in Pakistan. The speech involved a complex rhetorical exercise where the issues at stake were kept in balance through the use of a range of discourse strategies. Some of the sensitive issues that the speech had to balance include: the killing of a man without a trial inside a sovereign state not involved in the military operation (Inkster, 2011); the need for Obama to distinguish his international diplomacy from that of the previous administration while highlighting his own distinctive line of reasoning on the Middle East (Stevenson, 2011); and the necessity to highlight bin Laden's death as a significant milestone in the ongoing 'war on terror' (Torok, 2011). The need to legitimise the action and its motives were strong, as was the need to weaken any potential oppositional discourse. What follows is a selection of significant excerpts from the speech:

> It was nearly 10 years ago that a bright September day was darkened by the worst attack on the American people in our history. [...] Today, at my direction, the United States launched a targeted operation against that compound in Abbottabad, Pakistan. [...] After a firefight, they killed Osama bin Laden and took custody of his body. [...] The death of bin Laden marks the most significant achievement to date in our nation's effort to defeat al Qaeda. Yet his death does not mark the end of our effort. [...] We must – and we will – remain vigilant at home and abroad. [...] his demise should be welcomed by all who believe in peace and human dignity. [...] Tonight, I called President Zardari, and my team has also spoken with their Pakistani counterparts. They agree that this is a good and historic day for both of our nations. [...] The American people did not choose this fight. It came to our shores, and started with the senseless slaughter of our citizens. [...] as a country, we will never tolerate our

security being threatened, nor stand idly by when our people have been killed. [...] We will be true to the values that make us who we are. And on nights like this one, we can say to those families who have lost loved ones to al Qaeda's terror: Justice has been done. [...] The cause of securing our country is not complete. But tonight, we are once again reminded that America can do whatever we set our mind to. That is the story of our history, whether it's the pursuit of prosperity for our people, or the struggle for equality for all our citizens; our commitment to stand up for our values abroad, and our sacrifices to make the world a safer place. (http://www.whitehouse.gov/blog/2011/05/02/osama-bin-laden-dead)

This chapter focuses on a legitimisation strategy that Cap (2013) named *proximisation* and the extent to which this strategy is echoed in some Italian translations of Obama's speech, retrieved from the printed editions of *La Repubblica* and *Il Foglio* and the online versions of *Il Corriere*, *La Stampa*, *Il Manifesto* and *Il Foglio*. Cap (2013: 3) describes the phenomenon of proximisation as a communicative strategy upon which the entire war on terror discourse was built, 'a discursive strategy of presenting physical and temporally distant events and states of affairs [...] as directly, increasingly and negatively consequential to the speaker and their addressees'. On the level of discourse, this strategy works by inducing recipients to recognise any given danger as close to them, intensifying people's feelings of insecurity and fear (cf. Furedi, 2008: 651), and enticing them to favour any policy likely to guarantee a higher degree of protection. On the level of linguistic expression, proximisation strategies (cf. Bielsa & Bassnett, 2009: 116; Toury, 1995: 276) frequently involve deictic choices that activate assumptions about physical and social proximity. Proximisation strategies, moreover, play an important role in the discursive construction of national identities and political allegiances. When observed through the lens of translation, these strategies prove particularly problematic, since intercultural exchange may unmask discursive choices which would otherwise remain largely invisible and unquestioned. The main goal of this chapter is to analyse published press translations of Obama's speech in order to reveal the ways in which this practice inadvertently foregrounds discourse elements that were meant to be backgrounded.

Translating Proximisation

Cap (2008) analyses the Bush administration's legitimisation of the war against Iraq in 2003. Framed as a response to the 9/11 attacks, the administration based its legitimisation on the rhetorical construction of an in-group and an outsider group. This categorical distinction, however, poses problems in the process of translation, because the foreign recipients will not necessarily belong to the same in-group of recipients idealised in the American war discourse. In fact, the observation of translation choices often unveils and highlights discursive (i.e. proximisation) strategies that were left vague in the source text. Drawing on Bauman's (2012: 8) notion of liquidity and Baudrillard's (2010: 33–56) distinction across the power dimensions of domination and hegemony, I would like to highlight the role of translation in the shaping of a new globalised war discourse and the potential of translation analysis as a tool to enrich critical discourse analysis.

Within the context of capitalist modernity, Baudrillard asserts that '[c]lassical, historical domination imposed a system of positive values, displaying as well as defending these values', while '[c]ontemporary hegemony [...] relies on a symbolic liquidation of every possible value' (2010: 35). Domination implies the awareness of an ontological distinction between the dominators and the dominated, while in hegemony the dominated have accepted, in fact subconsciously internalised, the dominant ideology and have ceased questioning it. We can in this context envisage a politically transformative potential for translation, since what appears as hegemonic (i.e. *invisible*) in English may have become transformed into dominant (i.e. *visible*) in the translated Italian texts. This happens because the producers of the target text often have no other choice but to foreground the contradictions that are embedded in the hegemonic structure, contradictions which the source text authors had backgrounded through political discourse strategies. Translation may thus question the narrative and ideology of the discourse it attempts to re-verbalise, in our case the speech about bin Laden's death, and this questioning does not necessarily require a resistant translator (Tymoczko, 2010: 227–235). It is, in fact, the process of translation itself that may unveil the weak points of a new and thus *liquid* modern war discourse, which is why translation may occasionally play a modest role in the deconstruction of hegemony.

It could be argued that Baudrillard's work (2010) does not conceive of hegemony as opening up much room for dissent and resistance; this appears in stark contrast to Gramsci's conception of this powerful social force, underpinned by 'his disdain for any theoretical perspective that leads to passivity or fatalism' (Ives, 2004: 138). In agreement with Gramsci (see Ives, 2004), I consider hegemony as potentially questionable, and one of the most effective ways to question it is to deconstruct the underlying narrative of a specific ideological discourse (cf. Baker, 2006). Given that the production of a translation requires a deep understanding of the source text, the process of translation itself forces the translator to dig into the underlying discursive strategies inscribed in that source text. Any translational recognition, or indeed *deconstruction*, of these strategies releases a potential for more transparent communication in which the translated discourse may become more visible (i.e. *dominant*) than the invisible (i.e. *hegemonic*) ideological assumptions entailed in the original discourse.

The post-positivist and historical notions of *symbolic liquidation* (Baudrillard, 2010: 35) and *liquidity* (Bauman, 2012: 8) are employed here as a contrastive template that seeks to highlight the intrinsic weaknesses affecting *proximisation strategies* (Cap, 2013) within increasingly global narratives of war. Bauman's work revolves around the notion of liquidity and it demonstrates that power was traditionally negotiated within frameworks of *territorial* sovereignty because national security largely corresponded to the protection of geographical boundaries. The increasingly 'liquefying' normative matrix of modern society, where norms and value orientations undergo radical change, makes it virtually impossible to revert to inflexible territorial categories and narratives that for so long have determined the discourse of the social sciences (Bauman, 2012: 8). Territorial sovereignty and security became gradually eroded after the end of the *ancien régime*, up to an event which ensured 'that no one can any longer cut themselves off from the rest of the world' – that event being, of course, the attack on the Twin Towers in New York on 11 September 2001 ('9/11') (Bauman, 2002: 82). In his speech, Obama went to great lengths to remind his audiences of the fateful events unfolding on a day that Bauman considers pivotal to the idea of a liquid hegemonic space. We are dealing with the translation of a speech in which 9/11 is absolutely central. Since different languages tend to be identified with different nations, linguistic difference is an increasingly 'liquid' boundary. In a classical Western interpretation, translation may still mean carrying something across some boundary, but this boundary is gradually losing its significance, which will have an unavoidable effect on our notion of translation (for non-Western notions of translation, see Tymoczko, 2007).

Discourses of Power and Complexity

The investigation of sensitive political discourses in translation can benefit from interdisciplinary research in a variety of areas such as political studies, security science, social psychology or the digital economy (Cerny, 2013; Gollwitzer *et al.*, 2014; Inkster, 2011; Stevenson, 2011; Torok, 2011; Youngs, 2010). While in his speech Obama praises the Pakistani authorities and makes the case for an intelligence operation agreed upon by both countries, Inkster (2011: 6) points out that the raid 'amounted to an egregious violation of Pakistani national sovereignty'. Gollwitzer *et al.* (2014: 611) investigate American perceptions of justice and 'vengeful desire' in the aftermath of 9/11, and the extent to which bin Laden's assassination provided a sense of justice but also sparked a public desire to take further revenge. Youngs (2010) focuses on the notion of 'home front' and the impact of global media on modern warfare:

[t]he concept of the war on terror has been discursively constructed at the level of high politics, is widely contested, and has continued to shift

since the immediate after-math of the 9/11 attacks from standard security perspectives of external threats to the more complex sense of internal ones. (Youngs, 2010: 929)

The dwindling of the political effectiveness of territorial space has become a central topic in research on discourses of war. For Bauman (2002: 81), 9/11 was the 'symbolic end to the era of space', with the consequential 'annihilation of the protective capacity of space'. Similarly, Holmqvist (2012: 227) talks about 'shifting spatialities' and an 'absence of politics', arguing that modern wars are no longer narrated as conflicts between numerically identifiable enemy states. According to Holmqvist (2012), historical conceptions of nations as territorial space have given way to a new globalised consciousness, mainly because a shift in 'spatial imagination from linear statism to globality and supraterritoriality has involved a fundamental upheaval of political relationships and the way in which political agency is imagined'. In a similar vein, Torok (2011: 138) maintains that, as a result of the war on terror, 'we are clearly in a new global landscape', which engenders 'a "new kind of war" that embodies important cultural and discursive dimensions'. Significantly, the restrictions and violations of press freedoms since 9/11 provide evidence 'of a cultural shaping of messages in order to gain both domestic and international support for the war on terror [...] the lines between domestic and international audiences are becoming increasingly blurred' (Torok, 2011: 142). This qualitative change in international war diplomacy has obvious effects upon the processes and products of translation, and indeed on translation's potential to disturb and deconstruct hegemonic ideologies.

Obama's speech constitutes an example of a *post facto* legitimisation request (Chilton, 2004: 157). Chilton's model of cognitive discourse processing focuses on spatial, temporal and social deictic expressions, which can be defined as linguistic resources that prompt an addressee to cognitively link a specific deictic expression with situationally relevant features (Chilton, 2004: 56–58). Chilton draws on Lakoff and Johnson's (1980) seminal work on metaphors, and he investigates the ways in which social relations tend to be conceptualised and lexicalised in terms of space metaphors (e.g. 'close allies', 'distant relations', 'rapprochement', 'remote connections', 'outsiders'). Spatial representations play an important role in political discourse:

If politics is about cooperation and conflict over allocation of resources, such resources are frequently of a spatial, that is, geographical or territorial, kind. This is obvious in the case of international politics, where borders, territorial sovereignty and access are often at issue. Politics can also be about the relations between social groups, viewed literally or metaphorically as spatially distinct entities. Political actors are, moreover, always situated with respect to a particular time, place and social group. (Chilton, 2004: 57)

The word 'translation' itself can be considered a dead spatial metaphor (see also Tymoczko, 2007) and the process of translating is often described in terms of 'closeness' and 'distance' between 'source' and 'target' poles. A strong connection binds notions of space to that of translation (cf. Cronin, 2003: 42) and analysing translations through the lens of critical discourse analysis helps us to acknowledge the ways in which 'social space' is embedded in the very idea of translation.

Cap (2010) developed his proximisation concept for an analysis of political speeches that seek to legitimise pre-emptive action in remote countries, applying it primarily to Bush's speeches seeking to justify the war in Iraq. This analytical framework was also employed by Hart (2010), Dunmire (2011) and Amer (2009) in their investigations of (anti-)immigration discourse, political discourse and news discourse. Proximisation theory avails itself of the well known ontological *us* versus *them* divide, with *us* corresponding to entities *inside the deictic centre* (IDCs) and *them* to entities *outside the deictic centre* (ODCs). Three epistemological categories are crucial for this approach: the *spatial* aspect of proximisation, which construes ODC-instigated events as physically endangering the IDCs; the *temporal* aspect, which presents the events as momentous and historic for the IDCs; and the *axiological* aspect, which highlights a clash of values. The cumulative effect of these strategies is legitimisation. After the alleged possession of weapons of mass destruction on the part of Saddam Hussein's regime had been exposed as a disingenuous fantasy, the Bush administration's rhetoric moved from a primarily spatiotemporal proximisation towards a more universal axiological proximisation (Cap, 2010), in Cap's own words, towards 'a forced construal of a gathering ideological conflict between the "home values" [...] and the "alien", antagonistic values of the ODCs' (Cap, 2013: 94). An axiological strategy forcefully aims to entice the IDCs to perceive the ideological opposition as unacceptable and threatening, while the ODCs are construed as a threat to an imagined democratic world order (Cap, 2010: 131). In Obama's speech, proximisation strategies are clearly evident, but here the war is repeatedly portrayed as a crusade against the stateless organisation of Al Qaeda. Afghanistan is named only once and Iraq is entirely ignored, while references to Pakistan oscillate between the geographical place where bin Laden was found and friendly ruminations about the country and its people. The enemy is precisely located in geographical space, but the speech construes Al Qaeda as a deterritorialised global phenomenon capable of striking anywhere.

A critical analysis of politically sensitive texts in translation may fruitfully begin with an observation of significant linguistic-discursive elements included in the source text. Obama's speech contains linguistic choices that reinforce spatial, temporal and axiological proximisation. The speech opens with the trauma of 9/11, revisiting the tragedy in stark emotional imagery:

It was nearly 10 years ago that a bright September day was darkened by the worst attack on the American people in our history. The images of 9/11 are seared into our national memory – hijacked planes cutting through a cloudless September sky; the Twin Towers collapsing to the ground; black smoke billowing up from the Pentagon; the wreckage of Flight 93 in Shanksville, Pennsylvania, where the actions of heroic citizens saved even more heartbreak and destruction.

A cleft sentence marks the beginning of the narrative, and the discursive polarity is exemplified in a series of metaphors and metonymies: 'a bright September day' and 'a cloudless September sky' are diametrically opposed to images such as *darkened*, *seared*, *cutting* and *heartbreak*. Positive values are foregrounded through the collocation *heroic citizens* and the contrast between bright and dark. While in 2011 bin Laden and Pakistan were geographically distant from those inside the deictic centre, the memories of 2001 and of a geographically closer event are *temporally and spatially proximised* in the speech. In a further discursive twist, the time frame is moved forward to the present, with an account of the clash between those inside and those outside the deictic centre:

> Today, at my direction, the United States launched a targeted operation against that compound in Abbottabad, Pakistan. A small team of Americans carried out the operation with extraordinary courage and capability. No Americans were harmed. They took care to avoid civilian casualties. After a firefight, they killed Osama bin Laden and took custody of his body.

At this junction, proximisation has become axiological, it functions as a backgrounding strategy that aims to soften the act of shooting. The nominalised phrase 'After a firefight' conceals who started firing. The positive values attached to the IDCs are conveyed through the noun phrase 'extraordinary courage and capability' and the verb 'took care'. Even though the 'small team of Americans' is part of *our* group, they are deictically positioned through a third-person plural pronoun, which distances the speaker and the recipients from the act of killing. The following axiological move focuses on potential ideological and political clashes in the future. Obama praises the military operation and the killing of bin Laden, but underlines the continuity of the struggle:

> For over two decades, bin Laden has been al Qaeda's leader and symbol, and has continued to plot attacks against our country and our friends and allies. The death of bin Laden marks the most significant achievement to date in our nation's effort to defeat al Qaeda. Yet his death does not mark the end of our effort.

This passage exemplifies the fluid boundary between axiological and temporal proximisation. The present perfect tense employed in the first sentence has probably been chosen in order to frame bin Laden and his threat as still present. In addition, the speech reaches here the widest geographical and ideological inclusion of IDCs by repeating that the war is not against Islam and that the whole world should rejoice. The focus then narrows down again to American values, in an attempt to reinforce a feeling of patriotic belonging:

> The cause of securing our country is not complete. But tonight, we are once again reminded that America can do whatever we set our mind to. That is the story of our history, whether it's the pursuit of *prosperity for our people*, or the struggle for *equality for all our citizens*; our commitment to stand up for our values abroad, and our sacrifices to make the world a safer place. [...] Let us remember that we can do these things not just because of wealth or power, but because of who we are: *one nation, under God, indivisible, with liberty and justice for all*. [Emphasis added]

This last passage includes only US-Americans as inside the deictic centre. The words in italics are intertextual references to the American Declaration of Independence and to the Pledge of Allegiance to the Flag of the United States, which of course are likely to be lost on the recipients of translated texts. It is noteworthy that Bush's rhetorical strategy was based on conflict between *countries* (Chovanec, 2010), while Obama's is based on *people*, and hence proves much more liquid (to use Bauman's terminology). However, the entities constructed as inside the deictic centre do not remain the same throughout Obama's speech. Those inside the deictic centre are narratively constructed through a 'zooming out' perspective: the speech begins with an intimate family image of an 'empty seat at the dinner table' after the Twin Tower attacks, and eventually enlarges the group of people called upon to welcome bin Laden's demise to include 'all who believe in peace and human dignity'. After the inclusion of the whole world through the discursive removal of geographical and religious barriers, the focus regresses again towards the United States. Everybody can be inside the deictic centre, but Americans more than others, since 'we can do these things [...] because of who we are' – a subtle discursive strategy that generates an effect of domination. The implied narrative being, of course, that America is the leading global political force, that other countries are expected to recognise its superiority and that Americans are expected to act like the citizens of the wisest and most powerful country. This narrative works through a logic of political domination and through unacknowledged hegemony, that is, naturalised ideology, within its own symbolically 'liquefied' territorial space.

Who *We* Are and How We Translate *We*

Shortly after 9/11 the French broadsheet *Le Monde* and the Italian *Corriere della Sera* pandered to the hegemonic discourse through editorials that were both entitled 'We are all American'. The personal pronoun 'we' constitutes an effective rhetorical device in political discourse, and its translation appears to foreground what I would like to call *intentional ambiguities*. An analysis of the occurrences and referents of the pronoun 'we' provides insights into subtle textual manifestations of intentional ambiguity constructed by the writers of the source text (cf. Munday, 2012: 68–76). Moreover, an analysis of the pronoun's semantic ambivalence may be fruitfully linked to proximisation theory and the concept of social deixis.

In his discussion of Obama's first inauguration speech, Jeremy Munday asserts that this particular pronoun 'locates itself at the deictic centre of the communication'. With reference to the expression 'we the government', Munday differentiates between 'invoked inclusiveness' and 'implied exclusiveness', one referring to the 'government and/with the people' and the other to an exclusive 'we' that refers to a smaller group 'acting distinctly from the people but for their good' (Munday, 2012: 71). According to Munday (2012: 72), '[t]he fact that "we" generates these possible interpretations demonstrates its inherent ambiguity and the subjectivity of the response'. In the speech analysed in the present article, the usage of this pronoun is even more complex and blurred: the sentence 'We offered our neighbors a hand, and we offered the wounded our blood' refers to a wide group of Americans and other allied forces, while the sentence 'I met repeatedly with my national security team as we developed more information about the possibility that we had located bin Laden' refers to Obama's internal political circle, which represents a much smaller group. The first sentence constitutes an example of invoked inclusiveness and the second one signifies implied exclusiveness. This level of intentional ambiguity, however, can increase even further. For instance, in the statement 'over the last 10 years, thanks to the tireless and heroic work of our military and our counterterrorism professionals, we've made great strides in that effort. We've disrupted terrorist attacks and strengthened our homeland defense', it is hard to tell who are the referents of the pronoun 'we': Obama and military and counterterrorism professionals? Obama and his national security team? The government? Americans?

Chilton (2004: 157) analysed the implications of the usage of 'we' with reference to a speech given by President George Bush on 7 October 2001 in which he sought to justify military action against Iraq. For Chilton, Bush's speech constitutes another *post facto* legitimisation request in which Osama bin Laden was a prominent topic:

> In this type of speech by a political leader it is crucial to establish who is 'us' and who is 'them'. In fact it was an essential part of President Bush's discourse in this period to assert that there was no neutral or middle ground: leaders of other countries were told (since domestic broadcasts are directed also at non-Americans) to be either 'with us' or 'against us'.
> (Chilton, 2004: 159)

George Bush's discourse was meant to create an unambiguous antagonism (a good example is the phrase 'axis of evil', first employed during his
State of the Union Address on 29 January 2002). Obama's speech, on the
contrary, may, rather, be identified as a kind of 'liquid' discourse that leaves
the public with the impression that anyone can belong to 'our' group, notwithstanding nationality or religion. Of course, this strategy also implies
an antagonistic stance and it subtly places those who dare to question the
circumstances of bin Laden's killing on the side of Al Qaeda, with no space
left for the position of those who might be happy about his defeat but
doubtful about the way in which it was achieved. Yet Obama's discourse is
distinguished through a higher degree of ideological liquidity: its actors are
less recognisable, so anyone can be the enemy. In avoiding the weakness of
Bush's focus on national belonging, Obama's discourse creates an invisible
and placeless enemy: if the enemy originates from a territorially identifiable nation state, it is perceived as recognisable and easier to control; but if
the enemy is placeless, without geographical origin, it can be anyone and
might be able to strike from anywhere in the world. In a perverted sense,
this is the highest possible degree of proximisation, as the enemy might be
located much closer than the audience might dare to imagine!

These linguistic-discursive phenomena pose various issues in the
process of translation: in Italian, pronouns and possessive adjectives are
usually dropped and conveyed by other means, but the Italian translations
contain a higher number of explicitly phrased instances of *noi* ('we') and
nostro ('our') than one would expect in standard Italian. This additional
complexity in translation is due to the fact that Italian verb suffixes imply
the identity of the grammatical subject. For instance, the translation of
the sentence 'Over the years, I've repeatedly made clear that we would
take action within Pakistan if we knew where bin Laden was' as 'Nel corso
degli anni ho ripetutamente chiarito che noi avremmo agito in Pakistan
se avessimo saputo dove Bin Laden si trovava' (*La Stampa*) constitutes
a marked choice because 'we' has been translated with its literal Italian
equivalent *noi*. Here, standard Italian would work well without the
pronoun, yet including *noi* generates the implicature *we would take action,
while others would not*. This addition of an otherwise optional personal
pronoun renders the deictic positioning, that is, the identity of those at
the centre of the communication, even more complex and generates new
layers of interpretation.

The Italian news translations furthermore communicate an extra
tension of closeness and distance in terms of proximisation, because they
foreground a division between the United States and the rest of the world:
what was intended as a strategy of inclusion in the source text becomes
transformed into a strategy of inclusion *and* exclusion in the target texts.
Proximisation strategies indeed become weakened in the Italian target
texts because the recipients can no longer clearly identify themselves with
those inside the deictic centre. One sentence towards the end of the speech

constitutes the most significant example: 'But tonight, we are once again reminded that America can do whatever we set our mind to'. The sentence evokes the presence of some mystical higher truth that might bring about a political resolution. Three Italian translations include this sentence, all of which render 'we set our mind to' with exclusive reference to the subject 'America':

> Ma questa sera ci è stato ricordato che l'America può fare tutto ciò che si prefigge di fare. (*Il Foglio* – Alberto Muci)

> Ma questa notte ricorda a tutti noi ancora una volta che l'America può raggiungere qualsiasi obiettivo essa si ponga. (*La Stampat*)

> Ma questa sera ci viene ricordato ancora una volta che l'America può fare qualunque cosa si proponga. (*La Repubblica* – Emilia Benghi)

These translations highlight the semantic distinction that separates the two first-person plural pronouns in the source text and thus expose its hegemonic strategy. Unlike the recipients of Obama's English speech, the readers of the translation know unequivocally that it is America that 'is reminding them' and that they are not included among those who 'can do whatever they set their mind to'. The very reassuring message conveyed by the source text becomes somehow sinister in translation, conveying an ambivalent sensation of inclusion and exclusion. The fact that Obama's discourse may lose its effectiveness when translated into Italian appears to confirm the weakness of the very idea of proximisation in a globalised context (Bauman, 2002; Holmqvist, 2012). Proximisation strategies function smoothly alongside traditional military discourse where geographical distance and boundaries remain significant factors, not least because this discourse is still processed through enduring spatial (and thus hegemonic) nation-state categories. Modern international diplomacy, however, is characterised by globalised and thus supra-territorial discourses of war, and the contradictions between globalisation and spatial proximisation are bound to increasingly weaken traditional military discourse based on the logics of territory. It could be argued that the same happens when the source text recipient is an English-speaking person living outside the USA (for example an Australian citizen can be fully aware that 'we' in Obama's speech does not always include him or her); interestingly, however, the process of translation appears to further foreground political antagonisms.

Discourse in Translation

The practice of translating news texts suffers from time constraints and a lack of visibility and professional translation training (Bielsa & Bassnett, 2009; Schäffner & Bassnett, 2010). Only two translations from the analysed corpus mention the translator's name, both of which stem from the printed editions of *Il Foglio* and *La Repubblica*, the former signed by the journalist Alberto Muci and the latter by the professional translator Emilia Benghi. The textual characteristics in Benghi's translation are not present in any of the other versions, and her rendering of metaphors and avoidance of semantic deviations testifies to her professional experience. When, for instance, Benghi renders 'hijacked planes cutting through a cloudless September sky' as 'gli aerei dirottati che fendono il cielo terso' (back-translation: 'hijacked planes cutting through a terse/splendid sky'], Muci goes for 'gli aerei dirottati che attraversano il cielo di settembre senza nuvole' (back-translation: 'hijacked planes crossing the sky of September without clouds'). Similarly, in Benghi's translation 'the empty seat at the dinner table' becomes 'il posto vuoto a tavola all'ora di cena' (back-translation: 'the empty seat at the table when dinner time comes', while Muci opts for 'il posto vuoto al tavolo della cena' (back-translation: 'the empty seat at the table of the dinner'). It is hard to show through back-translations that Emilia Benghi's choices prove more idiomatic. Alberto Muci's translation cannot be classified as 'wrong', but an Italian reader is likely to perceive his translation of the speech as strange, due to a lack of idiomaticity. There is, for example, a subtle difference between *tavola* and *tavolo*: both mean table, but the first one refers to a table where people eat, and the idiomatic phrase 'a tavola!' means 'dinner's ready', thus evoking in Italian a much more specific image than *tavolo*, a word that simply refers to a piece of furniture.

Similar issues arise when translating possessive pronouns, which, as pointed above, in Italian are less frequent than in English. The translations of the possessive pronoun 'our' represent an important element in the construction of a polarised *us* versus *them* discourse, which has its experiential basis in the deictic positioning of those inside or outside the deictic centre. The 47 occurrences of 'our' in the source text correspond to 34 occurrences of the lemma *nostro* in *La Repubblica* and to 46 occurrences in *Il Foglio*. Emilia Benghi's translation in *La Repubblica* demonstrates that a standard Italian text does not usually feature the same amount of possessives found in English, so Alberto Muci's literal renditions in *Il Foglio* appear unconventional and deserve some closer observation. Five occurrences of the lemma *nostro* in Muci's Italian, however, have no corresponding occurrences in the source text (Table 10.1). Moreover, some English expressions that include the possessive 'our' were impossible to render with an Italian possessive. Translating the sentence 'America can do whatever we set our mind to' using *nostro*, for example, would result in a convoluted and non-idiomatic Italian expression. This means that English occurrences of 'our' that were lost in translation were counterbalanced by a corresponding number of the lemma *nostro* that were inserted into the translation, resulting in a target text that an Italian recipient would perceive as promoting a marked *us* versus *them* polarity.

Table 10.1 Five added occurrences of the lemma *nostro* in Alberto Muci's Italian translation of Barack Obama's speech

English source text	Possessives added in Muci's translation
no matter where we came from	nonostante la *nostra* origine
We've made great strides in that effort	i *nostri* sforzi ci hanno portato a fare grandi passi
we worked with our friends and allies	Abbiamo collaborato con i nostri amici e i *nostri* alleati
against our country and our friends and allies	contro il nostro paese, i nostri amici e i *nostri* alleati
we have never forgotten your loss	non abbiano mai dimenticato le *nostre* vittime [*sic* – this should be *vostre*]

Such translation choices could stem from the difficulties involved when asked to produce an idiomatic target text under a tight journalistic deadline; after all, Muci is a journalist rather than a translator. But such target text patterns may also be influenced by discourse strategies employed in the source text. Obama's speech spins an imaginary narrative of belonging and exclusion by strategically exploiting the 'liquid' boundary that separates national groups. The central deictic nucleus, US-Americans, remains the same throughout the speech, while the liquid boundary alternately expands to include all humanity (except Al Qaeda) and then shrinks back to the American people. The deictic centrality of 'us' as separate from 'them' is underlined by possessive pronouns, so the high frequency of the lemma *nostro* in Muci's target text constitutes a marked choice. What was constructed as a barely visible hegemonic proposition in the source text becomes a perceptible gesture of domination in translation, a gesture that could be interpreted as triggering the following implicature in the mind of an Italian reader: *We Americans are the central nucleus of global humanity who believe in peace and human dignity and we are the ones who should decide what is to be done to protect America and the rest of the world from terrorism.* It is indeed not unreasonable to argue that the Italian readers are fully aware of their ideological inclusion in some occurrences of *we* but excluded when *we* refers to an imagined American nation that is firmly positioned inside the deictic centre. Hence, the unusually large number of instances of the lemma *nostro* may indeed sensitise Italian readers to the political discourse strategies employed in the source text.

The translation published in *La Repubblica* displays a similar degree of ideological interference. Emilia Benghi, the professional translator, appeared more perceptive of the underlying political narrative and its discourse strategies. This version is characterised by one translation choice not found in any of the other target texts. Three Italian tenses correspond to the English simple past, of which the so-called *passato prossimo* (near past) is mainly employed in news discourse; the other two tenses are called *passato remoto* (remote past) and *imperfetto* (imperfect past), and these tend to be employed in narrative texts. The journalist Alberto Muci opted for the conventional *passato prossimo*, whereas Emilia Benghi used the unconventional *passato remoto*, which is a marked choice and thus highly recognisable for an Italian reader. Since English does not observe a similar distinction between these two past tenses, a professional translator into Italian is likely to compensate in this manner for other elements bound to be lost in translation. It is, however, essential to realise that these translations are both interlingual and intersemiotic, because the source text was mainly written to be heard, while the Italian translations were written to be read. Emilia Benghi seems to compensate for what the proximisation strategies partially lose in translation by inserting a narrative element that provides the speech with a slightly different tension. Here, the narrative flow of Obama's English remains more or less intact, evidenced through the efficient echoing of changes in rhythm and pace, metaphors, time expressions and metonymies (see Conoscenti, 2013).

Conclusion

President Obama's speech is challenging in the way it keeps various discursive and narrative elements in balance. The speech skilfully exploits the 'liquid' boundaries that separate those outside from those inside the deictic centre. A linguistic investigation of deictic space allows us to recognise the presence of proximisation strategies, and it also uncovers their limitations in an increasingly interconnected world. Translating this speech into Italian proved a difficult task, because proximisation strategies do not work as convincingly in the target text. Future research will benefit from investigation into the possible effects of translation into other languages, notably when the translated text relies heavily on proximisation strategies.

According to research in the social sciences, the erosion of 'classical' geographical notions of space has significantly weakened traditional discourses of war, with 9/11 being recognised as a pivotal historical milestone that signalled 'the end of the era of space' (Bauman, 2002: 81). Obama's speech may be considered a prime example of the war discourse that could well develop in forthcoming years. Since the practice of translation may foreground discourse elements that were meant to be backgrounded in a given source text, translators working on texts that aim to develop a 'liquid war discourse' can become agents of resistance, not because they are consciously following a translation strategy or actively promoting/resisting an ideological narrative, but simply because translation itself is bound to bring specific discourse strategies to the fore. As a consequence, translation choices are likely to highlight the weaknesses of a new war discourse that tries to strike a balance between a positive notion of an imaginary globalised togetherness and negative proximisation strategies. Such negative strategies, of course, are based on antiquated national fault-lines that continue to instil fear in their recipients.

References

Amer, M.M. (2009) 'Telling-it-like-it-is': The delegitimation of the second Palestinian Intifada in Thomas Friedman's discourse. *Discourse and Society* 20, 5–31.

Baker, M. (2006) *Translation and Conflict: A Narrative Account*. London: Routledge.

Baudrillard, J. (2010) *The Agony of Power*. Los Angeles, CA: Semiotext(e).

Bauman, Z. (2002) Reconnaissance wars of the planetary frontierland. *Theory, Culture and Society* 19 (4), 81–90.

Bauman, Z. (2012) *Liquid Modernity*. Cambridge: Polity Press.

Bielsa, E. and Bassnett, S. (2009) *Translation in Global News*. London: Routledge.

Bush, G. (2002) State of the Union Address, *Washington Post Online*, at http://www.washingtonpost.com/wp-srv/onpolitics/transcripts/sou012902.htm, accessed 19 July 2016.

Cap, P. (2008) Towards the proximization model of the analysis of legitimization in political discourse. *Journal of Pragmatics* 40, 17–41.

Cap, P. (2010) Proximizing objects, proximizing values. Towards an axiological contribution to the discourse of legitimization. In U. Okulska and P. Cap (eds) *Perspectives in Politics and Discourse* (pp. 119–142). Amsterdam: John Benjamins.

Cap, P. (2013) *Proximization: The Pragmatics of Symbolic Distance Crossing*. Amsterdam: John Benjamins.

Cerny, P.G. (2013) Reconfiguring power in a globalizing world. In S.R. Clegg and M. Haugaard (eds) *The Sage Handbook of Power* (pp. 383–399). London: Sage.

Chilton, P. (2004) *Analyzing Political Discourse: Theory and Practice*. London: Routledge.

Chovanec, J. (2010) Legitimation through differentiation: Discursive construction of Jacques Le Worm Chirac as an opponent to military action. In U. Okulska and P. Cap (eds) *Perspectives in Politics and Discourse* (pp. 61–81). Amsterdam: John Benjamins.

Conoscenti, M. (2013) Sprinkled metonymies in the analysis of political discourse with corpus linguistics techniques: A case study. In I. Poggi, F. D'Errico, L. Vincze and A. Vinciarelli (eds) *Multimodal Communication in Political Speech: Shaping Minds and Social Action* (pp. 258–275). Berlin: Springer Verlag.

Cronin M. (2003) *Translation and Globalization*. London: Routledge.

Dunmire, P. (2011) *Projecting the Future Through Political Discourse: The Case of the Bush Doctrine*. Amsterdam: John Benjamins.

Furedi, F. (2008). Fear and security: A vulnerability-led policy response. *Social Policy and Administration* 42, 645–661.

Gollwitzer, M., Skitka, L.J., Wisneski, D., Sjöström, D., Liberman, P., Nazir, S.J. and Bushman, B.J. (2014) Vicarious revenge and the death of Osama bin Laden. *Personality and Social Psychology Bulletin* 40 (5), 604–616.

Hart, C. (2010) *Critical Discourse Analysis and Cognitive Science: New Perspectives on Immigration Discourse*. Basingstoke: Palgrave Macmillan.

Holmqvist, C. (2012) War/space: Shifting spatialities and the absence of politics in contemporary accounts of war. *Global Crime* 13 (4), 219–234.

Inkster, N. (2011) The death of Osama bin Laden. *Survival: Global Politics and Strategy* 53 (3), 5–10.

Ives, P. (2004) *Language and Hegemony in Gramsci*. London: Pluto Press.

Lakoff, G. and Johnson M. (1980) *Metaphors We Live By*. Chicago, IL: University of Chicago Press.

Munday, J. (2012) *Evaluation in Translation*. London: Routledge.

Schäffner, C. and Bassnett, S. (eds) (2010) *Political Discourse, Media and Translation.* Newcastle upon Tyne: Cambridge Scholars Publishing.

Stevenson, J. (2011) Echoes of gunfire: bin Laden, the US and the Greater Middle East. *Survival: Global Politics and Strategy* 53 (3), 11–18.

Torok, R. (2011) The 9/11 Commission Report and the reframing of the 'war on terror' as a new type of warfare. *Journal of Policing, Intelligence and Counter Terrorism* 6 (2), 137–150.

Toury, G. (1995) *Descriptive Translation Studies and Beyond.* Amsterdam: John Benjamins.

Tymoczko, M. (2007) *Enlarging Translation, Empowering Translators.* London: Routledge.

Tymoczko, M. (2010) The space and time of activist translation. In M. Tymoczko (ed.) *Translation, Resistance, Activism* (pp. 227–254). Boston, MA: University of Massachusetts Press.

Youngs, G. (2010) The 'new home front' and the war on terror: Ethical and political reframing of national and international politics. *International Affairs* 86 (4), 925–937.

Part 4

Commercial Hegemonies in the Global Political Economy

11 Translation and Interpreting for the Media in the English Premier League

Roger Baines

Elite-Level Football, Power and Translation

The power that wealth confers on elite migrant athletes enables them to use translation as a means to participate in the negotiation of power (Baines, 2013). Elite-level migrant footballers in the English Premier League (EPL), particularly during the initial acculturation stages of their foreign career, may be involved in a range of translation and interpreting events. The situations in which these events occur come into three main categories: communicating with internal and external media (e.g. press interviews, press conferences, club media interviews, post-match interviews); professional activities within the football club (e.g. coaching, medicals, club community work, contract negotiations); and extra-professional activities (e.g. housing, healthcare, banking, arranging childcare). This chapter focuses on the first category, press interviews and press conferences that have been filtered through translation or interpreting. These two media activities reflect different power dynamics, which can be observed across two further sub-categories: press interviews and conferences where the interests of the elite migrant players and of the clubs are shared, and press interviews where those interests are divergent.

In his widely quoted paper on questions of power and translation, Fawcett (1995: 181) pointed out that 'the first expression of power in translation is, as has long been recognised, the decision whether or not to translate something and, if so, how much to pay for it'. Research into power dynamics in translation studies, however, has predominantly revolved around the various manipulations that support, negotiate or resist dominant ideological positions and interests rather than around questions of economic significance. Smart (2007: 6) describes sport as 'an economically significant, highly popular, globally networked cultural form'. Highly commercialised and mediatised elite sport, therefore, reflects globalised power relationships which are now primarily located in the marketplace rather than in political institutions (Savoie, 2010). This chapter concentrates on the economic and commercial determinants that govern the power dynamics of translation.

Elite-level football is an example of a globalised sport which, according to Sugden and Tomlinson (2002: 3), has become a very highly valued international commodity and also 'an important vehicle for the acquisition of wealth and status and the exercise of power'. Palumbo (2009: 88) defines power in translation as '[t]he ideological or political stance of those who, in various capacities, exercise control over the steps of the translation "chain" undergone by texts, thereby including the decision over what texts should be translated'. In elite football clubs, which employ players from a wide range of countries, press interviews and press conferences are overseen by club media managers and press officers, who are responsible for the texts (written and oral) that clubs provide to the media. Media managers exert power by dint of being entrusted with protecting and enhancing the status, reputation and wealth of their club and its players. As will become apparent, translation and interpreting, while facilitating communication with the media, can also destabilise the control that media managers have over the narratives that journalists publish about their club and players. The data presented here come from anonymised interviews with media managers from two EPL clubs, four interpreters (one via email), one translator and a migrant former player.

The steps in the translation chain are typically as follows: for an outlet external to a club, journalists submit questions in advance to the media manager, who may consult with a player's agent. The approved questions will then be translated by an interpreter in advance of an interview. During the event, the interpreter works bilaterally between English-speaking journalists and the non-English-speaking player, and the club media manager is usually present and can intervene. The journalists then write their articles based on the interpreter's text, or produce subtitles for broadcast in conjunction with the interpreter. The club may then ask to see the article copy before publication and reserve the right to request changes. For an internal publication outlet (e.g. club website, magazine or match-day programme), the translation chain is similar, but the scrutiny is less intense because the club's own staff provide the questions and, if necessary, edit the responses. For an interpreted press conference the chain is shorter, because the interpreter has no forewarning of specific questions from the journalists (though most questions can be predicted) and there is therefore little opportunity for a media manager to intervene before the interpreted text is produced and recorded. The interpreter may be briefed before the press conference on what to expect, and on what the responses to any difficult questions might be. The interpreter and the player meet at a media table in front of a much larger group of assembled journalists than in the press interview and the media manager invites questions; the interpreter relays questions and answers between player and journalists. Most journalists are monolingual and have to rely on the interpreter's text for their articles. Consecutive interpreting is the usual mode of interpreting during press conferences; simultaneous interpreting via interpreting booths is rare, but the clubs Arsenal in London and Manchester City in Manchester, for example, have these facilities.

Power, Globalisation and the Marketplace for Sport

There has been considerable research in sociology into questions of power in sport, in particular with reference to globalisation (e.g. Giulianotti & Robertson, 2007a; Lawrence & Rowe, 1986; Maguire, 2005; Sugden & Tomlinson, 2002), yet none of these studies makes more than a passing reference to translation or intercultural communication. The ideological stance of club media managers, who, as noted above, exercise control over published texts at various stages within the translation chain, is firmly grounded in economic considerations. What is at stake in the power dynamics during translation and interpreting processes at EPL clubs is the economic interests of clubs and players, and indeed wealthy migrant footballers may choose to use translation to influence media narratives. There are players who make little discernible attempt to adapt to the host culture, thus reinforcing their status as outsiders (Baines, 2013), yet while such attitudes would be disempowering for non-elite migrants, translation enables such elite migrants to actively participate in the negotiation of power. Globalised elite sport, in fact, provides a prime context for the analysis of the new power relationships promoted by globalisation, which tend to be largely located in the marketplace rather than in the domain of traditional power politics. Moreover, as Sugden (2002: 63) notes, 'we live in an age when the power and influence of the nation-state is being overridden by a network of international financial interests enmeshed through global communications networks'.

The predominance of the neoliberal marketplace in elite sport is a consequence of economic globalisation, where power is exercised and resisted through the principle of the deregulated free market and driven by policies that sustain private sector growth and wealth accumulation. Modern elite sport, in addition, encompasses the development of a globalised sports industry through the deregulation of state media control, the emergence of various media platforms that keep production at relatively low cost, and the recruitment of athletes with global appeal in order to increase profits (cf. Maguire, 2011). These conditions make it easier to develop income streams from media rights, sponsorship, merchandising and ticket sales (cf. Bridgewater, 2010). The economic dimensions of globalisation can be easily identified in the British football industry. The most relevant factors are the migration of high-profile athletes within a transfer market where fees have climbed dramatically over the past 20 years, the exponential growth of live media coverage and the vast income that this generates for clubs. The influx of foreign players increases the demand for translation and interpreting, and the generation of wealth through broadcasting rights creates the economic conditions that motivate clubs and players to exert control over the narratives that are disseminated by the media. The migration of elite athletes to places where they can earn the highest salaries (cf. Magee & Sugden, 2002; Maguire, 1996) is a consequence of globalisation processes which have broken down spatiotemporal and communication barriers.

An increased need for translation and interpreting is probably more marked in the UK than in other European countries because of the generally poor level of UK foreign language skills (CBI/Pearson Education, 2013: 26). The contrast in linguistic performance between any number of migrant players in the EPL who do adapt to the host culture and display high levels of fluency in English in interviews and media work (for example Thierry Henry, Vincent Kompany, Petr Cech) to the performance of some of the very rare British footballers or managers who work in non-English-speaking cultures is striking. Recent examples include Joey Barton (playing for Marseille in France) and Steve McClaren (managing FC Twente in Holland), who used the accommodation strategy of speaking English in press conferences with, respectively, strong French or Dutch accents. Linguistic accommodation is defined by Cogo (2009: 254) as 'adjusting speech to facilitate communication or changing one's speech to make it more intelligible or sometimes converging one's spoken habits to resemble those of one's interlocutors'.

Nevertheless, the need for translation and interpreting, especially during the initial period of adaptation to the host language and culture for migrant players, makes the context of the EPL a particularly fertile one in which to investigate economic power relationships in relation to translation. Since English clubs are the world's highest spenders on overseas players, the linguistic and cultural heterogeneity of EPL playing squads is very marked (e.g. £550 million was spent in 2013, an increase of 51% on 2012; FIFA, 2014). The Bosman ruling, a European Court ruling which enabled out-of-contract players to join a new club without the payment of a transfer fee, facilitated a steady yearly increase in non-English players from the 1994–1995 season. In that season, 69% of EPL players were English, whereas in the 2016–2017 season there were 65 different nationalities and only 31% of players were English (Sky Sports, 2017). The economic conditions of the EPL are summed up in the 2015 Deloitte annual review of football finances:

> England's top division has passed the £3 billion revenue mark for the first time and widened the gap to its nearest rival, the Bundesliga, to over £1 billion. The Premier League's virtuous circle of compelling content

attracting ever increasing broadcast revenues, which in turn attracts some of the best coaches and playing talent from around the world, complemented by capacity attendances at its stadia is a familiar one. (Jones, 2015: 2)

The material wealth of EPL clubs in great part derives from ever-increasing revenue from media contracts, making it 'the world's "most watched league", with a cumulative TV audience of 4.7 billion' (Brandwatch, 2013: 4). A live broadcast deal announced in February 2015 brought the 20 EPL clubs income of £5.1 billion, a 70% increase on the previous contract. According to UEFA, this deal would position the EPL as the most lucrative sports league in the world by 2017, surpassing the (non-soccer) National Football League in the United States (ESPN, 2015). In this economic context, the considerable power wielded by football club media managers is not at all surprising. The football industry is akin to corporate finance or politics, where the 'need to develop and promote a long-term "brand" image of the company or party to ensure continuing sales and electoral support' (Davis, 2007: 73) is crucial to media management. This means that the ways in which translation and interpreting are handled by football club media managers are vital in protecting a club's reputation and wealth.

Censorship and Translation in Football?

Interventions by media managers before the final edit of a translated or interpreted text are akin to acts of censorship. The 'censorial mechanisms' described by Toury closely reflect the practices of media translation in the English Premier League. According to Toury, such 'mechanisms are often resorted to post-factum, after the act of translation has been terminated, by way of [post]-editing, whether by the translator him-/herself or by some other agent', while frequently 'such a revisor is not even required to know the source language, and even if s/he does, it is not necessarily the case that s/he also falls back on it' (Toury, 1995: 278). Press interviews involve a combination of translation and interpreting, which gives media managers much more control over the editorial process than in the case of interpreted press conferences. As a result, examples of *post factum* intervention are not infrequent, as suggested by two media managers:

Media manager 1: When a player first comes over we would be very sympathetic to any interviews they do; they would be in their mother tongue with journalists probably from their home country. We also interview with our club media, for example, with an interpreter, all recorded making sure the player is happy. The player's agent plays a big role as well, so we make sure they are feeling comfortable with the interview as well, so we would show them the interview before it goes to print or show it to them on the website, making sure everyone is happy, there is no ambiguity around quotes, because this can happen with interviews which take place in other languages, which sometimes are spun around translation issues.

Media manager 2: We took him away for a club interview via his agent. Because he knew we were editing it, he had a degree of trust that if he did say anything foolish or inappropriate we would obviously edit it out. It also meant he could feel relaxed about how the questions were coming to him, take his time.

Although the media managers control text production, the player's agent also plays a part in this process. In this second example, for instance, the agent undertakes the interpreting task rather than a professional interpreter provided by the club. In the first example, the agent, while not providing the interpreting, is invited to scrutinise the text prior to publication. This sharing of power is mainly possible because the (economic) interests of the club, the player and his agent are also shared. While such a course of action doubtless creates a more comfortable, less risky, environment for the player and the club, it provides yet more evidence of the club mechanisms for remaining in control. This practice ensures in advance that translation is not going to be an issue or that there is space within the translation chain for any potential post-editing. For example, an interpreter noted that the player interview he interpreted for the club website was 'bolstered up' in the final text version 'because the player didn't give detailed answers' (Interpreter 4, 2016). The clubs also exercise control by choosing which player to put forward for interview (in Fawcett's terms, deciding whether or not to translate something) and by choosing the means of dissemination. *Post factum* editorial control for press interviews resides with the club, and certainly not with the translator. The one translator interviewed explained that the club intervenes after the translation process, by removing comments or questions deemed risky: 'It gets proofread at our end. What you might see is an element of censorship, not correction of a text but removal of anything you know…, and it doesn't take much for something to be deemed controversial within the context of an official club publication' (Translator, 2013). Kuhiwczak (2011: 360) describes censorship as 'a deliberate and conscious policy' because 'those who are in power implement censorship and give it legal and institutional legitimacy in order to protect their interests'. The interests that are being protected here are essentially economic.

It is relatively easy for media managers to intervene in the translation chain for press interviews, because they are conducted either in-house or with a limited number of journalists, with questions often being cleared in advance and responses edited prior to publication. Press conferences, however, are quite a different matter, because if there is to be any elimination of controversial material, it has to be pre-emptive rather than *post factum*. New players are usually introduced to the fans and the media at a press conference. One media manager described how interpreting in this kind of event is organised to ensure that player and club are comfortable:

Media manager 2: There is a massive expectation in football that, at the very least, when a player joins a club that the fans will hear from that player about why he has joined. The most preferred option is when an interpreter is introduced to the player, speaks to the player prior to any media activity, relays any information we or the player may have before any media activity and then sits next to the player and translates questions and answers with the player. That's the most reassuring solution for club and player.

The first step in the chain of communication allows the club to exchange information with the player before the press conference, potentially an opportunity to brief the player and the interpreter about what should and should not be said. One of the interpreters commented:

Interpreter 1: You would tend to have a briefing from someone from the press office beforehand, you know, if there were any hot-spots that they envisaged that they'd want you to steer clear of. I know it's something that makes club officials a bit jittery, especially these days when top clubs try and control everything. When you bring interpreters into the mix you're introducing an X factor to a certain extent.

A sense of disempowerment comes from the fact that the media manager is unable to screen questions in advance and to understand the language being used by the player and the interpreter. Another interpreter confirmed that such obstacles can be overcome much more easily in press interviews:

Interpreter 2: Interpreters have the final say over content and that's a loss of power for the person in charge and that can often be quite difficult. The media guys from the team, they breathe down your neck, watching like a hawk. They are so tense because they don't want to lose face, prestige and reputation. Clubs are not so keen on interpreters because it comes out before they've had a moment; they can't do it retrospectively.

A third interpreter reported a censoring intervention from a club media manager prior to a press conference. He recounted a situation where a player had changed his decision about which club to move to at the last minute of a transfer window, apparently for a better salary. This player was consequently being branded a mercenary by the media. Prior to the press conference at the new club to announce the player, the interpreter was informed about the official line, and unequivocally told 'if the player phrases it slightly differently to that, change it'. The interpreter added 'you could be the consummate professional and refuse to follow these instructions but you'd never work again' (Interpreter 3,

2014). If a club is not happy with the performance of an interpreter, it can request the services of a different agency the next time, given that '[t]he club controls the agencies very strongly and can punish by not using the agency' (Interpreter 2, 2014). All interpreters expressed a concern to avoid jeopardising future earnings by upsetting their employer, which further confirms the economic imperatives affecting translating and interpreting within the EPL. However, translators or interpreters who behave in this way challenge professional codes of ethics, as reported by Andrew Simpson when writing about his experience of working as an interpreter for Newcastle United:

> I am often called on to 'audit' interviews in French and iron out any potential areas that the club would not wish to be published in the media, or to assist in directing player responses, taking on a PR/media role in addition to my work as an interpreter. This is ethically difficult. (Simpson, 2014: 19)

The briefing of interpreters to prevent controversial statements from reaching the media, although rare, is a strategy that is not confined to press conferences. Media managers naturally develop relationships with journalists, so advance agreements can be put in place before press interviews in order to avoid the need for post-translation editing. For example:

> **Media manager 1**: If an English player is doing an interview with an English paper we would ask for copy approval, just for making things factually correct, but that is very difficult if a player has done an interview in another country. On the odd occasion we'd probably get a translator to have a look at it and then, yes, we would have the final say if we were unhappy, but you make that agreement with the journalist before the interview.

This media manager also talked about the approach to 'the mixed zone', the area players walk through after a match where journalists are assembled. Players decide whether they wish to give an interview, but the club will, again, try to exercise control:

> **Media manager 1**: We are a little reluctant to allow someone who has only just begun to speak English in TV broadcasts to speak to the newspapers. What we tend to do is either have an interpreter on a match day so that the player can speak through an interpreter. Or there's a couple of journalists that we work with regularly that are Spanish speakers so basically the interview is in Spanish and then you're relying on that interpretation/translation to be sound. But one thing we do stress is not to hang the player on any controversial line. You know, anything that could be critical of the opposition team or players. That's an unspoken agreement.

These examples show that there are unspoken or advance agreements put in place which have direct and indirect economic implications. If the agreement is not followed, then the journalist may not benefit from precious access to the club's players. But does control over translated content in the EPL indeed constitute censorship?

Norms and Translation in Football

Billiani (2009: 32) describes censorship as 'acting against what lies in the space between acceptance and refusal: the ambiguous, the composite and, more importantly, what disturbs identity, system and order'. This description applies to the interventions made by media managers in the translation chain before and after text production, designed to eradicate messages which could destabilise the club. The omission of unnecessary information for a particular audience, however, is a routine practice in media culture (cf. Bielsa & Bassnett, 2009). This kind of textual interventionism is standardised and ingrained in football clubs. It is deemed so significant to produce a discourse which does not endanger the economic strength of a club that what may appear to be deliberate censorship is perhaps the exercise of relatively unconscious normative control. As Hermans (1996: 30) notes, norms are a prescriptive form of social convention which 'derive their legitimacy from shared knowledge, a pattern of mutual expectation and acceptance, and the fact that, on the individual level, they are largely internalised'. Norm theory in translation studies allows scholars to describe the norms which differ across text types and historical periods (e.g. Chesterman, 1993, 1998; Hermans, 1991, 1996; Toury, 1995). The debates around translation norms largely focus on translators' textual practices and on norms which can be observed in the behaviour of other agents. Consequently, media managers who exert power by influencing translated or interpreted texts can be seen as displaying normative behaviour within the social context of media communications.

Some of the criticism of norm theory is germane to debates about power and translation in football. Pym, for example, complained that 'theorists and describers of translational norms spectacularly sideline questions concerning power relationships or conflictual social groups' (1998: 111, also highlighted by Baker, 2009: 193) and Baker stresses that norm theory does not take account of individual or collective resistance to norms, be it in the cultural, behavioural or textual domains:

> Norm theory encourages analysts to focus on repeated, abstract, systematic behaviour, and in so doing privileges strong patterns of socialization into that behaviour and tends to gloss over the numerous individual and group attempts at undermining dominant patterns and prevailing political and social dogma. Similarly, norm theory has nothing to say on the intricate patterns of interplay between repeated, stable patterns of behaviour and the continuous attempts at subverting that behavior, the interplay between dominance and resistance. (Baker, 2007: 152)

In order to analyse translation in conflict, Baker uses the critical tool of narrative theory, in part because 'by contrast to static power-insensitive concepts like norms, narrative theory recognises that dominance and resistance not only shape our discursive choices but are always in a relationship of tension' (2007: 167). In the context of elite sports, the most pre-eminent examples of resistance and subversion to the dominant norms of media manager control are unauthorised interviews conducted by football players in their first language, which come to the attention of media managers through translation. The most high-profile instances in which this resistance is visible in the media surrounds the transfer of players. An elite migrant player looking for a transfer or a salary increase will conduct an unauthorised interview in his native language and make comments which express his desire to leave his club or which are critical of his club or manager. When the comments are reported in the English media there is an immediate get-out clause to save face which is to blame poor translation, or to explain that the words were taken out of context. The player thus achieves his objective of alerting other clubs to his desire to leave or of bargaining for a higher wage, but does not necessarily damage his reputation in the eyes of his employer and the fans because he can blame translation. This strategy can be observed quite regularly (Baines, 2011), as a translator and a media manager both commented:

> **Translator**: The whole kind of 'blame it on translation' thing is a sort of standard gambit; you go and say something to the press back home in the knowledge that it will filter back and if you need to beat a retreat once it's out there, you say it wasn't me, it wasn't what I said.

> **Media manager 1**: It has been used with players and clubs to say, I didn't mean to say that, when probably they have kind of touched on a contro-versial subject. It comes back in English that X player has criticised X club. How do you prove it? I'm not comfortable with that tactic at all. We've had this in the past. We go to the player: 'Did you say this in a Spanish newspaper? It's in *The Sun* newspaper'. The player says 'No I didn't say that', so we go back to *The Sun* newspaper and say 'The player is adamant that he didn't say that. Where did you get it from?'

The media manager also noted that today many publications film inter-views for their websites, and this ready availability of a verifiable source text has diminished the practice of saying one thing in one language and denying it in another (see Giulianotti & Robertson, 2007b: 179).

What is remarkable in these incidents is that rarely is any effort made to find out what was really said and how it has been translated. The fact that these incidents are not examined in great detail is doubtless a conse-quence of sports news being abundant and fast-moving. It is the headline story which provides economic benefits to the media outlet, something which careful analysis of foreign language interviews and their translation could not achieve.

Mismatches between interests can also occur more innocently. In the following example, a former EPL player recounted an interview given in his home country where he negatively compared his English club's playing style to that of a club in his home country. Once the interview came to light through translation, he was hauled up in front of the manager:

> **Former EPL player:** I remember saying, well, we don't play the same system, it's not the same football, and that was interpreted from the point of view of my club in quite a bad way, in a bad way. I remember I was called to the manager's office and he said 'You can't say things like that'. I said 'I didn't say anything. I just said it's not the same way of playing football, not the same way of training and it was interpreted in the wrong way'. Translating from French to English, words don't mean the same, and yeah, I had my hands slapped.

The club deemed the player not to have had the organisation's interests at heart and exerted power by applying sanctions in the form of a fine, which shows that media managers are concerned with sustaining a narrative about their club to protect its status and reputation. They can do this because of the power that derives from their managerial position, but players communicating with the media independently of their clubs take back a measure of control and use translation as a tool to achieve their aims. Their power has a similar character to the power of media managers, since their status, reputation and wealth facilitate the circulation of narratives that suit their, and their agents', interests. To make an extreme comparison, a migrant cockle-picker unhappy with the way she or he is being treated does not have the status, let alone the resources, to arrange an interview in his or her home country, and even if such an interview were to take place it would not be of interest to mass media. This shows that, with translation as a 'bargaining tool', media managers and elite migrant players are able to affect public narratives.

Narrative Control and the Media

Various scholars have undertaken analyses of ideologically motivated manipulations of news texts in translation that reinforce particular discourses (e.g. Baker, 2006, 2007; Harding, 2012; Schäffner, 2012; Schäffner & Bassnett, 2010). What is of most relevance here is Baker's deployment of framing techniques within narrative theory to investigate translation and conflict. She defines framing as 'an active strategy that implies agency and by means of which we consciously participate in the construction of reality' (Baker, 2007: 107) and she shows how a range of reframing techniques are used in translation to activate narratives which support particular ideological positions. These include the choice of images, captions, titles, the use of paratexts, lexical choices and, particularly relevant for the purposes of this chapter, 'selective appropriation' (Baker, 2006: 50). In news reporting, additions and omissions tend to be evidence of intervention from outside forces, which often result from the pressure to adapt to certain public narratives. Narrative strategies used by club media managers to control texts mediated through translation and interpreting indicate similar methods of selective appropriation. Whether the interventions involve *post factum* intervention or pre-emptive management of the likely content of interviews, the overall purpose of the public relations work is to ensure the reinforcement of a larger narrative. Narratives embedded in the discourse of football media managers have historical roots that reflect a club's standing, reputation and status on a national and increasingly also global scale, considering that such narratives are frequently promoted by global media coverage and global branding. Davis observes the same practices of media control in corporate finance and politics, noting that there is 'ample evidence of overt control being exerted over news content on behalf of powerful groups and institutions in society' (Davis, 2007: 57). For him, the development of public relations and media management has been

> [a] fundamental tool during the steady shift towards neo-liberal (or 'neo-con') political, economic and military agendas since the Reagan–Thatcher years. Taxation systems, union legislation, welfare state management and employment law, have all been altered in ways that benefit large corporations and the wealthy. (Davis, 2007: 57)

Football club media managers and the public relations operations that wealthy football clubs now orchestrate are a good example of how powerful corporations exert control to generate a coherent body of statements which produce self-confirming accounts of reality. And such accounts frequently need to operate across linguistic boundaries. The power of the media to reinforce or contest the broad narratives of football clubs should not be underestimated. It may appear that media managers are the most powerful figures in the dynamics at work in the translational mediation of player interviews, yet club media managers are dependent on media outlets to disseminate the narratives, and the media themselves are implicated in wider mechanisms of social power, as van Dijk explains:

> Leading politicians, managers, scholars, or other professionals have more or less controlled access to [...] media discourse [...]. If such elites are able to control these patterns of media access, they are by definition more powerful than the media. On the other hand, those media that are able to control access to elite discourse, in such a way that elites become dependent on them in order to exercise their own power, may in turn play their own role in the power structure. (van Dijk, 1995: 12)

The examples of resistance to the power of media managers when the interests of a club, a player and his agent are divergent exhibit the same power dynamics as those between media managers and the media. The players who give unauthorised interviews to journalists from their home country in their native language are generally motivated by the desire to increase earnings or to force a move to another club. Even though such behaviour may adversely affect the public narrative about a club, it is underpinned by the same economic principles. Unauthorised interviews can produce sensational headlines which generate income, and these headlines can be enhanced through the selective appropriation of translated material. An interview conducted by the former Arsenal player Nicklas Bendtner in the Danish media is a case in point (Baines, 2011). Bendtner remarked in Danish that when he is playing at his best he should always be selected, yet he was inaccurately quoted as virtually demanding that 'I should start every game, I should be playing every minute of every match and always be in the team', which resulted in a manipulated narrative and thus a more lucrative news story. The news report in the tabloid *The Daily Mirror* translated his confidence in his abilities into arrogance under the heading 'Big 'ead Bendtner' (Baines, 2011: 103–105).

Conclusion

The argument that, in a globalised world, power resides more in the marketplace than in the political arena is by no means a new one. Translating and interpreting processes are just as interwoven into these market-driven power dynamics as other kinds of communication. First-hand accounts from the agents involved in the translation chains bring a new perspective to debates about power and translation in sport. The control that media managers exert over translated and interpreted media discourse is not, strictly speaking, censorship, but normative behaviour in a context where public relations are critical to the economic well-being of a club. This is indeed typical public relations behaviour in a marketplace where the monetary stakes are so high. Similarly, the behaviour of players who participate in unauthorised press interviews in languages other than English and then question the translation of those interviews tends to be underpinned by economic objectives. Self-confirming narratives that clubs promote uphold their status and reputation, which support a brand and the consumption of that brand. Any need for translation and interpreting renders the shaping and protecting of such narratives more challenging for media managers, and it also opens up ways in which players can contest them. The main vehicle for these narratives is the attitude of sports journalists to translated material. They follow unspoken agreements with club media managers to protect their access to the players and exploit the potential of translated texts to produce more lucrative stories. Such behaviour is just as economically motivated as the behaviour of club media managers and players. The pivots in this interlingual communication chain are translators and interpreters. Interpreters, in particular, also face situations which present economic and ethical challenges, when a club can exert pressure on them to protect its image. Shifting tensions between media managers, interpreters, translators, players/agents and the media over representation through translation and interpreting reflect conflicting power struggles. The goal of improving or protecting economic status, however, is a shared one.

References

Interviews

Interpreter 1 (2013), interviewed by author, 20 August.
Interpreter 2 (2014), interviewed by author, 17 July.
Interpreter 3 (2014), interviewed by author, 28 October.
Interpreter 4 (2016), private email, 7 November.
Media manager 1 (2013), interviewed by author, 19 July.
Media manager 2 (2014), interviewed by author, 4 February.
Former EPL player (2014), interviewed by author, 23 July.
Translator (2013), interviewed by author, 20 August.

Secondary sources

Baines, R. (2011) The journalist, the translator, the player and his agent: Games of (mis)representation and (mis)translation in British media reports about non-anglophone football players. In B. Maher and R. Wilson (eds) *Words, Images and Performances in Translation* (pp. 100–118). London: Continuum.
Baines, R. (2013) Translation, globalization and the elite migrant athlete. *The Translator* 19 (2), 207–228.
Baker, M. (2006) *Translation and Conflict*. London: Routledge.
Baker, M. (2007) Reframing conflict in translation. *Social Semiotics* 17 (2), 151–169.
Baker, M. (2009) Norms. In M. Baker and G. Saldanha (eds) *Routledge Encyclopedia of Translation Studies* (2nd edn) (pp. 189–193). London: Routledge.
Bielsa, E. and Bassnett, S. (eds) (2009) *Translation in Global News*. London: Routledge.
Billiani, F. (2009) Censorship. In M. Baker and G. Saldanha (eds) *The Routledge Encyclopedia of Translation Studies* (2nd edn) (pp. 28–32). London: Routledge.
Brandwatch (2013) *Analysis of Barclays Premier League Sponsorship*, at http://www.brandwatch.com/wp-content/uploads/2013/05/Brandwatch-Barclays-Premier-League-Report-May-2013.pdf, accessed 8 July 2014.
Bridgewater, S. (2010) *Football Brands*. Basingstoke: Palgrave Macmillan.
CBI/Pearson Education (2013) *Changing the Pace: CBI/Pearson Education and Skills Survey 2013*, at http://www.cbi.org.uk/media/2119176/education_and_skills_survey_2013.pdf, accessed 15 August 2013.
Chesterman, A. (1993) From 'is' to 'ought': Laws, norms and strategies in translation studies. *Target* 5 (1), 1–20.
Chesterman, A. (1998) Description, explanation, prediction: A response to Gideon Toury and Theo Hermans. *Current Issues in Language and Society* 5 (1–2), 91–98.
Cogo, A. (2009) Accommodating difference in ELF conversations: A study of pragmatic strategies. In A. Mauranen and E. Ranta (eds) *English as a Lingua Franca: Studies and Findings* (pp. 254–273). Newcastle: Cambridge Scholars Publishing.
Davis, A. (2007) *The Mediation of Power: A Critical Introduction*. London: Routledge.
ESPN Staff (2015) Premier League clubs to top NFL TV earnings by 2017 – UEFA report, at http://www.espnfc.co.uk/barclays-premier-league/story/2676914/premier-league-clubs-to-overtake-nfl-tv-earning-by-2017-uefa, accessed 1 November 2015.

Fawcett, P. (1995) Translation and power play. *The Translator* 1 (2), 177–192.

FIFA (2014) *Transfer Trends Revealed in FIFA TMS Annual Report,* 15 February, at http://www.fifa.com/aboutfifa/organisation/news/newsid=2266864, accessed 31 May 2014.

Giulianotti, R. and Robertson, R. (eds) (2007a) *Globalization and Sport.* London: Blackwell.

Giulianotti, R. and Robertson, R. (2007b) Recovering the social: Globalization, football and transnationalism. *Global Networks* 7 (2), 166–186.

Harding, S. (2012) How do I apply narrative theory? Socio-narrative theory in translation studies. *Target* 24 (2), 286–309.

Hermans, T. (1991) Translational norms and correct translations. In K.M. van Leuven-Zwart and T. Naaijkens (eds) *Translation Studies: The State of the Art* (pp. 155–169). Amsterdam: Rodopi.

Hermans, T. (1996) Norms and the determination of translation: A theoretical framework. In R. Álvarez and M.C. África Vidal (eds) *Translation, Power, Subversion* (pp. 25–51). Clevedon: Multilingual Matters.

Jones, D. (2015) Foreword. In A. Bull, A. Bosshardt, M. Green, C. Hanson, J. Savage, C. Stenson and A. Thorpe (eds) *Revolution: Deloitte Annual Review of Football Finance 2015 – Highlights,* at http://www2.deloitte.com/content/dam/Deloitte/uk/Documents/sports-business-group/deloitte-uk-arff-2015-highlights.pdf, accessed 1 September 2015.

Kuhiwczak, P. (2011) Translation and censorship. *Translation Studies* 4 (3), 358–373.

Lawrence, G. and Rowe, D. (1986) Introduction: Towards a sociology of sport in Australia. In D. Rowe and G. Lawrence (eds) *Power Play: Essays in the Sociology of Australian Sport* (pp. 13–45). Sydney: Hale and Iremonger.

Magee, J. and Sugden, J. (2002) 'The world at their feet': Professional football and international labor migration. *Journal of Sport and Social Issues* 26 (4), 421–437.

Maguire, J. (1996) Blade runners: Canadian migrants, ice hockey and the global sports. *Journal of Sport and Social Issues* 20 (3), 335–360.

Maguire, J. (ed.) (2005) *Power and Global Sport.* London: Routledge.

Maguire, J. (2011) The global media sports complex: Key issues and concerns. *Sport in Society* 14 (7–8), 965–977.

Palumbo, G. (2009) *Key Terms in Translation Studies.* London: Bloomsbury.

Pym, A. (1998) *Method in Translation History.* Manchester: St Jerome.

Savoie, D.J. (2010) *Power: Where Is It?* Montreal: McGill Queen's University Press.

Schäffner, C. (2012) Unknown agents in translated political discourse. *Target* 24 (1), 103–125.

Schäffner, C. and Bassnett, S. (2010) Politics, media and translation – exploring synergies. In C. Schäffner and S. Bassnett (eds) *Political Discourse, Media and Translation* (pp. 1–29). Newcastle: Cambridge Scholars Publishing.

Simpson, A. (2014) A league of its own. *The Linguist* 53 (3), 18–19.

Sky Sports (2017) Premier League has highest percentage of foreign players – UEFA report, 10 January, at http://www.skysports.com/football/news/11661/10725849/premier-league-has-highest-percentage-of-foreign-players-8211-uefa-report, accessed 3 November 2017.

Smart, B. (2007) Not playing around: Global capitalism, modern sport and consumer culture. In R. Giulianotti and R. Robertson (eds) *Globalization and Sport* (pp. 6–27). London: Blackwell.

Sugden, J. (2002) Network football. In J. Sugden and A. Tomlinson (eds) *Power Games: A Critical Sociology of Sport* (pp. 61–80). London: Routledge.

Sugden, J. and Tomlinson, A. (eds) (2002) *Power Games: A Critical Sociology of Sport.* London: Routledge.

Toury, G. (1995) *Descriptive Translation Studies and Beyond.* Amsterdam: John Benjamins.

van Dijk, T.A. (1995) Power and the news media. In D. Paletz (ed.) *Political Communication and Action* (pp. 9–36). Cresskill, NJ: Hampton Press.

12 How Global Conglomerates Influence Translation Practice: Film Title Translation in Turkey

Jonathan Ross

The Film Title as a Global Marketing Device

In *Translation and Globalisation*, Michael Cronin contends that '[t]he global age is characterised in its most banal form by the rise of giant multinational corporations and by the local consumption of global goods and images' (2003: 57). This certainly holds true for the film sector. Across the world, cinema, television, computer and mobile-phone screens are dominated by films produced and distributed by a handful of largely US-based companies, the so-called majors (Warner Bros., Sony Columbia, Walt Disney, Universal, 20th Century Fox, Paramount), which are owned by global media conglomerates. However, the versions of these films that audiences in different countries get to see are by no means identical. Whether motivated by (self-)censorship or the desire to conform to local norms and expectations, certain scenes may be removed, added or altered when a film is screened in a new territory (Gambier, 2003: 181). The modification of non-verbal visual elements, of course, is not the only way in which a film can be changed when exported to other countries, since the rendition of verbal elements through some form of audio-visual translation inevitably also leads to shifts.

The fact that audiences around the planet are exposed to variants of the 'same' film lends weight to the argument of Cronin (2003), Bielsa (2005) and others that grasping the impact of globalisation means more than just recognising the spread of cultural goods across the globe; it also entails appreciating the distinct forms in which global goods present themselves to local audiences. Consequently, we should not ignore the role of translation in the international flow of cultural goods, as so many theories of globalisation seem to do (Bielsa, 2005). In this chapter, I will not be looking at the translation of films themselves but rather at the translation of another kind of text that helps films to travel; this is the film title, one of the key marketing devices deployed in the film industry. Like the multimodal marketing texts in which they appear, such as posters, trailers, teasers and websites, titles can be regarded as what Gérard Genette calls 'paratexts', which 'offer the world at large the possibility of either stepping inside or turning back' (1987: 1f.). Genette devotes considerable space to titles attached to literary works (Genette, 1987: 55–103), but he has little to say about either film titles or the commercial environment in which the production of paratexts takes place. Christiane Nord (1993, 1995) has examined the translation of titles for printed works, but she too devotes little attention to film titles.

The current chapter deals with the choice of titles for film imports within the Turkish film sector in 2012. Whereas much of the existing literature on title translation offers an undifferentiating and relatively de-contextualised overview of translation practices, I wish to explore whether there are any significant differences between title translations carried out by three different types of distributor operating in Turkey:

- *major studios* – local branches of Warner Bros. and United International Pictures (UIP), the former based in the US, the latter a London-based joint venture of Paramount Pictures and Universal Studios;
- *major-linked independent distributors* – local companies with an ongoing agreement to distribute the products of a certain studio, for instance Tiglon Film, which formerly distributed the films of 20th Century Fox and Lionsgate;
- *independent distributors* – local companies that import and distribute films on an individual basis.

The Translation of Film Titles

According to Robert Marich (2009: 25), '[a]n evocative title can be the most effective single element of creative material in a broad marketing program'. Whenever people mention a title, they draw attention to the existence of a film and potentially help expand its audience, so the professionals who choose titles for films usually opt for ones that are easy to pronounce and memorise. This would explain why, when marketing the children's cartoon film *Ratatouille* internationally, the animation studio Pixar-Disney decided to retain the French title in countries that use the Latin alphabet but to indicate the local pronunciation of this title with vernacular phonetic notation. In our age, of course, titles of films are passed on not through spoken or printed discourse alone, for 'electronic word of mouth' via the internet also helps to publicise films (Hennig-Thurau *et al.*, 2004).

Despite the importance of the title for marketing films abroad, there is scant scholarly literature on the translation of film titles, with the academic discipline of film marketing studies showing even less interest than the translation research community (e.g. Kerrigan, 2010; van de Kamp, 2009). Several translation scholars (e.g. Bulut, 2001; Yin, 2009; Ying, 2007) propose taxonomies for the different procedures followed when translating film titles, including literal translation, non-translation, addition of explanatory subtitle and so on. Some researchers have conducted statistical analyses of patterns in title translation in certain territories over a certain period (e.g. Gärtner & Schlatter, 2001, on Brazil and Germany; Schubert, 2004, on Germany; Cioranu, 2010, on Romania; Berdis, 2013, on the Czech Republic). González Ruiz (2000, 2001) is one of the few who has pursued a contextualising, target-oriented approach, tracing the influence of religious-ideological and commercial pressures in the titling of foreign films in Franco's Spain. In Turkey, Doğan (2012) set out to ascertain whether members of the public responded to film-titling strategies in the ways in which film distributors expected them. She compared findings from surveys of cinema-goers with responses to a questionnaire for film distributors, gathering information from people involved in the *process* of choosing titles for film imports in Turkey instead of basing her judgements purely on translational *products*. Her research has provided novel insights into the 'real world' dimensions of film title translation.

One of the most interesting of these dimensions is the way the title interacts with other marketing materials, such as the images and tagline on a poster (Kerrigan, 2010: 130–140). Another point sometimes omitted or misrepresented in the literature on film title translation is the identity of those responsible for their translation. Several authors (e.g. Cioranu, 2010: 29; Yin, 2009: 173) maintain that this is done by the 'translators' of the film. Empirical research involving interviews and questionnaires, however, has revealed that the choice of titles usually falls to marketing experts rather than translators (Bravo, 2004: 227; Doğan, 2012; Gärtner & Schlatter, 2001: 85; Martí & Zapater, 1993: 85; Ross, 2013). What is more, only Doğan and I appear to have noted the control that the key people involved in film-making, including the executives of the financing studio, can have over the choice of titles in territories besides the one(s) where the film was initially produced. This is especially the case when the local distributor is allied to one of the majors, which are responsible for producing and distributing a large share of the films screened in Turkey, as in most countries.

Film Distribution: Majors and Independents

The majors are organised in the Motion Picture Association of America (MPAA). They belong to massive media and entertainment conglomerates such as Sony (Columbia Pictures) and Time Warner (Warner Bros.), which are also involved in cable and network television, publishing, the internet and music recording (Boyce, 2001: 214). The majors' success rests on their organisation into 'vertically integrated' structures, whose divisions, branches and subsidiaries manage all stages of the cinematic process. This enables them to cut costs and to ensure that all those engaged in the process have 'a common creative vision' and that the films have 'a coherent identity and message' (Kerrigan, 2010: 26). The clearest proof of the majors' power and success is the sheer number of films they produce and distribute. According to Marich (2009: 232), in an average year, productions from major studios account for around 97% of box-office takings in the US. In 2014, Kanzler observed that Turkey was the only film market in Europe where total ticket sales for local productions regularly outstripped those for US imports (2014: 1); in 2018, this continues to be the case. Since around 2003, Turkish cinema has been experiencing a renaissance, on a par with the golden age *Yeşilçam era* (between the 1950s and 1970s). In 2012, seven of the top 10 films in Turkey (and all of the top three) were local productions. However, 11 of the top 20 films and 51 of the top 100 films were made in the US by one of the major studios, and four of the seven most popular local productions were distributed in Turkey by UIP or Warner Bros., testifying to the conspicuous presence of the majors on Turkish screens too (these and all subsequent box-office data from Turkey are derived from the authoritative website boxofficeturkiye. com, accessed 24 March 2015).

In Turkey, foreign films – which largely means English-language US productions (Kanzler, 2014: 7) – reach cinemas through one of three channels. Firstly, a film by Warner Bros. or by one of the stakeholders in UIP will probably be distributed by the Turkish branch of Warner Bros. or UIP, respectively. Secondly, a foreign film may be distributed and marketed by an independent company that has agreed to serve as the local representative of a certain film-producing studio. Finally, a distributor might buy the rights to films on an individual basis, either directly from the production company or through an international sales agent (Kerrigan, 2010: 155). The process of title translation varies considerably, depending in part on the identity of the local distributor and on its relationship with the film-producing studio, aspects that have so far been neglected in the literature on film title translation.

Title Translation by Major Branches or Major-Linked Independent Distributors in Turkey

The titles of films commissioned by a major studio are normally chosen by film producers and directors in conjunction with company executives and marketing experts. Besides selecting a (usually) English-language title for the US and Canada, the studio will devise one or more English-language international titles, intended to serve as source texts for translated titles. These titles are then communicated to the studio's overseas offices, together with a plot synopsis, notes by the creative team, an American teaser and samples of posters. It is worth noting that in most countries local distributors use the posters prepared by the studio's US-marketing department. Tailor-made posters are produced (also in the US) only for countries like Japan, France, Russia and the UK which have a large cinema-going population and thus promise sizeable box-office revenues. Distributors in other territories may use these bespoke designs, the North American materials or the international versions, as long as they can justify their choice (Milli, 2014). Foreign distributors (and even American distributors) might not have the chance to see the finished film before they devise a title for it, which can lead to the selection of titles that fail to reflect the actual content of the movie (Berdis, 2013: 14).

It is usually the responsibility of the studio's regional headquarters – the London office in the case of UIP and Warner Bros. – to negotiate marketing issues like title choices with the studio's Turkish distributor. The regional office passes on instructions from the studio headquarters and creative team. It may inform the Turkish distributor that an original or international title should be retained verbatim. However, it may allow minor orthographic alterations, such as the replacement of the name *Shrek* with the Turkish *Şrek*. The regional office might demand a maximally literal translation, specify a range of 'acceptable' translation strategies or give the Turkish distributor (and, for that matter, subsidiaries of the studio in other territories) free range to translate as they see fit. As in the US, the task of drawing up a shortlist of possible title translations may be farmed out to an advertising agency (Özyiğit, 2011). In contrast to the US, though, market testing of titles appears to be nonexistent in Turkey, as in fact in the rest of the world (Kerrigan, 2010: 50). In Turkey, moreover, there is no institutional equivalent to the MPAA's Title Registration Bureau (see McCarthy, 2002), and copyright law protects titles only if they have a distinguishing character and are not in general use, so it is quite common for the same title to be used for several films in the same year (Ross, 2008).

Having selected a title, the Turkish distributor informs the London office. Unless the translated title is identical to the original, the distributor will provide a back-translation and explanation of the Turkish title. In consultation with the studio headquarters and creative team, the London office will then either approve or reject the Turkish distributor's choice. The latter may push for a certain choice of title, arguing that it is more familiar with the local film sector and film-going public; ultimately, though, it can market a film under a certain name only if it has the approval of the studio (Taçkın, 2015). Indeed, now that revenues for most Hollywood films outside the US outstrip domestic revenues (Eliashberg *et al.*, 2006: 650), the majors attach considerable importance to international marketing strategies, including the choice of titles for their films abroad. UIP-Turkey's marketing manager has acknowledged that the local naming strategy 'must be parallel to the strategy which is cleared by the studio'

(Özyiğit, 2011). The majors always have the last word, and their power to enforce the choice of certain titles rarely appears to be challenged by local branches or partners.

It is very unusual for a distribution company affiliated to a major to proceed with a title and marketing materials before having received approval for the translation. This occurred with Quentin Tarantino's *Inglourious Basterds* (2009), which was distributed in Turkey by UIP. Presumably to underline the wartime action genre of the film – 'genre-marking' being a very common practice in film title translation in Turkey (Ross, 2013: 257) – the title was initially translated as *İsimsiz Kahramanlar* (*Nameless Heroes*) and posters using this title were printed. But once UIP's regional office heard about the choice, it demanded that the title be changed (Karahan, 2014). The Turkish title was thought to present too unequivocally positive an image of the Jewish-American group of Nazi-hunters in World War II, whereas UIP wanted the title to tie in with the name that the group gave themselves: 'Basterds'. Furthermore, the choice of the original title (itself a modification of *Inglorious Bastards*, the English translation of a 1978 Italian war film *Quel Maledetto Treno Blindato*; literally, 'That Damned Armoured Train') had been very much associated with the director, Tarantino, who may have disapproved of the overly 'free' Turkish rendition. For this reason, the semantically closer translation *Soysuzlar Çetesi* (*Gang of Bastards*) was chosen and new Turkish marketing materials were prepared. The cost of producing these new materials, however, dented the profits UIP made on this film (Karahan, 2014).

Title Translation by Independent Distributors in Turkey

The process of title translation differs when a foreign film is distributed in Turkey by an entirely independent distributor. Such companies tend to distribute films by independent studios, whose wealth and leverage is in no way comparable to those of the majors. Their lack of economic firepower makes independent studios heavily dependent on financing from other companies, such as investors, distributors and television channels. In exchange for this funding, independent studios cede certain rights to their partners (van de Kamp, 2009: 51), for instance the right to choose a film title. In fact, when a Turkish distributor decides to buy rights to a particular foreign film from a non-major studio, it effectively claims ownership of it. According to Tolga Akıncı, head of distribution at the independent Medyavizyon, '[a] company buying a film can behave just as it wants. If we think of a film as a product, a good, that good is ours, so we can market it under whatever title we please' (Akıncı, 2011; my translation).

Very rarely, a small independent distributor in Turkey will agree to market a big-budget film produced by a large independent or major studio. In such circumstances, the production and distribution companies will make specific legal arrangements, which might give the studio ultimate control over the choice of title (Taçkın, 2015). However, this is more the exception than the rule, since Turkish independent companies usually distribute films made by smaller studios in the US or elsewhere. In this case, the foreign studio informs the Turkish distributor of the planned foreign title and provides it with materials such as a synopsis and sample posters, without setting any translation commission. Then, the Turkish distributor simply decides on the title and informs the studio of its choice, without requiring its approval.

Patterns in Title Translation in Turkey

Thus, the process of title translation depends on the type of local distributor and on this distributor's relationship to the foreign studio. But what impact (if any) does this process have on actual translational products, that is, the titles given to film imports? To offer at least a tentative answer to this question, I analysed the tactics used to translate the titles of the 230 foreign films among the top 300 releases in Turkey in 2012, drawing on a *typology of translation tactics* from a previous study of film title translation in Turkey and Slovenia in 2009 (Ross, 2013).[1] The 12 tactics comprising the typology are presented in Table 12.1, with examples from the Turkish context.

In this typology, the tactic 'transposition' means 'replacing one word class with another without changing the meaning of the message',

Table 12.1 Tactics used in translating film titles in Turkey in 2012

Translation tactic	Turkish film title	English literal back-translation of Turkish title	Original film title (from imdb.com)
Non-translation	*Skyfall*	Skyfall	*Skyfall*
Transcription	*Dr. Seuss Loraks*	Dr. Seuss Lorax	*Dr. Seuss' The Lorax*
Literal translation	*Açlık Oyunları*	The Hunger Games	*The Hunger Games*
Established idiomatic equivalent	Vur ve Kaç	Hit and Escape	*Hit and Run*
Transposition	*Sürücü*	Driver	*Drive*
Modulation	*Koruyucu*	Protector	*Safe*
Other minor semantic shift	*Zamana Karşı*	Against Time	*In Time*
Amplification	*Dehşet Kapanı*	Terror Trap	*The Cabin in the Woods*
Reduction	Korsanlar!	Pirates!	*The Pirates! Band of Misfits*
'Free' (semantic connection retained)	*Pamuk Prenses'in Maceraları*	The Adventures of Snow White	*Mirror Mirror*
'Free' (no apparent semantic connection)	*Can Dostum*	My Soulmate	*Intouchables*
Title with precedent	*Alacakaranlık Efsanesi: Şafak Vakti Bölüm 1*	The Twilight Saga: Dawn Part 1	*The Twilight Saga: Breaking Dawn – Part 1*

Table 12.2 Total frequencies of the deployment of the four most common tactics

Tactic	2012 (n=230)	2009 (Ross, 2013) (n=146)
Literal translation	101 (44%)	65 (45%)
Amplification	87 (38%)	44 (30%)
'Free' translation	70 (30%)	36 (25%)
Non-translation/transcription	54 (23%)	35 (24%)

while 'modulation' constitutes 'a variation of the form of the message, obtained by a change in the point of view' (Vinay & Darbelnet, 1958: 36). The tactic 'amplification' is understood as introducing details that are unformulated or implicit in the source text (adapted from Molina & Hurtado Albir, 2002: 510), a practice which other translation scholars call explicitation, addition, paraphrase or periphrasis. 'Reduction' includes omission and implicitation. It must also be noted that one translated title may incorporate more than one tactic, for instance non-translation plus the addition of a subtitle, which comprises both free translation and amplification. Therefore, the sum total of tactic deployments for each of the two years shown in Table 12.2 exceeds the number of film titles translated in that year. Table 12.2 gives the impression that film distributors generally opted for the same balance of tactics in both years. However, when we compare the tactics applied by individual independent distributors with those followed by major-linked distributors, a more complex picture emerges. According to the statistics (see Table 12.3), literal translation was a common method among all the distributors, but non-translation and transcription were resorted to with significantly greater frequency by the major studios' branches and by Tiglon than they were by the independents.

As indicated in Table 12.3, only a small proportion of UIP and Warner Bros. releases (17% and 8% respectively) had their titles translated 'freely', whereas the independents were more likely to resort to 'free' translation (between a quarter and a half of titles). Since 'free' title translations usually serve to give a clearer indication of the genre and film plots than original titles – for example *Ruhlar Oteli* (*Hotel of Spirits*) as a rendition of *The Innkeepers*, the title of a horror film – it is not surprising that a large proportion of the independents' titles involved amplification. Recourse to this semantic tactic was conspicuously less common in the case of Warner Bros. and UIP.

Blockbuster Titles as Brands

The generally accepted definition of a blockbuster is a film that grosses at least $100 million in box office receipts in the US (Eliashberg *et al.*, 2006: 647). Such films tend to enjoy brand status from the outset, since they are often marketed as continuations of popular film series, or

Table 12.3 Distributor-by-distributor frequencies of the deployment of the four most common translation tactics for titles of 2012 releases

	Local branch of major studio		Independent								
	UIP	WB	Tiglon	Pinema	M3 Film	Medya-vizyon	Chantier Films	Özen Film	Duka Film	Bir Film	Movie-box
No. of foreign releases (% of total foreign releases)	41 (17.8%)	24 (10.4%)	65 (28.2%)	33 (14.3%)	27 (11.7%)	14 (6.1%)	11 (4.8%)	8 (3.5%)	4 (1.7%)	2 (0.9%)	1 (0.4%)
Translation tactic											
Non-translation/transcription	15 (37%)	6 (25%)	18 (28%)	4 (12%)	4 (15%)	2 (14%)	2 (18%)	2 (25%)	0 (0%)	1 (50%)	0 (0%)
Literal	18 (44%)	15 (63%)	20 (31%)	15 (45%)	16 (59%)	3 (21%)	7 (64%)	6 (75%)	1 (25%)	0 (0%)	0 (0%)
'Free'	7 (17%)	2 (8%)	27 (42%)	14 (42%)	7 (26%)	6 (43%)	1 (9%)	1 (13%)	3 (75%)	1 (50%)	1 (100%)
Amplification	10 (24%)	5 (21%)	30 (46%)	17 (52%)	10 (37%)	9 (64%)	1 (9%)	0 (0%)	3 (75%)	1 (50%)	1 (100%)
Precedent	20 (49%)	13 (54%)	17 (26%)	6 (18%)	3 (11%)	3 (21%)	3 (27%)	3 (38%)	0 (0%)	0 (0%)	1 (100%)

they are based on well known cultural franchises such as television series, comics, books and video games. Only the majors and one or two large independent distributors possess the capital, infrastructure, experience and clout needed to distribute and market films of this kind. One reason why major-linked distributors are more likely to deploy the tactics of non-translation, transcription and literal translation is that a significant proportion of the films are big-budget productions designed to be globally recognised brands. Examples from 2012 are *Ice Age 4: Continental Shift* (the highest-grossing foreign film), which Tiglon translated literally as *Buz Devri 4: Kıtalar Ayrılıyor* ('Ice Age 4: The Continents Separate'), *Paranormal Activity IV*, whose title UIP retained verbatim, and the first part of the trilogy cinema version of Tolkien's fantasy novel, *The Hobbit: An Unexpected Journey*, which Warner Bros. rendered using a combination of non-translation and literal translation as *Hobbit: Beklenmedik Yolculuk*.

When we conceptualise such films as brands (cf. O'Reilly & Kerrigan, 2013), it becomes easier to understand why the companies that distribute them tend to be associated with certain title-translation tactics. In *Translating Promotional and Advertising Texts*, Ira Torresi (2010: 21–23) pinpoints four main ways in which brand names are rendered in a new target language. The first and most common is to use *non-translation*, followed by *transcription* and by making *minor changes* to the brand title in order not to violate taboos or introduce unwanted connotations. The application of *literal translation* may also serve to uphold a brand, since it assists film-viewers with knowledge of English to connect the Turkish title with a film they may well already know by another (English) name. This is indeed highly likely in today's digitally interconnected world, where people can access news about film releases in English before such information appears in their own language.

Several scholars have noted the rise in the use of non-translation in recent decades (Bravo, 2004: 227; Gärtner & Schlatter, 2001: 86; Martí & Zapater, 1993: 81; Nord, 1993: 48f.; Schubert, 2004: 251–253). As people everywhere deepen their knowledge of English, it becomes more likely that English titles, even in highly idiomatic and colloquial language, will be widely understood. In addition, the global spread of Anglophone (especially US) pop and youth culture (Schubert, 2004: 257) has made English appear ever 'cooler', especially among the young, the main film-viewing population in most countries (Kochberg, 1996: 38). Piller (2001) maintains, moreover, that the deployment of foreign languages in advertisements (particularly if one of the languages is English) helps to construct a *global consumer identity* in a world where multilingualism is valourised but English is dominant. Hence, employing an English word or phrase as or within a film title is a marketing strategy in itself (Piller, 2001: 163).

Although distributors of all types in Turkey sometimes retain English-language titles for film releases, this tactic is pronounced among distributors with major connections. A significant proportion of the films distributed by Warner Bros., UIP and Tiglon are conceptualised and marketed as international brands (see Table 12.3). Using a single title across the globe also brings the advantage that merchandise related to a film (toys, bed sheets, caps, mugs, etc.) can be produced in much bigger quantities for the entire world market, thereby enabling economies of scale (Bravo, 2004: 227). Additionally, a distribution company whose marketing is funded by a major studio will have access to a considerably larger budget than that available to Turkish distributors of independent and art-house films (Milli, 2014). A major-linked company can therefore distribute a significant quantity and variety of marketing materials, which can serve to forestall questions about the genre or film plot that an opaque foreign language title – such as *Skyfall* – may raise in the minds of potential viewers.

Major-Linked Distributors and Cross-cultural Power Play

When considering the translation tactics favoured by major-linked distributors, one also needs to bear in mind the international corporate power structures within which such distributors operate. As the apex of a hierarchical structure, the major studio can regulate the naming of films in 'overseas' territories even if local distributors resist this centralising position. As the former general director of Warner Bros.' Turkish branch conceded, 'it is hard to act "freely" in the titling of any Hollywood films' (Kaplanoğlu, 2014). The parent company, regional headquarters, Turkish subsidiary or contractual local distributor presumably share the aim of maximising box-office takings. However, there are inevitably occasions when the former two and the latter two disagree on how profits can be maximised and perhaps on other issues too. The 'creative talent' are likely to insist that the film be marketed (and thus titled) in a way that concurs with their vision of the film and with the image that they wish to project of themselves as individuals. Woody Allen, for instance, insisted as far back as 1978 that any contract between a studio making one of his films and the film's foreign distributors should include a clause advising distributors not to change the title without his express approval (Brisset, 2013). Studio executives will also be keen to promote the film in such a way that the reputation and values of the studio are upheld. However, due to cross-cultural and experiential differences, it might not always be possible to preserve the Hollywood-made marketing concept and still achieve box-office success; here particularly lies the potential for conflict between the film-makers and parent company on the one hand and the studio's local representatives on the other.

Mehmet Soyarslan, the owner and executive manager of the Turkish independent Özen Film, which represented 20th Century Fox in Turkey for 28 years, conceded that film producers in Hollywood sometimes insist on the retention of their English titles in Turkey (Soyarslan, 2009). Although unwilling to give any specific examples, possibly because he was still bound by non-disclosure agreements with former business partners (cf. van de Kamp, 2009: 102), Soyarslan emphasised that he occasionally resisted the demand from a major studio (presumably Fox) that the original English-language title of a film be used unchanged in Turkey (Soyarslan, 2009). Likewise, in her study of the marketing of Hollywood blockbusters in France, Danan (1995) emphasises that the US-based international marketing departments of two of the majors operating in the country, UIP and Warner Bros., were convinced that non-translation of titles was the way to push their brand films in that country in the mid-1990s. Around the time of the release of Steven Spielberg's blockbuster *Jurassic Park* (1993), UIP's London office even instructed UIP-France to convince the French publisher Laffont that new imprints of the book *Parc Jurassique* should carry the English title of the film. Similarly, UIP's headquarters insisted that *The Flintstones* be used as the French title for the feature-length version of this popular cartoon, even though the French marketing team warned that the English-language title would be a liability with the French public, because the television programme had appeared under the translated title *La famille Pierrafeu*. At first, the film was released with its English title, only to fail miserably, resulting in a re-release with the French title. This, however, seems to have been a rare triumph for the local branch, since in 1993 and 1994 UIP released about a third of its films in France under an English title, 'occasionally against the recommendation of the French team', while for Warner Bros. the figure even rose to around 50% (Danan, 1995: 138).

Independent Distributors and Title Translation: The Consequences of Commercial 'Freedom'

The translation decisions made by independent distributors appear to be quite different. In general, independents seem more prepared to stray from the source title. Moreover, a high proportion of amplification tactics (see Table 12.3) indicates a desire to produce a title with more explicit information about the film in question than the source title had provided. Certainly, the rather 'free' character of many title translations for independently distributed films has a lot to do with the films themselves and with the titles originally assigned to them. In most cases, the films distributed by Turkish independents are works by independent studios in the US or elsewhere. The titles of independent films, with their characteristic use of opacity, idiomatic language, word play or cultural-specific references, tend to pose more challenges to the translator than do mainstream Hollywood movies. One such example is the pun-based *What To Expect When You're Expecting*, which became *Dikkat Bebek Var* ('Watch Out – There's a Baby!'). Tuğçe Taçkın, who was responsible for marketing at Tiglon for four and a half years, has noted that, for Tiglon at least, specifying the genre of a film is the chief priority when translating the title:

We can't do word-for-word translations, because words don't have the same meanings in different languages. We take great pains to ensure that if it's a romantic film the title includes *aşk* [love] or if it's a horror film that it includes *ölüm* [death]. We were careful about this with the film *An Education* and opted for the title *Aşk Dersi* [*Lesson in Love*]. If we'd translated it as *Eğitim* [*Education*], this might have been the exact equivalent but it wouldn't have attracted an audience. (Cited in Keskin, 2010, my translation)

Tiglon's title choices may simply reflect a lack of creativity or derive from the practical imperative of finding a title in a short time. But such choices also need to be viewed in relation to the realities of the film sector in Turkey: independent companies distributing independent films do not have sufficient funds to conduct extensive marketing campaigns which they could use to clarify the genre and plot of films with obscure or non-translated titles. Deprived of this possibility, they tend to opt for spoiler titles aimed at members of the Turkish movie-going public who are fond of certain types of film. Such an approach is not unique to Turkey. As Kerrigan (2010: 101) notes, distributors of non-major films everywhere have to be able to compensate for a paucity of marketing materials by stimulating word of mouth; a key way of doing this is to create particularly effective titles, which to most independent distributors in Turkey appears to mean translating the title in such a way that it screams out the genre of the film.

The choice of titles by independent distributors can, however, also be explained through reference to power relations in the film industry. A greater proportion of independent titles are translated 'freely' simply because the distributors that create them enjoy greater freedom of choice. Having bought exploitation rights for the imported films, distributors like Tiglon, Medyavizyon and Pinema seemingly feel less tied to the original title (see Table 12.3). Questionnaire responses from a number of marketeers at Turkish independent distributors give the impression that these individuals set great store by using titles that sound 'correct' and natural in Turkish and appeal to the Turkish public, considerations that are less conspicuous in the discourse of marketeers working for the majors. When Pınar Özyiğit, UIP-Turkey's marketing manager, was asked 'When choosing film titles, to what extent do you try to create associations with existing titles in Turkish or with elements of Turkish culture?', she replied that she and her colleagues do not usually take Turkish films as a reference and expanded: '[o]ur references are the brand itself, target audience and global directions. We try to find a solution which combines all of them' (Özyiğit, 2011). By means of contrast, Ayşıl Özmen, responsible for marketing at the independent Chantier, commented: 'If there is a Turkish saying or expression that expresses the situation in or subject of the film, we prefer to use it' (Özmen, 2011).

Conclusion

An analysis of titles given to film imports in Turkey in 2012 suggests that there may be systematic differences between titles created by major-linked distributors and those devised by Turkey's independent importer distributors. The tactics deployed when translating titles undoubtedly reflect many other variables too, including the commercial value and genres of the films in question, the challenges posed by particular styles of titles, and the existence of local traditions in title translation, which may transcend differences between distributors (Gärtner & Schlatter, 2001; Ross, 2013). A former general director of Warner Bros.-Turkey (Kaplanoğlu, 2014) has good grounds for arguing that the blockbusters distributed in Turkey by Warner Bros. and UIP are titled the way they are because they are blockbusters, not because they are distributed by these companies.

It would be simplistic, moreover, to suggest that all the majors on the one hand and all the independents on the other behave similarly. At different times, independents like Tiglon and Özen have had ongoing arrangements with major studios and therefore have faced limitations to their freedom to choose titles for certain films. Even the six majors do not follow an identical strategy for the distribution and marketing of US films abroad. Both Danan (1995: 138), who examined the marketing of blockbusters in France, and van de Kamp (2009: 216), who focused on film and music distribution in the Netherlands, concluded that while Warner Bros. tends to demand uniform, universal marketing campaigns for its films, often entailing the non-translation of titles, the Columbia-Tristar Motion Picture Group (part of the Japanese-based Sony conglomerate) is more open to marketing campaigns that draw on local knowledge. Further empirical research on title translation, drawing on larger corpora of titles, is needed to confirm the existence (or non-existence) of patterns in the translational behaviour of particular distributors and types of distributor.

This empirical study has nonetheless offered a fresh perspective on film title translation by examining translational practices within the context of the film distribution sector in Turkey, a sector in which key agents of globalisation are heavily involved. The analysis of titles for foreign film releases in 2012 suggests that, compared with wholly independent Turkish distributors, UIP, Warner Bros. and Tiglon may be more inclined to apply the tactics of non-translation, transcription and literal translation, an inclination that I would link in part to the major studios' desire to protect their global brands. The fact that the distributors in Turkey employ these tactics, even if (judging from the comments of people like Mehmet Soyarslan) they may have doubts about their effectiveness and appropriateness for the Turkish setting, testifies to the control that the majors have over their local subsidiaries or partners. As such, the film-titling practices of 'dependent' distributors in Turkey exemplify the extent to which global (largely US-based) media conglomerations can shape decisions related to language in distant locales, influencing the production of texts both in English and in vernaculars. The contrasting preference of independent distributors for 'free' translation and amplification can be linked to a (perceived) need to target independent films at their niche audiences in Turkey. It can be seen, too, as a consequence of the greater freedom these distributors enjoy when choosing titles. Thus, certain titles selected by independent distributors are unmistakably 'facts of the culture which hosts them', as Gideon Toury has described translations in general (1995: 24). On the other hand, many title choices made by major-affiliated distributors can be understood much better within the context of the globalised entertainment sector, where translations are shaped not just by (target-)cultural factors but also by global marketing considerations and by the (economic) power of the conglomerates and individuals within the source culture who commission these titles.

Note

(1) Yves Gambier (2008: 78) recommends distinguishing between strategies and tactics: whereas he sees a *strategy* as a goal-oriented global approach to a translation task, such as rendering the text fluent according to the norms and conventions of the target language and culture, a *tactic* denotes a (conscious or automatised) routine employed on a local level during a translation (e.g. calquing or omission). For the present analysis, the term *translation tactic* refers to the different means by which foreign film titles are rendered for the Turkish market.

References

Questionnaire responses

Akıncı, T. (2011) (Former) director of theatrical distribution, Medyavizyon.
Özmen, A. (2011) Marketing and public relations department, Chantier Films.
Özyiğit, P. (2011) Marketing manager, UIP-Turkey.

Email correspondence

Kaplanoğlu, H. (2014, 28 September) Owner and managing director, Cinefilm, and former general director of Warner Bros.-Turkey.

Interviews

Karahan, M. (2014, 4 June) Audio-visual translator and translation manager for UIP and other distributors.
Milli, A. (2014, 26 September) Marketing manager, Disney-Turkey.
Taçkın, T. (2015, 27 March) PR and marketing manager at Medyavizyon, formerly responsible for PR, marketing and material acquisition at Tiglon.

Secondary sources

Berdis, V. (2013) English film titles and their Czech equivalents. BA thesis, Masaryk University, Brno, Czech Republic.
Bielsa, E. (2005) Globalisation and translation: A theoretical approach. *Language and Intercultural Communication* 5 (2), 131–144.

Boyce, G.H. (2001) *Co-operative Structures in Global Business: Communicating, Transferring Knowledge and Learning Across the Corporate Frontier*. London: Routledge.

Bravo, J.M. (2004) Conventional subtitling, screen texts and film titles. In J.M. Bravo (ed.) *A New Spectrum of Translation Studies* (pp. 209–230). Valladolid: Universidad de Valladolid.

Brisset, F. (2013) Woody Allen's French marketing: Everyone says *Je l'aime*, or do they? *InMedia* 3, at http://inmedia.revues.org/618#toc, accessed 9 March 2015.

Bulut, A. (2001) Çeviri araştırmalarında dilsel verilerin durumu [The status of linguistic data in translation research]. In *Üniversitelerarası XV Dilbilim Kurultay, 24–25 Mayıs 2001* (pp. 13–14). Istanbul: Yıldız Teknik Üniversitesi Basın-Yayım Merkezi.

Cioranu, R.A. (2010) Film titles in translation. *Translation Studies: Retrospective and Prospective Views* 3 (9), 29–33. (Special issue, 'Proceedings of the 5th Conference on Translation Studies: Retrospective and Prospective Views, 8–10 October 2010, "Dunarea de Jos", University of Galati', eds E. Croitoru, F. Popescu and S. Stan.)

Cronin, M. (2003) *Translation and Globalisation*. London: Routledge.

Danan, M. (1995) Marketing the Hollywood blockbuster in France. *Journal of Popular Film and Television* 23 (3), 131–140.

Doğan, P. (2012) The production and reception of titles for Hollywood film imports in Turkey. MA thesis, Boğaziçi University.

Eliashberg, J., Elberse, A. and Leenders, M.A.A.M. (2006) The motion picture industry: Critical issues in practice, current research, and new research directions. *Marketing Science* 26 (6), 638–661.

Gambier, Y. (2003) Introduction. Screen transadaptation: perception and reception. *The Translator* 9 (2), 171–190. (Special issue, 'Screen Translation', ed. Y. Gambier.)

Gambier, Y. (2008) Stratégies et tactiques en traduction et interpretation. In G. Hansen, A. Chesterman and H. Gerzymisch-Arbogast (eds) *Efforts and Models in Interpreting and Translation: A Tribute to Daniel Gile* (pp. 63–82). Amsterdam: John Benjamins.

Gärtner, A. and Schlatter, M. (2001) 'It could happen to you: 2 millionen $ Trinkgeld / Atraí do spelodestino': Die Titulierung von Kinofilmen im Deutschen und Portugiesischen (Brasiliens) [It could happen to you: The $2 million dollar tip / Attracted by destiny: the titling of cinema films in German and Brazilian Portugese]. *Lebende Sprachen* 2, 84–90.

Genette, G. (1987) *Paratexts: Thresholds of Interpretation* (J.E. Lewin, trans.). Cambridge: Cambridge University Press (1997).

González Ruiz, V.M. (2000) La traducción del título cinematográfico como objeto de autocensura: El factor religioso [The translation of the cinematic title as an object of self-censorship: The religious factor]. In A. Beeby, D. Ensinger and M. Presas (eds) *Investigating Translation: Selected Papers from the 4th International Congress on Translation, Barcelona 1998* (pp. 161–169). Amsterdam: John Benjamins.

González Ruiz, V.M. (2001) Ideología y traducción: Estudio de los títulos en castellano de las películas en lengua inglesa estrenadas en España durante el periodo de la dictadura franquista (1939–1975) [Ideology and translation: A study of the Castilian titles for English-language films released in Spain during the Franco dictatorship (1939–1975)]. PhD thesis, Universidad de Las Palmas de Gran Canaria.

Hennig-Thurau, T., Gwinner, K.P., Walsh, G. and Gremler, D.D. (2004) Electronic word-of-mouth via consumer-opinion platforms: What motivates consumers to articulate themselves on the Internet? *Journal of Interactive Marketing* 18 (1), 38–52.

Kanzler, M. (2014) *The Turkish Film Industry: Key Developments 2004 to 2013*. Strasbourg: European Audiovisual Observatory.

Kerrigan, F. (2010) *Film Marketing*. Oxford: Butterworth-Heinemann.

Keskin, E. (2010) Yabancı film adları Türkçeye neden farklı çevirilir? [Why are the names of foreign films translated differently in Turkish?]. *Zaman*, 'Cumaertesi' supplement, 6 March, at http://www.zaman.com.tr/haber.do?haberno=958364&title=yabanc%FD-film-adlar%FD-t%FCrk%E7eye-neden-farkl%FD-%E7evirilir, accessed 23 April 2011.

Kochberg, S. (1996) Institutions, audiences and technology. In J. Nelmes (ed.) *An Introduction to Film Studies* (pp. 7–59). London: Routledge.

Marich, R. (2009) *Marketing to Moviegoers: A Handbook of Strategies and Tactics* (2nd edn). Carbondale, IL: Southern Illinois University Press.

Martí, R. and Zapater, M. (1993) Translation of titles of films: A critical approach. *Sintagma* 5, 81–87.

McCarthy, E.R. (2002) How important is a title? An examination of the private law created by the Motion Picture Association of America. *University of Miami Law Review* 26 (4), 1071–1094.

Molina, L. and Hurtado Albir, A. (2002) Translation techniques revisited: A dynamic and functionalist approach. *Meta* 47 (4), 498–512.

Nord, C. (1993) *Einführung in das funktionale Übersetzen: Am Beispiel von Titeln und Überschriften* [*An Introduction to Functional Translation: Titles and Headings as a Case in Point*]. Tübingen: Francke.

Nord, C. (1995) Text-functions in translation: Titles and headings as a case in point. *Target* 7 (2), 261–284.

O'Reilly, D. and Kerrigan, F. (2013) A view to a brand: Introducing the film brandscape. *European Journal of Marketing* 47 (5/6), 769–789.

Piller, I. (2001) Identity constructions in multilingual advertising. *Language in Society* 30, 153–186.

Ross, J. (2008) When *Nights in Rodanthe* become *Storms of Love*: The creation of titles for imported films in Turkey. Unpublished conference paper, Third Asian Translation Traditions Conference, Boğaziçi University Istanbul, 22–24 October.

Ross, J. (2013) 'No *Revolutionary Road*s please – we're Turkish': The translation of film titles as an object of translation research. *Across Languages and Cultures* 14 (2), 245–266.

Schubert, C. (2004) Die Appellwirkung englischer Filmtitel und ihrer deutschen Neutitel: Techniken interkulturellen Transfers [The operative effect of English film titles and their German versions: Techniques of intercultural transfer]. *Arbeiten aus Anglistik und Amerikanistik* 29 (2), 239–259.

Soyarslan, M. (2009) Contribution to the panel *Türkiye Film Sektöründe Çevirinin Yeri* [The Role of Translation in the Turkish Film Sector], 7 May, Mithat Alam Film Centre, Boğaziçi University, Istanbul.

Torresi, I. (2010) *Translating Promotional and Advertising Texts*. Manchester: St Jerome.

Toury, G. (1995) *Descriptive Translation Studies and Beyond*. Amsterdam: John Benjamins.

van de Kamp, M. (2009) *Music and Film Majors in the Netherlands 1990–2005: Where Corporate Culture and Local Markets Meet*. Rotterdam: Erasmus Research Centre for Media Communications and Culture.

Vinay, J-P. and Darbelnet, J. (1958) *Comparative Stylistics of French and English: A Methodology for Translation* (J.C. Sager and M.-J. Hamel, trans. and eds). Amsterdam: John Benjamins (1995).

Yin, L. (2009) 'On the translation of English movie titles', *Asian Social Science* 5 (3), 171–173, at http://www.ccsenet.org/journal.html, accessed 23 April 2011.

Ying, P. (2007) Translation of film titles with the application of Peter Newmark's translation theory. *Sino-US English Teaching* 4 (4), 77–81.

13 Translated Chinese Autobiographies and the Power of Habitus in the British Literary Field

Pei Meng

Chinese Autobiographies and Translation

Autobiographical writings on Communist China have gained wide popularity in the British and North American book markets. The genre of 'writing Red China' (Grice, 2002: 103–126) emerged in the US as early as the 1950s, and it continued growing, especially from the 1990s, until around 2007. Testament to the lasting commercial success of this genre are bestsellers such as *Wild Swans* by Jung Chang (ST 1991; TT 2003), *Daughter of the River* by Hong Ying (ST 1997; TT 1998) and *To the Edge of the Sky* by Anhua Gao (ST 2000; TT 2011). These writings have set a successful precedent for subsequent autobiographical literature and its translation into English.

It is important to note right from the beginning, however, that some works subsumed under the generic label 'writing Red China' had originally been written and published in English. Only after they had proven popular with English-speaking audiences in Britain and North America were they translated and disseminated for a Chinese-speaking audience (see the two lists of primary references below). The best-known example is Jung Chang's *Wild Swans*, which narrates the experiences of three generations of women from one family during the political and military upheavals between the 1940s and 1970s. Two further noteworthy examples are *Life and Death in Shanghai*, by Nien Cheng (ST 1986; TT 1988), about the wife of an ambassador imprisoned during the Cultural Revolution (1966–1976), and *A Single Tear: A Family's Persecution, Love and Endurance in Communist China*, by Wu Ningkun (ST 1993; TT 2002), a gut-wrenching memoir about political persecution.

Literary success rests on the efficient interaction of a host of publishing networks which are instrumental in shaping the fate of translations.

The power relations within the publishing domain come into being with the selection of texts for translation into English and may influence translators' strategies in anticipation of readers' expectations (Merkle, 2006; Milton & Bandia, 2009). This chapter sketches the influence of one particular literary agent with respect to the introduction of Chinese autobiographies into the British book market, considering selection processes as a set of 'functions of social relations based on competing forms of capital tied to local/global power' (Inghilleri, 2005: 143). From the vantage point of such institutional 'power play', it is useful to start with an interrogation of the publishing procedures and agent dispositions that influence practices of selection.

Literary agents closely cooperate with publishers in searching for and promoting books and authors for a given target audience (Gordon, 1993). They are important mediators in the selection and production of translations for a foreign market, but thus far they have 'enjoyed very little visibility in the literary field' (Buzelin, 2005: 209). Overlooking the role played by the literary agent in regulating the literary system, with its numerous rewards and sanctions, may result in downplaying the networked and economic dimensions of the translation process, two factors which help explain the commercialisation of translations as cultural commodities in literary markets. This chapter, therefore, approaches translation from the perspective of social agents and their interactions within commercial imperatives that constrain translation activities. The discussion draws on Pierre Bourdieu's concepts of field, capital and habitus in order 'to make descriptive theoretical approaches more "agent aware"' (Gouanvic, 2005: 142), a sociological perspective which tends to be overlooked by poly-system theory (Hermans, 1999: 132–136). The concept of *habitus* circumscribes an unspecifiable set of largely unconscious (pre-)dispositions, preferences, modes of thinking and behaving, and the rules, norms and values that underpin them, all of which are specific to a field within which individuals operate (Bourdieu, 1993: 5–6). The concept of *field* can be seen as a metaphorical space of activities where a certain type of capital circulates (Bourdieu, 1990a: 14), and the notion of *capital* describes the various rewards – material, symbolic, cultural, social – that agents aim to acquire and consolidate within a particular field (Bourdieu, 1991: 229–231). It is within and across the contexts of specific fields and through the individual's habitus that 'social agents establish and consolidate their positions of power in social space, where all have a stake in the acquisition of specific forms of capital' (Inghilleri, 2005: 135).

Bourdieu (1977: 95) defines habitus as 'an acquired system of generative schemes objectively adjusted to the particular conditions in which it is constituted'. A habitus functions as a 'structuring' and 'structured' psychosocial mechanism, and it involves the internalisation of norms (Gouanvic, 2005; Simeoni, 1998: 21–22). Investigations of translated literature, however, need to take into account that the 'recontextualization of habitus is required not just within specialized fields but in fields of power' (Gouanvic, 2005: 149). When we try to make sense of the multi-dimensional nature of translation as a set of cultural and economic practices, therefore, empirical research should focus not only on the objective structure of a sociocultural field within which translations arise, but also on the trajectory of the social agents who contribute to the making and unfolding of these practices (Hanna, 2005: 168). This in turn necessitates a focus on the different types of capital that social agents have at their disposal within translational fields (Thoutenhoofd, 2005: 237). This chapter raises and addresses a number of questions on the ways in which the genre 'writing Red China' was introduced into the British cultural context and why texts with certain thematic orientations tend to be translated more than others, with special reference to the role of literary agents and economic power relations in the British publishing system. An important related question is whether the analytical concept of habitus is capable of explaining underlying power dynamics more convincingly than the concept of translational norms.

Creating a Market for 'Writing Red China'

The publication of translations in the British literary field during the 1980s was an uncertain and risky business. At the time, it was difficult to anticipate a readership for translated literature, especially when it involved the introduction of new genres from an unfamiliar cultural area such as China. Any translation commission, for instance, entails significant production costs, which is why few in the literary field would be willing to 'gamble' on translations. Moreover, in the case of China, this difficulty was exacerbated by the country's long cultural and political isolation and its bad human rights record (Ching, 2008). Under these circumstances, involvement with a Chinese translation project could be a risky adventure. At the same time, however, publishing translations repre-sented an uncharted territory which could potentially generate handsome profits within an untapped market. On the whole, Chinese semi-fictional literature had the potential to compensate for an almost complete lack of knowledge about certain historical events in China, a country that for many in the so-called 'West' remained surrounded by a veil of mystery and exoticism. In spite of its status as a crucial historical moment, for instance, the Cultural Revolution remained at the time relatively unreported from the viewpoints of cultural insiders and eyewitnesses. In addition, the fact that autobiographical writing operates upon the implicit claim to relay an authentic voice through the eyes of an insider did offer an opportunity to create literary and commercial success.

The eventual opening up of the British market for the translation of Chinese autobiographies can be traced back to the success story of Jung Chang's *Wild Swans*. Originally published by the author in cooperation with a literary agent, LA,[1] in 1991 for the British market, its phenomenal success brought about a sudden realisation that there was a big untapped market with great potential for commercial exploitation. Since then, LA has opened the door for many other Chinese authors, enabling them to exploit new market opportunities for which *Wild Swans* had paved the way.

The publishing network analysed here can be described as part of an 'investment game' geared for the introduction of Chinese writing into the British literary field. Investment games are underpinned by what Bourdieu calls *illusio*, an individual's 'feel for the game' (Bourdieu, 1990a: 61), which involves a 'tacit recognition of the value of the stakes of the game and ... practical mastery of its rules' (Bourdieu & Wacquant, 1992: 117). Those competing for the stakes of the field believe that the game merits investment (Bourdieu, 1990a); in other words, they believe to a considerable extent in its 'profitability'. Embedded within a competitive publishing network, LA played a formative role in the literary and commercial aspects of the translation process as he opened a gateway for Chinese autobiographies by introducing them to publishers in the UK. Therefore, it is worth dwelling on his decisive role in creating a market for translated Chinese autobiographies.

The role of literary agents has been gradually shifting over the last few decades; it is now seen as part and parcel of literary production, and the remit of their work has been extended to handling a wider range of business-related tasks (Gordon, 1993). Literary agents closely cooperate with publishers, supporting them also in their commercial, financial and administrative activities. These two 'power players' exert control over literary production, wielding significant tutelary power over authors and their work by monitoring and protecting literary value and rights (Finkelstein & McCleery, 2005: 94–97). A primary responsibility for the literary agent is to scout for potentially profitable books to sell to publishers, which inevitably puts them in the position of being the arbiters and evaluators of literary manuscripts, whereby they become 'the source of the valuation of copyright' (Gillies, 1993: 22). A spontaneous 'feel for the game', manifested in a 'feel for the right book', is an essential dimension of any literary agent's habitus. Their ability and reputation (or symbolic capital in Bourdieu's terms) for 'digging out' a potentially marketable book is put to the test before the first words have even been translated.

Selecting Chinese Autobiographies for the Literary Translation Market

Literary agents play a critical role in the initial selection and commissioning of suitable translations. This process greatly affects the way selected works are translated and received, with significant implications for the image and representations of modern Chinese society. The book selection process in the British publishing field, however, is fairly flexible, with no cut and dried rules or rigidly structured procedures. This section discusses the selection processes for the translation of the Chinese auto-biographical genre 'writing Red China', taking two *biographies*, two *autobiographies* and two *semi-autobiographies* as prime examples, each of which passed through a slightly different selection route. It is important to note that four of these authors were living in the UK during the writing and translation process. In fact LA's enthusiasm for and interest in their projects had led him to commission a series of Chinese autobiographical works that had not even been written yet, with the storylines still brewing in the authors' heads. The two semi-autobiographies, however, had been written in China before the translations were initiated in the UK.

Xinran's two biographies *The Good Women of China* (ST 2002; TT 2002) and *Sky Burial* (TT 2002) centre around the suffering and misery of Chinese women during and after the Cultural Revolution. The author wrote the Chinese texts in the UK, and while the Chinese version of *The Good Women of China* was published in China *after* the English transla-tion had come out, *Sky Burial* has not yet been published in its Chinese original. Such an approach to selecting literary models for translation demonstrates the economic and cultural power of the literary agent, who controlled the entire writing, translation and publication process in this particular instance. Moreover, it reminds us of the complexities of the translation and publishing processes, which cannot be reduced to sim-plistic source–target binaries, as has frequently been done in translation studies research.

Ma Jian's autobiography *Red Dust* (ST 2002; TT 2001) was first published in English translation. The book is situated in the post-Mao China of the 1980s, recounting the author's flight from political persecu-tion. During his first encounter with LA, Ma Jian stressed the potential literary value of his earlier novel *The Noodle Maker* (ST 1991; TT 2004), yet LA was mainly interested in Ma Jian's experiences of travelling around China in the 1980s. LA interpreted these journeys as symbolic self-discoveries, and Ma Jian's accounts of poverty-stricken and forgotten places could potentially 'market' the author as a liberal and rebel at odds with the Communist regime. LA believed that the book's unique selling point was its resemblance to Jack Kerouac's bestseller *On the Road* (1958), especially in view of Ma Jian's exploratory journey through secretive places and his depiction of heroic and anti-conventional protagonists who challenge the status quo. Literary agents need to maintain a close eye on audience expectations and future revenues, and the association of Ma Jian's Chinese travels with Kerouac's drug-fuelled odyssey exempli-fies the significance of accruing cultural and economic capital within a literary field.

A second autobiography, Hong Ying's *Daughter of the River* (ST 1997; TT 1998), relives the author's childhood experiences in Chongqing during the Great Famine (1958–1961) and the Cultural Revolution, leading up to the Tiananmen demonstrations. This autobiography was commissioned by LA in the UK for its Chinese and English versions after the publication of *Summer of Betrayal* (ST 1992; TT 1997), the same author's first published novel in English translation since she arrived in the UK. The Chinese version of *Daughter of the River* was published by Erya Press in 1997 and won the Best Book Award of the Taiwanese *United Daily News Reader* in the same year. It was followed by an English translation published in the UK in 1998.

Another approach to scouting for future bestsellers is to monitor books on the Chinese literary market with potential appeal to a British readership. Zhou Weihui's semi-autobiography *Shanghai Baby* (ST 1999; TT 2001), for instance, mainly grabbed LA's attention because it was banned in China in 2000 for its pornographic and homosexual content. The book was initially rejected by six major publishers in London because they did not believe in its commercial success, but Constable and Robinson eventually acquired the foreign rights, bringing them a comfortable reward of around 200,000 sold copies in the first year. Prior to the publication of *Shanghai Baby*, LA also explored the possibility of publishing works by Mian Mian, another leading female author in the UK whose writing had been labelled as 'sensationalist' in China in the 1990s (Ferry, 2003: 656). His enthusiasm for this kind of literature was based on the simple consideration that sex sells, while the banning of a book, as in the case of *Shanghai Baby*, pandered to the eternal appeal of the forbidden and mysterious. LA spotted the marketability of sexual explicitness, underground romance and political dissidence for the British market quite early, and his selection of *Shanghai Baby* surely was not accidental, so the book's success can be credited to his commercial acumen and his 'feel' for successful translations.

Like Zhou Weihui, Guo Xiaolu belongs to a young generation of writers who narrate their semi-autobiographies in the third-person singular. Guo Xiaolu's *Village of Stone* (ST 2003; TT 2004) is based on her childhood in a fishing village, which stands in striking contrast to the Beijing city life of her adolescence. It is a story set against the backdrop of the transitional modernisation processes in China that caused significant social and cultural upheavals during the 1990s. Emboldened by the huge success of *Wild Swans*, Guo Xiaolu selected the only semi-autobiographical texts out of her six books that had been published in China, and presented 10 translated pages to LA, who subsequently forwarded the sample to several publishers – and he immediately landed the book with the major publisher Random House. The author's anticipation of the British reading public's cultural preferences played a major role in this successful pitch. Yet, although it appears that *Village of Stone* was Guo Xiaolu's selection and that she was the active agent on this occasion, the decision to invest in the book ultimately depended on the literary agent's professional judgement.

The Literary Agent's Habitus

The endorsement of a literary translation in the UK includes devising a plan to minimise potential economic failure. Any risk calculation for an investment in a foreign autobiography is, of course, based on assumptions and predictions about sociocultural factors. The ability to identify the relevant economic and sociocultural factors for the potential success or failure of a given literary work is intimately related to the literary agent's habitus and 'feel' for the right book. Professional knowledge is central to the constitution of the literary agent's habitus, a durable yet flexible predisposition that may be seen to encompass three individual and collective dimensions.

Firstly, literary agents need to possess a solid *socio-historical knowledge* of the various fields involved in literary production. In the case of translations, this involves knowledge about the literary and publishing fields of both China and the UK and an awareness of literary trends and cultural sensibilities. In spotting the marketability of *Shanghai Baby*, LA showed a good cultural understanding of the taboo-laden 'New Generation Literature' in the Chinese literary field of the 1990s.

Secondly, the ability to open up a new market niche is dependent on a good deal of *practical knowledge*, based on skills such as liaising with publishers and anticipating the expectations of potential readers. Solid practical knowledge proves especially important for publishing ventures that involve the introduction of a new literary genre such as 'writing Red China' into a foreign literary market.

Thirdly, *commercial acumen and good editing skills* are crucial in order to enable a literary agent to successfully pitch the economic, cultural and literary value of a new project to a publisher. For example, LA spent three months creating a presentable translation draft of Xinran's *The Good Women of China* before he eventually managed to sell it to the publisher. This type of knowledge about how to make a strong commercial case for a book, in conjunction with editorial work, rests on a set of habitual dispositions and a flexible 'take' on situations that allow literary agents to anticipate the expectations that publishers might have of a translated textual narrative.

The formation of the literary agent's professional habitus is embodied in cumulatively acquired knowledge and skills that are attuned to the requirements, stakes and logic of a specific field. These 'generative dispositions', as Bourdieu (1977: 95) notes, are not fully conscious, although the weighing up of risks and the setting of goals happen at a conscious level based on the literary agent's interests and strategies. The manner in which LA selected the six Chinese texts and the ways in which he interacted with various parties show that his individual strategies cannot be seen as purely conscious actions which follow or resist sociocultural and behavioural norms mainly located in a given target culture (cf. Toury,

1995). These strategies are 'designed to locate the source of their practice in their own experience of reality' (Bourdieu, 1990a: 60), an observation that relates to a literary agent's practical sense of dealing with projects according to the internal logic of a literary field. Yet, while the conscious selection of specific Chinese autobiographies was made from within a location and a field, a literary agent does not 'choose the principle of these choices' (Bourdieu & Wacquant, 1992: 45), precisely because the cultural options for any selection are not *only* made available by target cultural norms (as suggested by Toury, 1995), but because 'it is habitus itself that commands this option' (Bourdieu & Wacquant, 1992: 45). Ultimately, the major functions of the habitus appear to support the formation and maintenance of new knowledge, professional expertise and the stakes in a given field's power dynamics.

Habitus and the Power of Convertible Capital

The decision-making processes in a publishing field can be regarded as spheres of negotiation where the key players include experts in the areas of publicity, marketing and sales (Graham, 1993: 128). Most of the time, however, final decisions are made between literary agents and publishers, who do not always agree on potentially sellable books or project strategies. Even after the successful publication of Ma Jian's *Red Dust*, Random House was hesitant to take on Xinran's *The Good Women of China*, which was eventually sold to Chatto and Windus, and Random House also rejected Zhou Weihui's *Shanghai Baby* despite LA's well established reputation in the publication of Chinese autobiographical writings. The rejection of *Shanghai Baby* rested on the presumption that British readers were more inclined to read, as Davies (1995: 13) notes, 'books that fit into a tried and tested pattern in terms of the market need they are fulfilling'. However, based on his own research on this new and daring trend in female Chinese writing, LA concluded that sociocultural differences should be seen as a positive factor in terms of investment. While this situation highlights the complexity of collaborative and competitive relations within the publishing network, LA's insistence may be seen to conform to the 'no risk, no gain' logic in the business field. After LA's massive success with *Shanghai Baby* had become apparent, *voilà*, Random House decided to acquire Xinran's biography *Sky Burial* and Guo Xiaolu's semi-autobiography *Village of Stone*. The economic, symbolic, social and cultural capital that LA had gained from previous successful book selections was eventually recognised by some publishers.

The habitus becomes shaped through professional experiences that increase practical chances or an 'objective probability' of success (Bourdieu, 1990b: 20–21), conforming to a set of dispositions that enable individuals in the literary field to adjust their expectations and decisions on publishing projects. These dispositions are determined by ideological positions and the various forms and degrees of capital at an individual's disposal. A literary agent's professional habitus is shaped through numerous communicative interactions and their underlying economic and ideological interests. Hence, a dynamic process of local negotiations is bound up with global relations of power and hegemony. These power dynamics are linked to institutional and discursive dimensions that cannot be fully explained in terms of individual subjectivities and behaviours, although they are also manifest at the micro-level of communicative interaction in the translation process. Two dimensions of power play are at stake in this network of text selection, publishing, translation production and dissemination: at the macro-level, the English language constitutes a hegemonic medium of communication that remains attached to an enduring cultural and economic imperialism within the 'Western imagination' (cf. Said, 1994); and at the micro-level, individual agents tend to reproduce the economic dominance of 'the West' in relation to everyone else within the global marketplace. To put this in practical terms, in order to convert cultural-artistic capital into economic capital on a highly profitable scale, one needs to gain a foothold and a niche within the Western marketplace and appeal to its customers. At the heart of this power play stand publishers and literary agents who are able to shape the visibility and profitability of translated works within a global capitalist consumer market.

Strictly speaking, economic capital is the primary form of capital for publishers and literary agents. The profit generated from successful books is convertible to other forms of capital, which facilitates the further accumulation of economic capital. Bourdieu stresses the variable levels of concentration of economic, cultural, symbolic and social forms of capital within their corresponding fields (e.g. the dominance of economic capital in the publishing field), while there may also be a high degree of convertibility between the different forms of capital (Bourdieu, 1977: 177–178). An obvious example of convertibility relates to a literary agent who has benefited from multiple forms of capital. A literary agent acts as a mediator who handles conflicting demands and opportunities on an author's behalf. This mediating activity may inspire the formation of a very specific form of capital, which may be described as *mediating capital*, which takes on special significance when the literary agent is successful in negotiating the interests of an author across cultural barriers. LA's culture-specific knowledge, for instance, enables him to interact efficiently with Chinese writers and thus to achieve good outcomes. His mediating capital, along with his 'feel' for suitable books, has made him an indispensable business partner for many publishers, and this is reinforced by his role as an important facilitator for foreign authors attempting to enter the British literary field.

The successful selection and introduction of Chinese autobiographical writings within the British literary field and the ensuing financial gains have enhanced LA's symbolic capital, that is, the recognition of his literary expertise. His increased symbolic capital stems to a significant degree from the belief in the economic value attached to the works he introduced into the literary market. Any attempt to exploit the potential success of a translation involves the introduction of a literary work into another cultural system, and in this process LA's enhanced symbolic capital was capable of being converted into mediating and, of course, economic capital. A literary agent attempting to introduce a translation into a new sociocultural environment comes to act as a proxy literary critic, and she or he needs to be an astute arbiter of what may count as literary value from the perspective of a publisher's economic evaluations and of a prospective foreign readership's aesthetic expectations.

Conclusion

The habitus of literary agents and their collaboration with publishers strongly impact on the selection and translation of Chinese autobiographical writings. Their introduction into the British literary field and commercial market involves the interactions of a range of social agents situated within different institutional contexts. The criteria for selecting the genre 'writing Red China' for a foreign market were less based on the genre's artistic licence or a perceived need to showcase Chinese literary culture; rather, they appeared to be determined by British cultural and ideological attitudes. In essence, the selection criteria were determined by market forces that facilitated the accommodation of this type of literature within the British target culture as principally factual 'eye-witness narrations'. Chinese autobiographies were framed as market commodities, with commercial revenue over-riding literary value. In fact, the prioritisation of market demands and thus financial profits largely shapes the attitudes and dispositions of the major players within the publishing field.

In a way, a given habitus constitutes the result of structural tendencies within a given field which are shared and contested by the people involved in the selection, translation and publishing process. The habitus of a literary agent is constituted by an understanding of prevailing cultural and ideological dispositions. LA demonstrated a carefully judged understanding of the tastes and commercial calculations of other literary professionals and of a prospective British readership. In particular, his 'knack' for spotting the right Chinese books, in conjunction with the economic rewards for his efforts, eventually 'translated' into a boosted reputation in the professional field (symbolic and cultural capital) and a widened social network in the publishing and literary fields (social capital), which in turn enhanced any long-term prospects of landing additional lucrative contracts (economic capital). The fact that the selection process constitutes the first and crucial step in the literary translation process implies its ideological and market-driven nature and, in turn, its significant role in anticipating and (re)constructing representations of contemporary Chinese culture and society.

Note

(1) The overall discussion is based on interviews with one British literary agent, here denoted LA, as well as other professionals in the field. For reasons of confidentiality, sources are anonymised.

References

Primary sources

Texts first published in Chinese and their English translations

Guo Xiaolu 郭小橹 (2003) *Wo Xinzhong de Shitouzhen* 我心中的石头镇 [*Village of Stone*]. Shanghai: Shanghai Wenyi Chaubanshe.

Guo Xiaolu (2004) *Village of Stone* (C. Cindy, trans.). London: Chatto and Windus.

Hong Ying 虹影 (1992) *Beipan Zhixia* 背叛之夏 [*Summer of Betrayal*]. Taiwan: Wenhua xinzhi Publisher.

Hong Ying (1997) *Ji'e de nÜ'er* 饥饿的女儿 [*Daughter of the River*]. Taibei: Er Ya Chubanshe.

Hong Ying (1997) *Summer of Betrayal* (A. Martha, trans.). New York: Grove Press.

Hong Ying (1998) *Daughter of the River: An Autobiography* (G. Howard, trans.). London: Bloomsbury.

Ma Jian 马建 (1991) *Lamianzhe* 拉面者 [*The Noodle Maker*]. Hongkong: Tiandi Publishing Company.

Ma Jian (2004) *The Noodle Maker* (D. Flora, trans.). London: Chatto and Windus.

Zhou Weihui 周卫慧 (1999) *Shanghai Baobei* 上海宝贝 [*Shanghai Baby*]. Shenyang: Chunfeng Wenyi Chubanshe.

Zhou Weihui (2001) *Shanghai Baby* (H. Bruce, trans.). London: Robinson.

Texts first published in English and their Chinese versions

Gao Anhua 高安华 (2000) *To the Edge of the Sky*. London: Viking.

Gao Anhua (2011) *Tian Bian* 天边 [*To the Edge of the Sky*]. Taibei: Xinrui Wenchuang Press.

Jung Chang 张戎 (Zhang Rong) (1991) *Wild Swans: Three Daughters of China*. London: Simon and Schuster.

Ma Jian 马建 (2001) *Red Dust* (D. Flora, trans.). London: Chatto and Windus.

Ma Jian (2002) *Hong chen* 红尘 [*Red Dust*]. Hong Kong: Hong Kong Mingchuang chubanshe.

Nien Cheng 郑念 (1986) *Life and Death in Shanghai* (Cheng Naishan and Pan Zuojun, trans.). New York: Penguin Books.

Nien Cheng (1988) *Shanghai Shengshi Jie* 上海生死劫 [*Life and Death in Shanghai*]. Beijing: Chinese Culture Publishing Company.

Wu Ningkun 巫宁坤 (1993) *A Single Tear: A Family's Persecution, Love and Endurance in Communist China* (Wu Ningkun, trans.). New York: Atlantic Monthly Press.

Wu Ningkun (2002) *Yi Dilei: Cong Sufan dao Wengge de Huiyi* 一滴泪: 从肃反到文革的回忆 [*A Single Tear: A Family's Persecution, Love and Endurance in Communist China*]. Taibei: Taiwan Vision Press.

Xinran 欣然 (2002) *Zhongguo hao nÜren* 中国好女人 [*The Good Women of China*]. Taibei: Dakuai Wenhua Chuban Gongsi.

Xinran (2002) *The Good Women of China: Hidden Voice* (T. Esther, trans.). London: Chatto and Windus.

Xinran (2004) *Sky Burial* (T. Esther and J. Lovell, trans.). London: Chatto and Windus.

Zhang Rong 张戎 (Jung Chang) (2003) *Hong: Sandai Zhongguo Nvren de Gushi* 鴻: 三代中國女人的故事 [*Wild Swans: Three Daughters of China*] (Zhang Pu, trans.). Taibei: Taiwan Zhong Hua Book Company.

Secondary sources

Bourdieu, P. (1977) *Outline of a Theory of Practice* (R. Nice, trans.). Cambridge: Cambridge University Press.

Bourdieu, P. (1990a) *In Other Words: Essays Towards a Reflexive Sociology*. Cambridge: Polity Press.

Bourdieu, P. (1990b) *The Logic of Practice*. Cambridge: Polity Press.

Bourdieu, P. (1991) *Language and Symbolic Power* (G. Raymond and M. Adamson, trans.). Cambridge: Polity in association with Basil Blackwell.

Bourdieu, P. (1993) *The Field of Cultural Production: Essays on Art and Literature*. Cambridge: Polity Press.

Bourdieu, P. and Wacquant, L. (1992) *An Invitation to Reflexive Sociology*. Cambridge: Polity Press.

Buzelin, H. (2005) Unexpected allies: How Latour's network theory could complement Bourdieusian analyses in translation studies. In M. Inghilleri (ed.) 'Bourdieu and the Sociology of Translation and Interpreting', special issue, *The Translator* 11 (2), 193–218.

Ching, F. (2008) *China: The Truth About Its Human Rights Record*. London: Rider.

Davies, G. (1995) *Book Commissioning and Acquisition*. London: Blueprint.

Ferry, M.M. (2003) Marketing Chinese women writers in the 1990s, or the politics of self-fashioning. *Journal of Contemporary China* 12 (37), 655–675.

Finkelstein, D. and McCleery, A. (2005) *An Introduction to Book History*. London: Routledge.

Gillies, M.A. (1993) A.P. Watt, literary agent. *Publishing Research Quarterly* 9 (spring), 20–34.

Gordon, G. (1993) Literary agents. In P. Owen (ed.) *Publishing Now* (pp. 165–172). London: Peter Owen.

Gouanvic, J.-M. (2005) A Bourdieusian theory of translation, or the coincidence of practical instances: Field, 'habitus', capital and 'illusio' (J. Moore, trans.). In M. Inghilleri (ed.) 'Bourdieu and the Sociology of Translation and Interpreting', special issue, *The Translator* 11 (2), 149–166.

Graham, J. (1993) Publicity. In P. Owen (ed.) *Publishing Now* (pp. 126–133). London: Peter Owen.

Grice, H. (2002) *Negotiating Identities: An Introduction to Asian American Women's Writing*. Manchester: Manchester University Press.

Hanna, S. (2005) Hamlet lives happily ever after in Arabic: The genesis of the field of drama translation in Egypt. In M. Inghilleri (ed.) 'Bourdieu and the Sociology of Translation and Interpreting', special issue, *The Translator* 11 (2), 167–192.

Hermans, T. (1999) *Translation in Systems: Descriptive and Systemic Approaches Explained*. Manchester: St Jerome.

Inghilleri, M. (2005) The sociology of Bourdieu and the construction of the 'object' in translation and interpreting studies. In M. Inghilleri (ed.) 'Bourdieu and the Sociology of Translation and Interpreting', special issue, *The Translator* 11 (2), 125–145.

Kerouac, J. (1958) *On the Road*. London: A. Deutsch.

Merkle, D. (2006) Towards a sociology of censorship: Translation in the late-Victorian publishing field. In M. Wolf (ed.) Übersetzen –*Translating* – *Traduire: Towards a 'Social Turn'?* (pp. 35–44). Wien: LIT.

Milton, J. and Bandia, P. (2009) Introduction: Agents of translation and translation studies. In J. Milton and P. Bandia (eds) *Agents of Translation* (pp. 1–18). Amsterdam: John Benjamins.

Said, E.W. (1994) *Culture and Imperialism*. New York: Vintage Books.

Simeoni, D. (1998) The pivotal status of the translator's habitus. *Target* 10 (1), 1–39.

Thoutenhoofd, E. (2005) The sign language interpreter in inclusive education: Power of authority and limits of objectivism. In M. Inghilleri (ed.) S'Bourdieu and the Sociology of Translation and Interpreting', special issue, *The Translator* 11 (2), 237–258.

Toury, G. (1995) *Descriptive Translation Studies and Beyond*. Amsterdam: J. Benjamins.

Conclusion: Translation, Power and Social Justice

Stefan Baumgarten and Jordi Cornellà-Detrell

This book aspires to achieve a balance across political, cultural and socio-economic viewpoints on power and translation. This volume has touched on a range of issues, including agency, media power, translation policy and, above all, translation, understood as a form of commodity exchange. The underlying premise of all the chapters is that relations of domination and hegemony in translation are channelled through embodied disposi-tions, the (re)production of social identities, techno-scientific rationality and the political thrust of capital.

Domination involves the *more visible* aspects of the power struggle, with oppression functioning as social and exploitation as economic forms of domination, whereas hegemony constitutes a *less visible*, naturalised manifestation of power that is trickier to identify (cf. Gramsci, 1999: 306). Jean Baudrillard contends that the intensification of hegemonic power along the circuits of technology and finance capital 'relies on a symbolic liquidation of every possible value' (Baudrillard, 2010: 35; see also Cristina Caimotto in Chapter 10 of the present volume), but it is perhaps Edward Said (1993: 158) who most fittingly characterises the nature and dynamics of hegemonic relations as a 'self-forgetting delight in the use of power'. A kind of 'self-forgetting delight' is evident at every junction of the libidinal, digital and political economies of translation.

New media and technology are increasingly transforming social iden-tities and relationships, thereby changing the way we perceive and process information. The exponential growth and therefore 'cheapening' of infor-mation flow, multiplied by the use of automatic translation, has resulted in an unnavigable ocean of data, too vast to be 'translated' into knowledge. In an age dominated by algorithms and economic cost–benefit considera-tions, more information does not necessarily lead to more knowledge or better-informed decisions; rather, this surplus can be theorised as 'directly destructive of meaning and signification' (Baudrillard, 1994: 79).

The information overload we are witnessing has compromised our sen-sitivities to crucial ethical values such as truth and authenticity, granting higher degrees of tolerance of misleading or inaccurate claims about the social and natural world. Traditional media, with their (comparatively) higher degree of pluralism, neutrality and ethical standards, find it difficult to compete with a decentralised cyberspace ruled by algorithms that generates information flows at vertiginous speeds. The information excess and growing massification of automated messages also threaten to detach communication and language from their quintessentially human potential. The virtual world has, indeed, more undesirable bearings on the environment than is often acknowledged, given that the energy and devices required to support the continuous growth of cyberspace are anything but immaterial (Cronin, 2016: 96). The 'ecosystem of information', like that of translation, has been severely disrupted, and it will be necessary to develop strategies to ensure that old ways to manipulate information, and to control and justify inequality, do not continue or even multiply under new technological conditions. In order to fight this growing anarchic cacophony, Cronin proposes a low-tech approach to translation, one which places much more attention on the *whats* and *hows* of translation, an approach that emphasises means and processes over calculated end results, therefore rejecting a purely instrumental and commodified vantage point (Cronin, 2016: 32). José Lambert, in Chapter 8, examines the circulation of discourses on a global scale, and he not only warns us against the homogenisation of messages across the international circuits of information, but also urges us to pay more attention to the strategies that are used to conceal translated communication. Often, translation is rendered invisible in order to obscure the origins of a given discourse and to reinforce the myth of hermetically sealed and monolingual cultures.

Luc van Doorslaer, in his analysis in Chapter 3 of linguistic rights and territorial power relationships, similarly emphasises that the key role played by translation in complex multilingual societies remains unacknowledged. Language and translation policies tend to be subordinated to hegemonic nationalist and (increasingly) neoliberal discourses, and the topic of translation policy has, surprisingly, received very little attention (cf. Reine Meylaerts's investigations of translation policy and multilingualism – Meylaerts, 2010, 2011). Language and translation policies have a tendency to disregard linguistic, cultural and socio-economic imbalances, which has a negative impact on the communicative interaction between authorities and their citizens. Hence, if *linguistic justice* (van Parijs, 2011) is to be attained, a more robust development and implementation of translation and linguistic policies will be needed.

Translation and interpreting are, in many ways, contributing to *social justice*, an ideal broadly applied to research and initiatives aiming to facilitate equality and diversity in order to promote social, economic and environmental sustainability (Freysinger *et al.*, 2013). Such an ideal, to be sure, is unlikely to be met without free and equal access to knowledge and information (Jansen *et al.*, 2011). The attainment of social justice will require, to phrase it in socio-economic terms, a globally balanced libidinal, digital and political economy of translation that ensures equality in the production and sharing of information and thus contributes to sociocultural stability. These interconnected translational economies need cross-cultural mediators with an acute local and global awareness of the ways in which they participate in the creation and circulation of knowledge; it needs translators with the ability and nous for subtle reflection on the ways in which their practice might reinforce or challenge local and global inequalities.

In Wales, translation played a central historical role in addressing cultural and political imbalances. Marion Löffler's analysis in Chapter 5 of translation into a colonised language reveals that translators into Welsh have long used their craft to negotiate and contest colonial dominance, reassembling, rewriting and reconstructing texts in order to oppose source culture values. Their invisibility allowed them to safely express political views and produce resistant, subversive translations which counteracted English hegemony, and domestication strategies allowed them to erase traces of English values in the texts and contribute to their native textual tradition. It is well known that translational tendencies *into* English – such as keeping translators invisible and domesticating texts to adapt to an Anglophone target audience – increase the hegemonic power of Anglophone values (Venuti, 1998), yet in Löffler's analysis of political translation from English into Welsh these tendencies actually function as strategies that *resist* domination and hegemonic power.

Cristina Caimotto in Chapter 7 equally, yet perhaps in more subtle ways, underlines the transformative potential of translation, its capacity to deconstruct underlying ideological discourses and to promote more transparent and equitable modes of communication. This transformative cross-cultural potential does not require translators to become conscious agents of resistance, because it is embedded in the very practice of translation: the unavoidable semiotic, structural and semantic differences between languages may bring to light discursive choices that were supposed to remain invisible and unquestioned in the text. The construction of polarised *us* versus *them* discourses, for instance, often loses its effectiveness when translated into another language, as logical and discursive contradictions embedded in the source text may, so to speak, 'scramble' their way to the foreground. Caimotto's chapter downplays (but does not exclude) the role of agency, suggesting that, by the very nature of language, counter-hegemonic and resistant strategies are already embedded and therefore at play in the very act of translating.

As discussed by Agnieszka Pantuchowicz in Chapter 2, the power of translation lies in the fact that the translational act makes it evident that meaning is always contingent and negotiable. Translation challenges the transparency and apparent internal consistency of the source text, putting into question the concept of an apparently untainted original and revealing that ideological discourses and the structures of language are always part and parcel of any act of communication. It is for this reason that the idea of loss in translation should be rejected, because loss implies the possibility of having access to an unquestionable truth; instead, we should embrace the possibilities of gain, the ability of translation to estrange, defamiliarise and reveal new avenues for meaning-making, interpretation and representation.

Translation's meaning-making potential is further highlighted by Karen Bennett in Chapter 4, who contends that, since our perceptions are limited by categories present in our language and culture, translations have the ability to develop new layers of meaning not present in what is commonly dubbed the source text. The case of the Bible demonstrates that translations are palimpsests formed by layer upon layer of superimposed discourses, that every translation is at the same time a source and a target text. And discourses, like translations, are negotiated on a regular basis, in a continuous power struggle for the imposition of meaning, in line with or in opposition to changing sociocultural conditions and values. Since language has no direct access to any external reality, meaning is always mediated by the structures of language, ideological discourses, power flows and (hierarchical) networks consisting of a multitude of agents. Therefore, as Christina Schäffner argues in Chapter 9, translation is a socially situated practice embedded in specific institutional ideologies and values. The cultural turn placed the agendas of social and institutional powers at the centre of research in translation studies and highlighted the more committed and proactive role of translators, but Schäffner reminds us that translation products are subject to the intervention of institutions, power structures and other agents who are not always immediately perceptible.

Translation activist groups and individuals are certainly contributing to a more equitable distribution of information resources, by, for instance, making available in other languages alternative media accounts or other repressed voices. Social justice, however, requires not just an increase in translation growth, but also in ethical sustainability. Translation technologies, in this sense, may have a significant liberating and democratising potential, but in a neoliberal context where freedom and democracy tend to be equated with deregulation and privatisation, the protection of desirable ethical values and core human rights cannot be taken for granted. On a primary level, 'sustainable' translations contributing to the achievement of social justice should be accessible to everyone and therefore reside in the public domain. Unlike global corporate information flows, which, as several chapters in this volume demonstrate, require anonymity and submission to corporate goals, a sustainable information flow would highlight the role of translators, who would be recognised for their expertise and adequately rewarded for their work. In contemporary society, power has been gradually displaced from the political arena to the techno-capitalist marketplace, which is why far more research is needed on the practices of media control in the corporate world.

Roger Baines in Chapter 11 and Jonathan Ross in Chapter 12 open up space for new lines of research on corporate control, showing that translation plays a key role in market-driven power dynamics. The regulation of translation and interpreting in the English Premier League and of title choices by major American film corporations are instances of new and emergent regimes of power. Forged in the marketplace rather than in the traditional political sphere and grounded on the principles of economic growth and market deregulation, these neoliberal regimes transcend geographical and political boundaries. In a corporate context, translation and interpreting are overseen by company executives and marketing experts, whose role it is to build and maintain the organisation's reputation and thus primarily to serve economic interests. Pei Meng's analysis in Chapter 13 of the crucial role of literary agents in the selection and production of translations also highlights the need to pay close attention to the networked and economic dimensions of the translation process. The task of the literary agent is to identify potentially profitable books and oversee the translation and publication process, but key players in the areas of publicity, marketing and sales also participate in decision-making. Ultimately, literary success is the result of efficient interaction between different actors. Beyond their symbolic and cultural capital, literary agents need to be familiar with commercial imperatives and the ideological discourses circulating within the publishing industry.

Social justice in translation would imply a more democratic and thus dialogical relation between translator and translated, to the benefit of the whole community, which takes precedence over the capitalist logic of commodity exchange. While Toury's idea to regard translation solely as a fact of the target culture (2012: 17–34) helped to free translation and its study from narrow conceptions of equivalence across texts, this perspective can have counterproductive effects, as it may justify the appropriation of knowledge. As demonstrated by Marion Löffler in Chapter 5, this appropriation can work both ways, but translational relationships are in many cases clearly asymmetrical. They are rooted not only in socially grown and thus politically and ideologically charged hierarchies, but above all in the material and thus socio-economic conditions of everyday life. Cristina Gómez Castro in Chapter 7 offers an example of political enforcement on a massive scale: during Franco's dictatorship (1939–1975), Spanish society and culture were both dominated by strict mechanisms of state control, which had an enormous impact on translation practices. In order to ensure ideological uniformity, publishers were frequently forced to suppress certain elements from texts, a situation that was ultimately internalised by members of the corporate and cultural establishment and which led to the naturalisation of self-censorship.

If a more symmetrical, and thus hierarchically equal, relation between translators and translated is to be achieved, the former will have to be heard; they will have to become empowered to raise concerns regarding the shape and potential uses of the translated text. Such an empowerment must be driven by a thorough knowledge of historical, intercultural and economic conditions, so in their daily work translators will have to see through the faultlines of tradition, cultural memory and experience; they will need to thoroughly appreciate the contexts of the text, where it originated and where it is supposed to be transplanted. As discussed by Yajima and Toyosaki (2015: 110–115), such a perspective promotes true intercultural dialogue and will empower both the translator and the trans-lated. In Chapter 6, Maria Sidiropoulou and Ozlem Berk Albachten offer a fitting example of such empowerment. They examine the ways in which a book focusing on a traumatic population exchange between Turkey and Greece was translated into Turkish and Greek. The fact that the source text was in English became unimportant during the translation process: what mattered was how to approach the personal and collective memories that the book would elicit among the reading public in both countries. The experience of the 1923 population exchange, initially interpreted from a foreign perspective, was translated into Greek and Turkish languages and cultures, and this required the implementation of a number of discursive strategies to ensure that the text would not unnecessarily stir traumatic memories. Independently of each other, both translators adopted a strategy of reconciliation which, without downplaying human suffering, stressed intercultural affinities and acknowledged that pain was shared. This example shows that pursuing social justice may have a strong bearing on translation practices: since inequality is based on (socially constructed) differences such as gender, class, ethnicity, nationality, sexuality and also economic capital, avoiding such deeply ingrained biases will require trans-lational approaches that establish new horizons of representation, new ways to represent individuals, communities and cultures.

Social justice is linked to a notion which has already gained much credit in translation studies, that of ethics (Baker & Maier, 2011; Bermann & Wood, 2005; Drugan & Tipton, 2017; Kenny, 2011; McDonough-Dolmaya, 2011; Pym, 2001). There is, however, a fundamental difference between the two concepts. Ethical concerns tend to be subjugated to private property rights, which do not guarantee or take precedence over justice or ecological sustainability, and ethical compliance seems to demand acquiescent and complicit translators, who reproduce a text according to Western standards. As pointed out by McMurtry (2011: 14), ethical requirements tend to be linked to the rights that rule economic and political institutions, which is why they appear disconnected from the life of human beings or ecosystems: 'The rules and rights by which we live are ungrounded in life and life value and the slow-motion collapse of planetary life infrastructures signals this across domains'. The ecosystem is at risk and, as Cronin (2016: 10) argues, it is important to discuss how translation can be re-conceptualised in order to promote and develop ecological ideologies which contribute to the protection of biocultural diversity. In the face of an impending ecological catastrophe, both social justice and translation must include an ecological dimension. Translators and texts are part of larger networks of relations, which include other living organisms and the physical environment. The ecological viewpoint stresses that languages, cultures and the economic arena are not isolated, self-contained entities, because the relations between them are flexible, dynamic and constantly subject to change. The aims of this emerging paradigm are varied: they can be as diverse as translating ecological texts overlooked in the past, re-translating works where nature had been misrepresented or, even, modifying and appropriating texts that originally did not include an ecological dimension (Badenes & Coisson, 2015: 360). An additional objective is to analyse the ways in which nature has been represented in translation and how this has affected our perception of our relationship with the environment.

The ethics of difference propounded by resistant and activist translators and scholars, influenced by post-colonial thinking, addresses issues at the core of social justice. Scholars such as Spivak (1992) and Venuti (1998) have rightly emphasised the ethnocentrism of the Western conception of ethics, which reflects deeply ingrained Western values that, intentionally or not, often exert violence on the translated text by erasing otherness and imprinting extraneous values on them. What is more, translation ethics, as generally understood by professional associations, companies and scholars, tends to be a concept primarily subordinated to the economics of property rights, which engenders the commodification of cultural resources and which maintains perceptible structures of social and economic domination. Against this background, it is difficult to consider ethics as a straightforward tool for social change and liberation, because it simply reproduces and reinforces the current libidinal, digital and political order. While traditional ethical concerns based on the notion of fidelity have been challenged, the guides and codes of practice of professional associations and the contracts issued by translation companies still present faithfulness and impartiality as the benchmarks against which ethical compliance is measured (Inghilleri & Maier, 2009: 102; van Wyke, 2013: 549). The key difference between the concepts of ethics and social justice is that the latter is relevant not only to the final translated product, but also to its effects, invoking in this way the responsibility of the translator towards society as a whole. To make it easier to share information and build on previous knowledge, translators promoting social justice have adopted copyright systems outside the realms of the capitalist logic, such as the Creative Commons, which operates through an alternative logic of exchange that resists the commodification of life.

Baker (2006) and Tymoczko (2010), by taking an activist perspective, have highlighted the responsibility on the part of translators in the face of conflict and injustice and the need to consider their own social and political agendas. The activist perspective has attracted a fair amount of criticism: who is to decide what constitutes a resistant translation and what has to be resisted? Equally important, how can the results of such a resistant translation be measured? These are valid points, but they do not invalidate the premise upon which the idea of resistance in translation is based: the fact that power dynamics are always at play in linguistic usage and that the idea of neutrality in communication is an ideological construct that responds to vested hegemonic interests. This is a complex issue that cannot be resolved in absolute terms but only on a case-by-case basis. As discussed by Yajima and Toyosaki (2015: 99), translation may have positive economic effects and therefore improve distributive justice; at the same time, however, the reliance on translated information may establish strong relations of dependency between societies that actually reinforce asymmetrical relations of power. Problematic as the idea of activist or resistant translation may be, we cannot simply return to the notion of equivalence, nor ignore the fact that translation agents are not neutral mediators who work in a vacuum, but active social agents with their own value systems who participate in the creation of meaning and whose actions are embedded in constantly fluctuating power dynamics.

Ultimately, what is needed is a critical perspective which explores how the power relationships established between science, technology, culture, society and the economy determine the ways in which translated communication is produced, disseminated and consumed across cultural and linguistic boundaries. Since these relationships, at least in the current neoliberal socio-economic order, accentuate inequalities and promote unsustainable development – and thus seriously hamper social justice – it is also paramount to explore how translation can contribute to a new libidinal, digital and political economy which is not at the service of hegemonic values, but of knowledge, understood as a cooperative effort for the benefit of the whole of humanity.

References

Badenes, G. and Coisson, J. (2015) Ecotranslation: A journey into the wild through the road less travelled. *European Scientific Journal*, 356–368, at http://eujournal.org/index.php/esj/article/view/6544/6269, accessed 1 July 2018.

Baker, M. (2006) *Translation and Conflict – A Narrative Account*. London: Routledge.

Baker, M. and Maier, C. (2011) Ethics in interpreter and translator training: Critical perspectives. *The Interpreter and Translator Trainer* 5 (1), 1–14.

Baudrillard, J. (1994) *Simulacra and Simulation* (S.F. Glaser, trans.). Ann Arbor, MI: University of Michigan Press.

Baudrillard, J. (2010) *The Agony of Power* (A. Hodges, trans.). Los Angeles, CA: Semiotext(e).

Bermann, S. and Wood, M. (2005) *Nation, Language, and the Ethics of Translation*. Princeton, NJ: Princeton University Press.

Cronin, M. (2016) *Eco-Translation: Translation and Ecology in the Age of the Anthropocene*. London: Routledge.

Drugan, J. and Tipton, R. (2017) Translation, ethics and social responsibility. *The Translator* 23 (2), 119–125.

Freysinger, V.J., Shaw, S.M. and Henderson, K.A. (2013) *Leisure, Women, and Gender.* State College, PA: Venture Publishing.

Gramsci, A. (1999) *The Antonio Gramsci Reader – Selected Writings 1916–1935* (D. Forgacs, ed.). London: Lawrence and Wishart.

Inghilleri, M. and Maier, C. (2009) Ethics. In M. Baker and G. Saldanha (eds) *Routledge Encyclopedia of Translation Studies* (2nd edn) (pp. 100–104). London: Routledge.

Jansen, S., Pooley, J. and Taub-Pervizpour, L. (2011) *Media and Social Justice.* New York: Palgrave Macmillan.

Kenny, D. (2011) The ethics of machine translation. Paper presented at the New Zealand Society of Translators and Interpreters Annual Conference 2011, 4–5 June, Auckland, at http://doras.dcu.ie/17606/1/The_Ethics_of_Machine_Translation_pre-final_version.pdf, accessed 12 September 2017.

McDonough-Dolmaya, J. (2011) The ethics of crowdsourcing. *Linguistica Antverpiensia* 10, 97–111.

McMurtry, J. (2011) Human rights versus corporate rights: Life value, the civil commons and social justice. *Studies in Social Justice* 5 (1), 11–61.

Meylaerts, R. (2010) Multilingualism and translation. In Y. Gambier and L. van Doorslaer (eds) *Handbook of Translation Studies* (vol. 1, pp. 227–230). Amsterdam: John Benjamins.

Meylaerts, R. (2011) Translational justice in a multilingual world: An overview of translational regimes. *Meta* 56 (4), 743–757.

Pym, A. (2001) Introduction. In A. Pym (ed.) 'The Return to Ethics', special issue, *The Translator* 7 (2), 129–138.

Said, E. (1993) *Culture and Imperialism.* New York: Vintage Books.

Spivak, G. (1992) The politics of translation. In M. Barrett and A. Phillips (eds) *Destabilizing Theory: Contemporary Feminist Debates* (pp. 177–200). Cambridge: Polity Press.

Toury, G. (2012) *Descriptive Translation Studies and Beyond* (revised edn). Amsterdam: John Benjamins.

Tymoczko, M. (ed.) (2010) *Translation, Resistance, Activism.* Boston, MA: University of Massachusetts.

van Parijs, P. (2011) *Linguistic Justice for Europe and for the World.* Oxford: Oxford University Press.

van Wyke, B. (2013) Translation and ethics. In C. Millán and F. Bartrina (eds) *The Routledge Handbook of Translation Studies* (pp. 448–560). London: Routledge.

Venuti, L (1998) *The Scandals of Translation: Towards an Ethics of Difference.* London: Routledge.

Yajima, Y. and Toyosaki, S. (2015) Bridging for a critical turn in translation studies: Power, hegemony, and empowerment. *Connexions: International Professional Communication Journal* 3 (2), 91–125.

Index